More Praise for *The New Entrepreneurial Leader*

"This book is an exemplar of the new wave of thinking about how to develop the next generation of entrepreneurs, leaders, and managers for the 21st century. The discussion is framed by tractable concepts and is grounded in practical application. You will gain a valuable perspective on what matters and how to deliver transformational learning to students."
—**Robert F. Bruner, Dean and Charles C. Abbott Professor of Business Administration, Darden School of Business, University of Virginia, and author of *Deals from Hell***

"In a world overwhelmed with problems, we desperately need more entrepreneurial problem solvers—whether that's young people starting companies from scratch or change agents inside big companies launching breakthrough initiatives. This remarkable book showcases the newest thinking from Babson College, one of the world's most-admired centers of entrepreneurial education, about two timeless questions: what makes entrepreneurs special, and what are the most effective ways to teach aspiring entrepreneurs to succeed? The best education doesn't just tell you what you need to know; it changes how you think. This powerful book does just that."
—**William C. Taylor, cofounder and Founding Editor, *Fast Company*, and author of *Practically Radical***

"In *The New Entrepreneurial Leader*, Babson extends its own leadership in management education. Indeed, this book effectively argues that 21st-century management *requires* entrepreneurial leadership. Larger companies should require this book for every executive."
—**Stephen Spinelli, President, Philadelphia University, and cofounder, Jiffy Lube International**

"This book builds on Babson's thirty years of pioneering researching and teaching entrepreneurship. It challenges conventional business education by arguing convincingly that the entrepreneurial mindset is key to success in our incredibly complex world—not just for entrepreneurs but also for managers, whether they operate in businesses or nonprofit organizations, in highly advanced or in emerging economies. It is a must-buy book."
—**Guy Pfeffermann, CEO and Chairman of the Board, Global Business School Network**

"More than thirty years ago, Babson College was the first institution to teach entrepreneurship as a discipline, and once again, with the publication of *The Entrepreneurial Leader,* Babson has demonstrated that it is an innovator in management education. This is a thought-provoking book that provides very practical insights on ways to teach future entrepreneurs how to think and act more critically and analytically, strive for greater self- and social awareness, and achieve outstanding results."
—**William D. Green, Chairman, Accenture**

"This book provides a vision for developing leaders who aspire to create social, environmental, and economic value simultaneously. It offers practical advice on how to transform management education to realize this vision."
—**Liz C. Maw, Executive Director, Net Impact**

"This is a book that was long overdue...the chapters that discuss the challenges of defining metrics for CSR and the difficulty of linking CSR to corporate social performance have the potential to impact the content of our business curriculum."
—**Dr. Norean Sharpe, Associate Dean, Undergraduate Programs, McDonough School of Business, Georgetown University**

"Reinvention is essential and must be done with guts and in a vigorous manner. In *The New Entrepreneurial Leader*, you will find a viable approach to reinvent management education. This book is a must-read for all who run, teach in, or plan to attend a business school."
—**Kevin C. Desouza, Associate Professor and Director, Institute for Innovation in Information Management, University of Washington, and author of *Intrapreneurship***

The New
Entrepreneurial
Leader

The New Entrepreneurial Leader

Developing Leaders Who Shape

Social and Economic Opportunity

Danna Greenberg

Kate McKone-Sweet

H. James Wilson

and Babson College Faculty

Berrett–Koehler Publishers, Inc.
San Francisco
a BK Business book

Berrett-Koehler Publishers, Inc.
235 Montgomery Street, Suite 650, San Francisco, CA 94104-2916
Tel: (415) 288-0260 Fax: (415) 362-2512 www.bkconnection.com

Ordering Information

Quantity sales. Special discounts are available on quantity purchases by corporations, associations, and others. For details, contact the "Special Sales Department" at the Berrett-Koehler address above.

Individual sales. Berrett-Koehler publications are available through most bookstores. They can also be ordered directly from Berrett-Koehler:
Tel: (800) 929-2929; Fax: (802) 864-7626; www.bkconnection.com.

Orders for college textbook/course adoption use. Please contact Berrett-Koehler:
Tel: (800) 929-2929; Fax: (802) 864-7626.

Orders by U.S. trade bookstores and wholesalers. Please contact Ingram Publisher Services, Tel: (800) 509-4887; Fax: (800) 838-1149; E-mail: customer.service@ ingrampublisherservices.com; or visit www.ingrampublisherservices.com/Ordering for details about electronic ordering.

Berrett-Koehler and the BK logo are registered trademarks of Berrett-Koehler Publishers, Inc.

Printed in the United States of America

Berrett-Koehler books are printed on long-lasting acid-free paper. When it is available, we choose paper that has been manufactured by environmentally responsible processes. These may include using trees grown in sustainable forests, incorporating recycled paper, minimizing chlorine in bleaching, or recycling the energy produced at the paper mill.

Library of Congress Cataloging-in-Publication Data
Greenberg, Danna.
  The new entrepreneurial leader : developing leaders who shape social and economic opportunity / Danna Greenberg, Kathleen McKone-Sweet, H. James Wilson, and Babson College Faculty. — 1st ed.
       p. cm.
  Includes bibliographical references and index.
  ISBN 978-1-60509-344-4 (hardcover : alk. paper)
1. Leadership—Psychological aspects. 2. Entrepreneurship. I. McKone-Sweet, Kathleen. II. Wilson, H. James. III. Babson Center for Entrepreneurial Studies. IV. Title.
  HD57.7.G7434 2011
  658.4'092—dc23
                                                                    2011019416

16   15   14   13   12   10 9 8 7 6 5 4 3 2

Cover design by Richard Adelson.
Interior design and composition by Gary Palmatier, Ideas to Images.
Elizabeth von Radics, copyeditor; Mike Mollett, proofreader; Medea Minnich, indexer.

*To the Babson community
for its dedication to educating students and
developing entrepreneurial leaders*

Contents

Foreword

BABSON COLLEGE'S CURRENT CURRICULUM IS ROOTED IN AN intellectual journey that started more than three decades ago. At that time most schools relied heavily on the scientific method to train general and functional managers for jobs in a vibrant and growing corporate sector in the United States, Europe, and Japan. The entrepreneur as an economic actor was largely ignored. Recognizing this gap, Babson was the first to focus on the study of entrepreneurship as a discipline.

We introduced an entrepreneurship program, held business plan competitions, created an entrepreneurship center, hosted the first research conference in entrepreneurship, and began the systematic development of entrepreneurship faculty and intellectual capital, such as the Symposia for Entrepreneurship Educators and the Global Entrepreneurship Monitor. These were all innovations in management education that helped make Babson the recognized leader in the academics of entrepreneurship.

Introducing the entrepreneurship program allowed us to look systematically at the entrepreneurial experience. An important insight was that that experience, which spans new venture from cradle to grave, could be a powerful educational means of training business professionals regardless of whether they started a new venture. We also learned that entrepreneurs see business problems in a more holistic way than do managers, who often see issues in terms of functional domains.

These insights gave birth to two important curricular innovations. The first was a new undergraduate course in which students had to start and close a business during their freshman year, donating the profits to a charity of their choice. At the graduate level, the master's in business administration (MBA) program was reorganized around the life cycle of a business. The second innovation was an integrated curriculum in which disciplines were not only introduced to match the venture life cycle but also focused on interdisciplinary problem solving. Many of the classes and the programs developed during this phase are referenced in this book.

The third stage of our intellectual journey began in the past few years with the recognition that entrepreneurs think and act differently; that is, entrepreneurship most fundamentally is a method and a mindset of leadership that could and should be used when leading all types of organizations. This fresh focus on the method and the mindset of entrepreneurial leaders is precisely what the book's authors imply by developing "the new entrepreneurial leader." Of course, much of the credit for recognizing the power of this conceptualization of leadership belongs to our students and alumni, who report the benefits of entrepreneurial thinking and methods in their decision-making and leadership approach. Although many of our graduates choose to work for large corporations, they tell us how being exposed to entrepreneurial thinking and methods informed their decisions and career paths.

This 30-plus-year evolution of Babson's programs coincides with great changes in the world in which we live. These changes have given rise to serious doubts about the efficacy of the traditional model of business education as well as an increasing realization that the answer may lie in entrepreneurship of all kinds. Consider some of the changes that have taken place recently.

We live in an increasingly crowded world in which the divide between the haves and the have-nots is growing. This divide requires job creation at rates that are not possible for most businesses and governments. The result is high youth unemployment, which poses a challenge to the stability of "have-not" countries and is a national security issue for the "have" countries. Moreover, this economic gap is generating significant national security issues across all continents. For example, *Businessweek* described the 2011 uprisings in the Middle East as the result of the "youth unemployment bomb" (Coy 2011).

The magnitude of unemployment challenges one of the basic assumptions of business education—that graduates will find work in the corporate sector. But if the need of the day is to turn out employment *creators* and not employment *consumers,* we need more entrepreneurial leaders. This is becoming increasingly apparent to public- and private-sector leaders. President Barack Obama convened an entrepreneurship summit in 2010 as a symbol of positive engagement across the world, Secretary of State Hillary Clinton has made entrepreneurship a key element of US foreign policy, and Goldman Sachs has invested $500 million for a "10,000 Small Businesses" initiative in 2011.

In more-affluent countries, significant change is under way as well. The underlying structures that once ensured some stability in our jobs and corporate careers are giving way to "a gig economy," where short-term project-based work is becoming the norm. In this situation workers need to continuously network to create opportunities across organizations and industries. Perhaps most significantly, they will pursue these opportunities across geographies as well, as the so-called BRIC (Brazil, Russia, India, and China) countries become new hubs of global business activity and innovation.

Often the business challenges arising from these shifts are not neatly packaged or amenable to the rational and analytical skills that business schools are so good at developing in students. We must be motivated to change management education to develop leaders who are not paralyzed by the emerging or unknowable facets of the world, where reliable and relevant data are not yet available. We must develop leaders who can also *create* social and economic opportunity.

Our message is that students can learn to become cognitively ambidextrous. On one hand they apply an entrepreneurial mindset and methodology to experiment with new ideas and act in new environments; on the other they apply deep functional knowledge and detailed analysis to plan future actions. Students can learn to act creatively within unknowable portions of the world while learning more-traditional competencies for cases in which information is relevant and accessible. Future leaders must discern the knowable from the unknowable, understand the approach that works in each case, and adapt their actions and analyses accordingly.

As management educators we too can become practitioners of this approach, especially as we try to answer fundamentally unfamiliar or messy questions: How do we infuse social and environmental responsibility into the curriculum? How do we globalize education? How do we prepare students to lead in a complex and ever-changing world?

This book offers an integrated way to look at these questions, encouraging you to think about social and environmental sustainability alongside analytics and profits, to consider multiple ways of making decisions and leading organizations, and to examine the importance of self- and social awareness. We are still in the early stages of integrating these themes into our own curriculum, so the following pages do not offer the final word. Instead we hope this is the beginning of a conversation.

Shahid Ansari, Provost of Babson College
Leonard Schlesinger, President of Babson College

Reference

Coy, P. 2011. "The Youth Unemployment Bomb." *Businessweek*, February 2. http://www.businessweek.com/magazine/content/11_07/b4215058743 638.htm.

INTRODUCTION

Entrepreneurial Leadership: Shaping Social and Economic Opportunity

W E BELIEVE IN THE POTENTIAL OF GLOBAL INNOVATIONS THAT can yield both social and economic opportunity, and we believe that management education can, and should, play a transformational role in this movement. Management educators can do this by developing a generation of *entrepreneurial leaders* who engage a different *logic* of business decision-making based on a fundamentally different *rationale* for the existence of business. Profit maximization and shareholder value creation, long considered an adequate basis for businesses, are no longer sufficient (Porter and Kramer 2011). Maximizing the common good and minimizing social injustice and environmental impact is the order of the day.

We don't come to this position lightly. Over the past two years, we have conducted extensive research in collaboration with a

The ideas presented in this introduction are based on a white paper that was developed at Babson on the next generation of management education reform (Greenberg, D., K. McKone-Sweet, J. DeCastro, S. Deets, M. Gentile, L. Krigman, D. Pachamanova, A. Roggeveen, J. Yellin, D. Chase, and E. Crosina. 2009. *Themes for Educating the Next Generation of Babson Students: Self and Contextual Awareness, SEERS, and Complementary Analytical Approaches to Thought and Action.* Babson working paper).

cross-disciplinary team of faculty. During this process we have investigated our own approach to management education as well as that of other schools in the United States and around the world. We have conducted an extensive literature review that has taken us across diverse fields such as management education, cognitive psychology, and financial valuation. Finally, we have conducted two global studies involving more than 1,500 companies to understand the practical relevance of the concepts we were developing to real decisions that leaders make. This effort has led us to this viewpoint of how and why society needs entrepreneurial leaders today more than ever.

Entrepreneurial leaders are individuals who, through an understanding of themselves and the contexts in which they work, act on and shape opportunities that create value for their organizations, their stakeholders, and the wider society. Entrepreneurial leaders are driven by their desire to consider how to simultaneously create social, environmental, and economic opportunities. They are also undiscouraged by a lack of resources or by high levels of uncertainty. Rather they tackle these situations by taking action and experimenting with new solutions to old problems, as our industry research shows (Wilson and Eisenman 2010). Entrepreneurial leaders refuse to cynically or lethargically resign themselves to the problems of the world. Rather through a combination of self-reflection, analysis, resourcefulness, and creative thinking and action, they find ways to inspire and lead others to tackle seemingly intractable problems.

It is important to note that *entrepreneurial leadership* is not synonymous with *entrepreneurship*. It is a new model of leadership. Entrepreneurs, and the specific discipline of entrepreneurship, are often focused on new venture creation. Entrepreneurial leaders, on the other hand, also pursue opportunities outside of startup ventures.

- Entrepreneurial leaders work in established organizations, introducing new products and processes and leading expansion opportunities.

- Entrepreneurial leaders work in social ventures, tackling societal problems that others have ignored.

- Entrepreneurial leaders build engagement in social and political movements, and they change existing services and policies in non-governmental organizations (NGOs) and in governments.

These leaders are ready to challenge, change, and create new ways to address social, environmental, and economic problems through these different organizations. Entrepreneurial leaders are united by their ability to think and act differently to improve their organizations and the world.

As management educators, we have the opportunity and the responsibility to be a force for change as we redesign—and even reinvent—management education and development programs to foster entrepreneurial leadership. In this book we introduce the three principles that form the basis of entrepreneurial leadership, and we provide examples of how faculty members from different disciplines are modifying their pedagogy to develop entrepreneurial leaders. Before we discuss further entrepreneurial leadership and how we suggest reshaping management education toward entrepreneurial leadership, we bring this concept to life through the case of Clorox and the launch of Green Works.

Clorox and the Launch of Green Works

Clorox's product line dates back to 1913 with the introduction of bleach. Over time the company built its reputation by creating products that effectively cleaned and disinfected, thanks to its synthetic, chemical-based formulas (Cate et al. 2009). Clorox's hallmark brands include Pine-Sol and Formula 409—some of the most toxic, though effective, cleaning products on the market. By 2005 the company had grown to more than $5 billion in revenue; and except for minor improvements to established products, Clorox had not released a new brand in 20 years. While other industries might have been moving toward environmentally friendly products, the cleaning products industry remained primarily a chemical industry. Of the $12 billion spent each year on cleaning products, the "natural" category accounted for only 1 percent of the industry at the time. Furthermore there were considerable consumer barriers to green cleaning products, including perceptions of efficacy, availability in stores, and price.

If we were to end the case here and ask most managers and management students to evaluate whether Clorox should enter the "natural" cleaning products market, we believe that most would argue against the decision. In a case discussion, participants might cite as reasons against the new product line the small size of the natural-products segment relative to the whole industry, Clorox's lack of product innovation, the brand reputation of Clorox, and the consumer barriers to entry. A conventional business analysis approach would accurately result in the conclusion that entering the natural-products market segment would be a high-risk decision without a substantial financial reward for Clorox. As Jessica Buttimer, the marketing manager for Green Works, said, the market was "too small, too emerging, and the size of those barriers were too large" (O'Leary 2009).

Yet Clorox and its leadership team did not use a traditional management decision-making approach. Green Works began as a product line when a team of entrepreneurial leaders at Clorox, who had a different worldview of business, used an alternative decision-making approach in which they started by taking action, rather than just analysis, to build the new brand. Although this work was undertaken by many entrepreneurial leaders at Clorox, we focus primarily on the actions of Suzanne Sengelmann and Mary Jo Cook, who lead the transformation of the Green Works product line.

In 2005 Sengelmann and Cook had a unique job-share arrangement as the vice president of new business for Clorox's laundry home care division. The two oversaw a small team that was isolated from the rest of the division, and they were charged with being entrepreneurial and innovative as they imagined new opportunities for laundry home care.

Sengelmann and Cook began by engaging in discovery work with consumers in the area of cleaning products. They knew that many consumers were raising concerns that the chemicals they used to clean their houses were worse than the germs and the dirt they were cleaning. Labeled "chemical-avoiding naturalists," this market segment wanted to get toxic chemicals out of their homes but also wanted a product that worked. Their interest in natural cleaners was based in their concern about the health and the well-being of their families and less in their interest in preserving the natural environment (Cate et al. 2009).

Beyond their professional interest in this growing market segment, Sengelmann and Cook had personal passion for moving forward with natural cleaners. Both women were mothers of young children and heard frequently from concerned friends and community members about the impact of chemicals on children's development and the possible links between chemicals and autism and attention-deficit hyperactivity disorder (ADHD). Cook had been involved in recycling initiatives long before they became fashionable, and both women had a personal interest in the environment. The personal passion the women brought to the project was essential for invigorating their energy to tackle the challenges they would face over the next three years as they brought Green Works to market. As Sengelmann stated, "For any good idea, you need personal passion" (Sengelmann 2010).

While Sengelmann and Cook believed in natural cleaning products, they also knew that the business opportunity for Clorox depended on creating a natural product that worked as well as if not better than the chemical products. Sengelmann and Cook connected with an internal group of chemists who had been experimenting with biodegradable plant- and mineral-derived cleaning formulas. Under the leadership of Sumi Cate, research and development (R&D) manager of "Project Kermit," this skunkworks group had been testing alternative ways to perfect a natural cleaning product that worked. Partnering with this team, Sengelmann and Cook continued forward, shaping this social and economic opportunity for Clorox.

In early 2006, less than a year after Sengelmann and Cook had begun their discovery work, the corporate new ventures team came to them to discuss the potential market for natural cleaning products. The corporate team was responsible for identifying the next big idea across divisions and had recently discovered a European natural cleaning product that they believed worked. The corporate team brought this shell of an idea to Sengelmann and Cook. When they saw the passion and the knowledge that the women brought to the concept, they asked them to run with it. Here again we see the importance of passion, as a tenet of the corporate new ventures team was to hand off new ideas only to team leaders who had personal passion for a concept. Thanks to this practice, Sengelmann and Cook caught the idea from new ventures and began to move forward to create the new value proposition.

Yet even with their shared passion, Sengelmann and Cook continued to face challenges. First and foremost, as their R&D partners tested the European natural cleaning products, they found that they weren't as effective as the corporate team had suggested, but another break arose a few months later. In the summer of 2006, there was a "shift in the supply and quality of technologies available," and Sumi Cate and the "Project Kermit" team were able to develop a natural cleaning product that could compete with the effectiveness of established chemical brands. The team would eventually create five products that were 99 percent petrochemical-free and matched or beat standard cleaners in consumer tests (Kamenetz 2008).

Sengelmann and Cook sought the help of Jessica Buttimer, a marketing manager in their group, to lead the effort to bring the project to market. Sengelmann and Cook were strategic in choosing Buttimer, as they knew she also had a personal connection to the product line. Buttimer was a mother of young children, an active hiker, and a supporter of local organic markets. She too had been hearing from neighbors about the desire for Clorox to produce more environmentally friendly cleaners (Neff 2009). Buttimer's personal passion fueled the effort and the innovative thinking she brought to the project.

As the R&D group made progress on creating a full product line of high-quality natural cleaners, these entrepreneurial leaders had to tackle two marketing challenges that at first glance seemed in direct opposition: On the one hand, they could use the Clorox brand name to build consumer confidence in the products' effectiveness. On the other hand, the brand name also introduced a new market challenge: convincing consumers that Clorox was introducing a product that was, in fact, natural. "There were a lot of greenwashing reports starting to surface and the consumers were skeptical," said Buttimer (Kamenetz 2008).

Again these three women acted their way into an innovative solution. Using their networks, they built a partnership with an environmental group that might have been seen as an adversary—the Sierra Club. Although the Sierra Club did not typically endorse products, especially ones from big companies, these entrepreneurial leaders were able to create a unique opportunity for both Clorox and the Sierra Club (Makower 2008). Values and passion again played into the success of the partnership. Carl Pope, the executive director of the Sierra Club, stated, "I think this [partnership] has worked well because in the Bay Area there is a kind of common set of attitudes . . . Because of their [Clorox's] common Bay Area roots, the communication has really been a pleasure. There really is an ability to just talk like when I was talking with one of my fellow environmentalists" (Michels 2008). The result of these shared values and eased communications was an agreement whereby the Sierra Club logo would appear on the

Green Works label and the Sierra Club would receive undisclosed financial compensation.

This team of entrepreneurial leaders finally had a natural cleaning line that worked and that consumers could trust. Through their established marketing channels, they tackled the other challenges related to cost (most green cleaners were twice the cost of Clorox's current products) and inconvenience (most natural cleaners were available primarily in specialty stores). Because of Clorox's power with suppliers and retailers, the women were able to place their products in mainstream stores at a price that was just a 20 to 25 percent premium over traditional cleaning products. They also created innovative grassroots marketing campaigns to connect with the values and the passions of the "chemical-avoiding naturalist" market segment through a reverse graffiti initiative and the use of social media sites such as Facebook and YouTube.

In December 2007 Clorox launched Green Works, its first new product line in 20 years. Within the first six months of 2008, Green Works became the market share leader, with an estimated 42 percent market share. Currently, Green Works has 10 products, and the brand is a significant reason why sales of natural cleaning products doubled over the past two years. The Sierra Club also benefits from its partnership with Clorox; based on 2009 revenues, Clorox gave $645,000 to support its conservation efforts (Duxbury 2010).

These entrepreneurial leaders were successful because they pursued this project in an unconventional way. Starting from their passion and values and a unique action-oriented, network-based approach to pursuing opportunities, Sengelmann, Cook, and Buttimer led the Green Works transformation. The uniqueness of their approach is echoed by Buttimer, who considered herself "part of a small, social brand in Clorox that doesn't have all the data of established brands but continues to try to connect with consumers in new and different ways" (Neff 2009).

Entrepreneurial Leadership in the Clorox Case

These leaders' actions at Clorox epitomize our conceptualization of entrepreneurial leadership. As entrepreneurial leaders, Sengelmann, Cook, and Buttimer combined a different way of acting predicated on a different worldview.

The first unique element of being entrepreneurial leaders is that these women's actions were rooted in their understanding of themselves and the communities in which they lived. Sengelmann and Cook's actions began out of their own value systems, founded in their personal histories. Rather than leaving at home their interest in the environment and their families, they carried their values to their corporate job. These women then tapped their personal social networks to pursue opportunity. Through their understanding of their community and the local perspective, they were able to consider how Clorox could tailor natural cleaning products to meet the needs of these consumers.

While these women were passionate about the social and environmental need for natural cleaning products, they were also passionate in their pursuit of economic value. They recognized that Clorox would require a business case for the brand, and they worked to develop it. As entrepreneurial leaders, they understood the importance of connecting social and environmental sustainability with economic sustainability.

Starting from their passion and this unique view of business, these entrepreneurial leaders relied on an action-oriented decision-making approach to bring the Green Works product line to market. Rather than start with traditional analysis, Sengelmann and Cook took steps to solve critical problems that could put an end to the natural-product line. For example, a key challenge for Green Works was gaining consumers' trust that it was an authentically green product line. Clorox looked to a broad array of external partners and built an innovative relationship with an organization that might have been seen as an adversary to the product, the Sierra Club. Traditional analytical techniques would not have led to the creation of such a partnership. Through their action orientation and value-based approach, this team has been credited not just with changing the industry but with changing how Clorox does business (Neff 2009).

As this example shows, even large, established companies that lack a history of innovation can pursue breakthrough ideas that create social, environmental, and economic value simultaneously. To do this they need entrepreneurial leaders who begin the process of value creation by engaging a different method of making decisions and taking action that is rooted in a different worldview of business.

The Principles of Entrepreneurial Leadership

Entrepreneurial leadership involves a new model of thought and action, which begins with a fundamentally different worldview of business and applies a different decision-making logic. The good news is entrepreneurial leadership is not based on an innate set of personality characteristics. Rather, entrepreneurial leaders have developed unique mental models that support the power of human action to create and build a better world. Exhibit 1.1 depicts the three principles that underlie this mental model, all of which are discussed in more detail in this section.*

---

*The identification of these three principles as the basis of the mental model underlying entrepreneurial leadership came out of extensive work of a Babson task force. The goal of this task force was to identify what the next generation of management students needs to know. Engaging a grounded research approach that included interviewing faculty, survey research with alumnae and students, and reading pedagogy and theory across diverse management and liberal arts disciplines, this task force arrived at this model of entrepreneurial leadership.

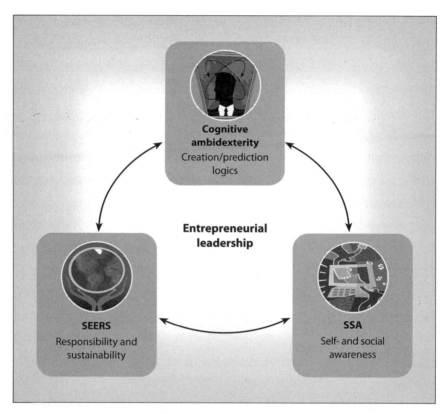

Exhibit I.1 The three principles of entrepreneurial leadership

We call the first principle, which introduces this different way of thinking and taking action, *cognitive ambidexterity*. Entrepreneurial leaders need to learn to be cognitively ambidextrous, engaging both prediction logic and creation logic in their decision-making approach. When an organization's future goals and environment reflect the past, entrepreneurial leaders can apply traditional analytical models to predict and manage the situation. When the future is unknowable and bears little resemblance to the past, however, entrepreneurial leaders must learn how to create the future through action and experimentation. Through cognitive ambidexterity, entrepreneurial leaders learn to balance and engage both of these decision-making approaches.

Guiding this different way of thinking and acting is a fundamentally different worldview of business and society. This different worldview starts from understanding a different value base for business that we refer to as *social, environmental, and economic responsibility and sustainability (SEERS)*. Entrepreneurial leaders must know how to navigate social, environmental, and economic value creation and the inherent tensions and potential synergies therein. Moreover they must learn to engage social, environmental, and economic value creation simultaneously rather than sequentially.

Beyond SEERS, entrepreneurial leaders also leverage their understanding of themselves and the social context to guide effective action. This third principle of entrepreneurial leadership we refer to as *self- and social awareness (SSA)*. Through an authentic and insightful understanding of their own sense of purpose and identity and of how they are affected by the context around them, entrepreneurial leaders make more-effective decisions in uncertain and unknowable circumstances.

While each of these three principles is rooted in existing theory, we go beyond existing ideas as we show the inherent connections among the three principles. Hence we redefine each principle using terminology that reflects these relationships. Furthermore, while other management educators have talked about the importance of each of these principles individually, what is also unique about our concept of entrepreneurial leadership is the integration of the three principles.

If entrepreneurial leadership is the key to unlocking social and economic opportunity, as management educators we needed to consider how to alter existing pedagogy to further develop the mindset of an entrepreneurial leader. To begin creating this pedagogy, we asked a series of questions, including: How do we develop entrepreneurial leaders who engage this unique way of decision-making that combines analysis and action? How do we develop entrepreneurial leaders who consider social, environmental, and economic opportunity in all that they do? How do we develop entrepreneurial leaders who lead from their passion? In our research we recognized quickly that current models of management education fall short in teaching the principles of entrepreneurial leadership.

First, as Mintzberg (2004, 464) points out, management education is too analytical and focused on concepts and quantitative modeling. While these approaches may be useful for teaching leaders to manage uncertain situations, they are not applicable to solving the complexities of today's *unknowable* world. The only way to lead in an unknowable environment is through action. To develop these skills, we need to teach students how to use creativity, experimentation, and action to harvest opportunities (Datar, Garvin, and Cullen 2010). Management education has also been criticized for the lack of emphasis on ethics and social responsibility (Holland, 2009). Our overemphasis on shareholder value creation has come at the expense of social and environmental needs (Ghoshal 2005; Khurana 2007). To develop entrepreneurial leaders who lead with a different worldview, we need a new basis for understanding value creation beyond profit maximization.

Finally, to develop entrepreneurial leaders we need to be teaching our students how to use self-awareness and social awareness in their management approach. To date, we have not paid enough attention to developing leaders who are reflective of themselves and of the world around them (Mintzberg 2004). Entrepreneurial leaders need to connect to their values and passions if they are to inspire and create social and economic opportunity (Fleischmann 2009).

If we don't consider new paradigms for educating management students in new ways of thinking, in new worldviews, and in the importance of self-awareness, we are unlikely to meet the challenge of educating a generation of leaders who will be a positive force for change. As highlighted above, we are not the only ones who see these challenges in management education. Other authors have laid out in great depth the weaknesses of management education models (i.e., Datar, Garvin, and Cullen 2010; Mintzberg 2004; Moldoveanu and Martin 2008). Actions such as the introduction of an MBA oath; increased emphasis on ethics, leadership, and corporate social responsibility; and the use of design thinking are all important steps in the right direction—but they are just that: steps. None of these steps provides management educators with a comprehensive new way of educating leaders who will be able to generate social and economic opportunity in today's unknowable environment.

Management Education That Fosters Entrepreneurial Leadership

In this book we lay out a comprehensive paradigm for how to revise, and perhaps even reinvent, management education and development to mold entrepreneurial leaders who will shape social and economic opportunity. In each section we explore in depth the three principles behind this mental model of entrepreneurial leadership. More importantly, we provide concrete examples of how management educators across all disciplines can integrate these ideas into their courses—and even their entire curriculum—to develop tomorrow's entrepreneurial leaders.

Many of our colleagues who are shaping entrepreneurial leaders developed the ideas and examples herein. We recognize these important contributions with a byline at the start of specific chapters. Chapters without assigned authorship were written by the principal authors of this book.

The following is an overview of the chapters to come.

Part I. A New Way of Thinking and Acting: Developing Cognitive Ambidexterity

In part I we explain the concepts behind cognitive ambidexterity and describe how to develop this mindset in entrepreneurial leaders. The principle behind cognitive ambidexterity is that entrepreneurial leaders must rely on varied yet complementary analytical approaches to thought and action to create and implement solutions that are socially, environmentally, and economically sustainable.

On the one hand, entrepreneurial leaders must understand how and when to use the analytical approaches that have always been central to management education. *Prediction logic,* our phrase to describe the use of a traditional analytical approach, is an extension of the scientific method in which students learn to think, evaluate, and then act to move an organization toward predefined goals. The premise underlying prediction logic is that one can protect against or control the future through detailed analysis. Students learn how to practice data mining, market research, and traditional statistical tools to identify and develop opportunities. A prediction approach is most applicable for situations in which the goals are predetermined, the issues are clear, the causes and the effects are understood, and the data are reliable and available. A prediction approach assumes that an uncertain future can be predicted and that decisions can be made based on those predictions.

Yet entrepreneurial leaders also find themselves in situations where novelty or complexity limits their predictive capabilities. In fundamentally new or complex circumstances in which traditional cause-and-effect relationships are unknown, it is not always possible to gather the appropriate data or to use historical trends to engage a prediction analytical approach. In these situations of unknowability, entrepreneurial leaders must learn to apply a different logic that is based in action, discovery, and creation. We label this complementary decision approach *creation logic.*

With creation logic students learn that the future is created, not predicted. In unknowable situations action is needed to generate data and insight, to further assess the problems and the opportunities, and to select the next course of action. With creation logic students learn to examine who they are, what resources they have access to, and which context they are operating in as they identify a course of action (see also Keifer, Schlesinger, and Brown 2010). Students also learn that as they begin this course of action they will work with a network of stakeholders, including both allies and adversaries, with whom they will co-create their goals. As surprises arise—and they will be in an unknowable environment—students learn how to adapt to or overcome them. Thus creation logic teaches students how to make decisions by beginning with thoughtful action that gives rise to new data and information, which can then be analyzed to guide future action.

All entrepreneurial leaders need to employ both creation and prediction logics and become adept at cycling between the two as they introduce new ideas and initiatives. Continuously alternating between creation and prediction approaches enables individuals and organizations to effectively innovate and manage change. Teaching entrepreneurial leaders cognitive ambidexterity involves not only showing them the underlying theories and methods but also giving them opportunities to apply and alternate between them.

Chapter 1 outlines the two logics in more detail and provides innovative exercises for how to introduce entrepreneurial leaders to the frame of cognitive ambidexterity. The next two chapters highlight each of the approaches that make up cognitive ambidexterity. Chapter 2 focuses on creation logic and introduces a number of courses that have been developed to teach undergraduates and experienced managers how to be cognitively ambidextrous in their approach to innovation and entrepreneurial leadership. Chapter 3 highlights the importance of analytics (a mode of prediction logic) and the role it plays as a complement to creation logic for entrepreneurial leaders of startups and small firms. Through a number of examples of prediction logic courses, we illustrate how management educators can frame courses that enable entrepreneurial leaders to develop cognitive ambidexterity.

Part II. A New Worldview: Social, Environmental, and Economic Responsibility and Sustainability

As mentioned, one of the principles that makes entrepreneurial leaders unique is that this new way of decision-making is based on a fundamentally different worldview. In part II we explore how to develop entrepreneurial leaders who have this unique worldview, by focusing specifically on the concept of social, environmental, and economic responsibility and sustainability and innovative ways to help entrepreneurial leaders understand the importance of this unique view of business and society.

Emerging global, social, environmental, and economic realities oblige us to teach leaders to consider issues beyond profit creation and shareholder value maximization. Entrepreneurial leaders need to develop a more complex understanding of the relationships among social, environmental, and economic value creation. The traditional business paradigm that focuses exclusively on economic value creation, or that depicts social and environmental value creation as secondary to economic value creation, is no longer valid. Individuals and organizations are increasingly being held accountable for the social, environmental, and economic outcomes of their actions.

Entrepreneurial leaders must operate out of a different worldview of business in which they understand the inherent tensions and the potential synergies that exist among social, environmental, and economic value creation. To do this they must also learn how to assess the interests, rights, and powers of a widely diverse group of stakeholders. Rather than ask whether a sustainable solution to a particular challenge is possible, entrepreneurial leaders need to learn how to develop, implement, and measure the effects of responsible and sustainable solutions. In teaching SEERS we develop entrepreneurial leaders with a worldview focused on simultaneously managing social, environmental, and economic value creation rather than the traditional sequential model.

Chapters 4 and 5 emphasize social and environmental value creation. In chapter 4 we discuss the SEERS worldview and introduce a number of ways that management educators are teaching students to consider social and environmental issues as they connect to complex business decisions. Chapter 5 focuses on environmental sustainability and responsibility and offers suggestions on how to develop materials on environmental issues that integrate information from a broad array of disciplines and that engage students in thinking about the scientific, legal, ethical, and cultural implications of their actions.

The next two chapters turn our attention to the complex economic aspect of SEERS. As we introduce entrepreneurial leaders to social and environmental value creation, we also have to teach them how to consider these issues in light of established financial models and theories of wealth creation. Chapter 6 focuses specifically on the accounting and financial perspectives and some of the challenges and the opportunities that these perspectives provide for students as they pursue social and economic opportunities. We discuss some of the unique ways in which we can educate external decision-makers and entrepreneurial leaders to consider accounting standards and begin the process of developing standards to support a SEERS perspective.

In chapter 7 we further examine the financial challenges of adopting a trifold view of value creation and some of the struggles that entrepreneurial leaders may face as they adopt this unique worldview. The chapter provides a framework for evaluating SEERS investments with financial analytical rigor and for preparing entrepreneurial leaders to engage in SEERS practices that are aligned with shareholder value.

Part III. Self- and Social Awareness to Guide Action

Part III focuses on how to develop entrepreneurial leaders' self-awareness and social awareness and teach them to lead from their passions. The third principle of entrepreneurial leadership involves developing a critical understanding of themselves and the societal context of business opportunities. This understanding provides the basis for engaging *a new way of knowing* based on a more expansive view of business. By starting with a critical understanding of their own perspectives and of the world around them, entrepreneurial leaders are better prepared to apply diverse perspectives as they respond to situations that are uncertain and unknown. They are also better prepared to effectively co-create an ongoing course of action and to negotiate the uncertain and ambiguous results that can arise from their decision-making.

Finally, entrepreneurial leaders who have developed this richer understanding of perspective are able to engage a more sophisticated understanding of the world—one that enables them to see the social, environmental, and economic implications of action. To develop this sense of being, entrepreneurial leaders must be able to explore these critical questions: *Who am I? What is the context in which I am situated? Whom do I know, and to what does that give me access?* Understanding these questions enables entrepreneurial leaders to make responsible choices as they choose a path of action in both unknowable and uncertain situations.

Chapter 8 focuses on teaching entrepreneurial leaders to understand the question *Who am I?* and using this understanding to choose an appropriate course of action. Entrepreneurial leaders must understand their own identity, in terms of their values, drives, and background, and be honest and open about their capabilities and limitations. An introduction of self-assessment and professional development work is essential to changing how entrepreneurial leaders understand themselves and take action toward their career aspirations as well as how they develop and coach others to do the same. Such personal growth enables entrepreneurial leaders to develop the skills and the insight to involve their organizations—and the individuals within the organizations—in a new approach to generating social and economic opportunity that is connected to their personal passions and abilities.

Chapter 9 focuses on the question *What is the social context in which one is operating, and how does this affect action?* This chapter considers how entrepreneurial leaders must understand the influence of context on action. Action is governed by the rules of one's context. If entrepreneurial leaders don't understand the cultural and ethical environment, they are more likely to disengage stakeholders and create unfavorable outcomes. A clear understanding of historical, cultural, and societal background enriches entrepreneurial leaders' understanding of the opportunities that lie before them, as well as the implications their actions can have on the world around them.

Finally, chapter 10 considers the question *Whom do I know?* and explores how entrepreneurial leaders build and leverage relationships to co-create opportunities. The discussion begins with the importance of social networks to entrepreneurial leaders and goes on to consider the use of social media to build rich networks. We then highlight some of the ways we have been teaching entrepreneurial leaders to leverage the opportunities that social media affords them. For entrepreneurial leaders to develop these networks for co-creation, they must begin by understanding themselves and their context so that they have the knowledge base from which to effectively build the networks that will underlie their future partnerships.

Part IV. Management Educators as Entrepreneurial Leaders

In part IV we look at specific approaches to implementation. Chapter 11 looks at innovating the case method to teach the underlying principles of entrepreneurial leadership. By reorienting case discussions using the Giving Voice to Values curriculum, educators can move students toward action, self- and social awareness, and SEERS.

In Chapter 12, the final chapter of the book, we introduce specific actions for faculty and administrators to reorient an entire curriculum around these three principles. The core question in this chapter is

How can management educators introduce systemwide changes to reorient student learning toward educating entrepreneurial leaders? Drawing from our own experience, we offer emerging approaches that address this question.

In sum, we invite you to read further and explore this model of entrepreneurial leadership and the various ways to alter your course and curriculum. We are excited and optimistic, as we believe that entrepreneurial leadership provides the long-awaited, pathfinding approach to creating social and economic opportunity around the world.

References

Cate, S. N., D. Pilosof, R. Tait, and R. Karol. 2009. "The Story of Clorox Green Works—in Designing a Winning Green Product Experience Clorox Cracks the Code." *PDMA Visions Magazine,* March. http://www.pdcinc.com/files/Visions_March09.pdf.

Datar, S., D. A. Garvin, and P. G. Cullen. 2010. *Rethinking the MBA: Business Education.* Boston: Harvard Business Press.

Duxbury. S. 2010. "Boost in Clorox Green Works Sales Means Green for Sierra Club." *San Francisco Business Times,* March 2. http://www.bizjournals.com/sanfrancisco/stories/2010/03/01/daily42.html?s=print.

Fleischmann, F. 2009. "What Is Entrepreneurial Thinking?" Paper delivered at St. Gallen University, Switzerland, October 4, 2009.

Ghoshal, S. 2005. "Bad Management Theories Are Destroying Good Management Practices." *Academy of Management Learning and Education* 4 (1): 75–91.

Holland, K. 2009. "Is It Time to Retrain B-Schools?" *New York Times,* March 14. http://www.nytimes.com/2009/03/15/business/15school.html.

Kamenetz, A. 2008. "Clorox Goes Green." *Fast Company,* September 1. http://www.fastcompany.com/magazine/128/cleaning-solution.html.

Keifer, C., L. Schlesinger, and P. B. Brown. 2010. *Action Trumps Everything: Creating What You Want in an Uncertain World.* Duxbury, MA: Black Ink Press. http://www.actiontrumpseverything.com.

Khurana, R. 2007. *From Higher Aims to Hired Hands: The Social Transformation of American Business Schools and the Unfulfilled Promise of Management as a Profession.* Princeton, NJ: Princeton University Press.

Makower. J. 2008. "Clorox Aims to Show That "Green Works." *Futurelab,* January 14. http://www.futurelab.net/blogs/marketing-strategy-innovation/2008/01/clorox_aims_to_show_that_green.html.

Michels, S. 2008. "Extended Interview: Clorox CEO and Sierra Club Chief on Green Products." *PBS NewsHour.* http://www.pbs.org/newshour/bb/business/july-dec08/clorox_08-15.html.

Mintzberg, H. 2004. *Managers Not MBAs: A Hard Look at the Soft Practice of Managing and Management Development.* San Francisco: Berrett-Koehler.

Moldoveanu, M. C., and R. L. Martin. 2008. *The Future of the MBA: Designing the Thinker of the Future.* New York: Oxford University Press.

Neff, J. 2009. "Women to Watch 2009: Jessica Buttimer: Global Domain Leader, Clorox Green Works." *Advertising Age,* June 1. http://adage.com/womentowatch09/article?article_id=136909.

O'Leary, N. 2009. "Marketer of the Year '09." *Brand Week,* September 14. http://login.vnuemedia.com/bw/content_display/special-reports/marketer-of-the-year/e3id4e011604f3ec58298aaaf76043e0321.

Porter, M. E, and M. R. Kramer. 2011. "Creating Shared Value: How to Reinvent Capitalism—and Unleash a Wave of Innovation and Growth." *Harvard Business Review,* January/February, 62–77.

Sengelmann, S. 2010. Phone interview with Danna Greenberg. October 21.

Wilson, H. J., and E. Eisenman. 2010. *Report on Business Uncertainty: 2010 Global Survey Results.* Babson Executive Education working paper.

PART I

A New Way of Thinking and Acting: Developing Cognitive Ambidexterity

Cognitive Ambidexterity: The Underlying Mental Model of the Entrepreneurial Leader

Heidi Neck

IN 2003 JIM POSS WAS WALKING DOWN A BOSTON STREET WHEN HE noticed a trash vehicle in action. The truck was idling at a pickup point, blocking traffic, smoke pouring out of its exhaust, and litter was still prevalent on the street. *There has to be a better way,* he thought to himself. In investigating the problem, Poss learned that garbage trucks consume more than 1 billion gallons of fuel in the United States alone. The vehicles average only 2.8 miles per gallon, and they are among the most expensive vehicles to operate (BigBelly Solar 2010). In the early 2000s, municipalities and waste collection services were considering more-fuel-efficient vehicles and better collection routes to reduce their overall costs and environmental footprint. Poss was not convinced that this was the right approach.

Through interactions with diverse stakeholders, he turned the problem upside down. He considered that the answer might not be about developing a more efficient collection process but about reducing the need for frequent trash collection. As he considered this solution, he discovered multiple benefits: if trash receptacles held more trash, they would not need to be emptied so often; if trash did not need to be collected so often, collection costs and associated pollution would be reduced; and if receptacles did not overflow, there would be less litter on the streets. There were many advantages to this approach.

By applying the solar technology he used at work, Poss envisioned how a new machine might better manage trash. His initial concept of a solar-powered trash compactor was dismissed in favor of other ideas for environmentally friendly inventions, including a machine that would generate electricity from the movement of the ocean. Nonetheless the problem and the potential solutions continued to occupy his mind. Poss said, "I took pictures of trash cans on my honeymoon" (Simpson 2007).

He began to involve others, choosing a team based on who he knew might be interested within his social network. "We are motivated in part because we care about the environment and in part because we know this can be financially successful" (Xing 2007). Poss and his assembled team experimented with a variety of options and finally returned to the solar-powered trash receptacle—the BigBelly— an innovation that provides clear solutions to the problems he noted on the city street that day. The current version can hold up to five times more trash than traditional receptacles. As a result, it dramatically decreases the frequency of trash pickup and cuts fuel use and trash truck emissions by up to 80 percent.

Entrepreneurial leaders such as Jim Poss need the skills and the knowledge to define the world rather than be defined by it. To achieve this, entrepreneurial leaders must identify, assess, and shape opportunities in a variety of contexts—ranging from the predictable to the unknowable. They use creative and innovative approaches to create value for stakeholders and society. They create opportunities using a method of observing, acting, reflecting, and learning that is a constant and ongoing process. This is the method Poss used when observing a waste collection problem, pondering new technology-based solutions, reflecting on the possibilities, and creating the BigBelly solution.

In this chapter we introduce the way of thinking and acting that underlies entrepreneurial leadership: *cognitive ambidexterity*. Cognitive ambidexterity presumes two different approaches to thought and action: prediction logic and creation logic. To be an effective entrepreneurial leader, one must be skilled in both prediction and creation logics and able to cycle between them. It was through the use of both prediction and creation logics that Poss was able to create economic and environmental value; he literally turned garbage into an opportunity.

This chapter explains cognitive ambidexterity in more detail and provides examples of how to develop entrepreneurial leaders who engage cognitive ambidexterity. To do this, however, management education must move beyond teaching entrepreneurial leaders *what* to think to teaching them *how* to think.

Cognitive Ambidexterity: Linking Prediction and Creation Approaches

Entrepreneurial leadership requires cognitive ambidexterity—a way of thinking and acting that is characterized by switching flexibly back and forth between prediction and creation approaches. The prediction approach, which is based on analysis using existing information, works best under conditions of certainty and low levels of perceived uncertainty. Creation, on the other hand, involves taking action to generate data that did not exist previously or that are inaccessible. It is most effective in environments characterized by extreme uncertainty or even unknowability.

In some instances prediction and creation logics are portrayed as incompatible methods of thought and action. In theory and in practice, this distinction is artificial. Through conscious effort, one way of thinking can be used to inform *and* progress the other way of thinking, making the approaches complementary. Moreover, by engaging prediction and creation approaches, entrepreneurial leaders are able to create greater value than if they had tried only one of these approaches.

Consider the example of Yvon Chouinard, who founded the outdoor apparel company Patagonia in 1974. When asked how he knows if he's making the right move, he responded, "If you study something to death, if you wait for the customer to tell you what he wants, you're going to be too late, especially for an entrepreneurial company. That comes from Henry Ford: Customers didn't want a Model T, they wanted a faster horse" (Wang 2010, 23). Chouinard takes action first (the creation approach) and uses data from his actions and experiments to make decisions (the prediction approach). His cognitive ambidexterity is producing impressive results. Patagonia is still a private company, 100 percent owned by Chouinard, with approximately 1,300 employees and $315 million in sales for 2009. In addition, Patagonia continues to receive numerous awards for its emphasis on social and environmental responsibility and sustainability (Wang 2010).

Framing Cognitive Ambidexterity for Entrepreneurial Leaders

To understand the abstract concept of cognitive ambidexterity, we developed an exercise that enables entrepreneurial leaders to *experience* the difference between the prediction and creation ways of thinking. The exercise we describe is based on Sarasvathy's (2008) seminal work on effectuation, where the contrasting metaphors of a quilt and a jigsaw puzzle expose the differences between effectual and causal thinking, which are akin to creation and prediction logics (see exhibit 1.1).

This exercise can be used at the beginning of any course that discusses entrepreneurial leadership. At the start of the course, students are least comfortable with one another, the professor, and the course content. In this way course participants simulate the experience of being in an unknowable world. The exercise begins as the professor

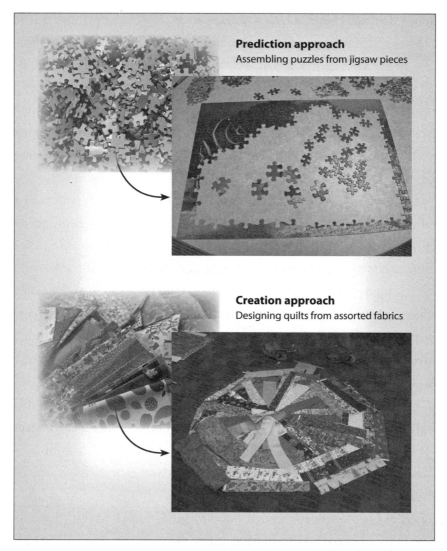

Prediction approach
Assembling puzzles from jigsaw pieces

Creation approach
Designing quilts from assorted fabrics

Exhibit 1.1   Exercise to introduce cognitive ambidexterity

asks students to count off into groups of six. The professor tells students that this is a time-limited competition. Groups are instructed to go to their assigned table, which has the directions.

At each table participants read the instructions, which indicate that their task is to complete a 300-piece jigsaw puzzle as quickly as possible. While the initial setup may be a little chaotic, order quickly appears at each table, as most students have experience doing jigsaw puzzles. Group members use their experience as they begin to separate edges from center pieces, search for corners, and use the picture on the box to begin assembling the puzzle.

After five to 10 minutes, the professor announces that one volunteer is needed from each group. The volunteers leave the puzzle area and are brought to a large, empty room. In one corner of the room are hundreds of pieces of fabric of different colors, textures, and sizes. The group of volunteers are again confused and concerned. The instructor tells them that each student will now become a quilt leader responsible for designing a quilt that will be judged. Quilt leaders are told that they don't need to sew; they can simply place fabric on the ground and start designing the quilt. They begin the process by choosing six pieces of fabric, selecting a space in the room to create the quilt, and laying their pieces down. The quilt leaders are also told that over the next 45 minutes, other volunteers will be brought into the room and will be invited to join in designing quilts.

The quilt leaders get to work, and in five minutes six more volunteers join the quilt-making room. These volunteers are told to select six pieces of fabric and join any team they want. Every five minutes a new group of volunteers leave the puzzle-making area and enter the quilt-making room. As more people join the effort, some quilts grow larger or become more creative. Soon the entire class moves from putting together puzzles to designing quilts. Though participants don't yet realize it, they have just experienced the prediction and creation logics of cognitive ambidexterity.

The Jigsaw Puzzle as Prediction Logic

Assembling a jigsaw puzzle is analogous to prediction logic within cognitive ambidexterity. The puzzle box itself offers a number of known variables, including the number of pieces inside and a picture of the solved puzzle, both of which can be used to reduce uncertainty around the level of difficulty and potential time to completion. The process begins by establishing the goal: complete the puzzle. The second step is to acquire resources to achieve that goal: open the box and get the puzzle pieces. The third step is to analyze everyone's experience with puzzle building and to design a process for completing the puzzle. This might involve separating pieces by color, doing the edges first, and so on. The fourth step involves measuring progress and making adjustments by reviewing the box cover and revising the plan. Finally, the project is complete when all the pieces are connected to match the picture on the box. Participants start with a clear goal and follow a linear process to completion.

Prediction logic, which is vividly illustrated by the experience of assembling a jigsaw puzzle, is the established analytical approach taught by most management educators. The concepts and the teaching methods that underlie this approach provide students with the tools, frameworks, and processes for analyzing the causes and predicting the effects of a given event or action. Through this approach management students learn how to predict the outcome of actions using observation, experience, analysis, and reasoning. They learn that through rigorous analysis of the causes and the effects of a situation, they can make decisions that yield the intended results.

The six principles that guide the use of a prediction approach are shown in the following sidebar. Like putting together a jigsaw puzzle, a prediction approach is applicable in organizational situations in which goals are predetermined, issues are clear, and data are reliable and available. In these circumstances entrepreneurial leaders focus on assessing the situation, defining the problems and the opportunities, diagnosing the problem, evaluating alternative actions using established frameworks and tools, and identifying the best solution or plan to reach established goals. This sequential process of assess, define, diagnose, design, and act assumes that we can predict the future based on past experiences.

Principles of a Prediction Approach
to Thought and Action

1. Goals are predetermined and achievable given known information.

2. Enough information is known for rigorous analysis and testing.

3. Tools and frameworks are available to guide decision-making.

4. Optimal solutions are identifiable within a given set of constraints.

5. Through analysis, risk can be minimized or mitigated to achieve optimal returns.

6. Outside organizations are seen as competitors and barriers to future growth.

Adapted from Dew et al. 2008; Greenberg et al. 2009; and Sarasvathy 2008.

In management education prediction logic has been the dominant paradigm for teaching everything from accounting to organizational behavior to entrepreneurship. To develop their cognitive ambidexterity, entrepreneurial leaders will still need to be taught the prediction approach. They need to learn established tools and frameworks for following a rigorous, analytical decision-making process.

Yet the ambiguity of today's business environment means that a prediction approach to leadership is not enough. In complex situations where cause-and-effect relationships are unknown or uncertain and where information is ambiguous, a prediction approach must be complemented by the creation approach based in action, discovery, and shaping opportunities. Entrepreneurial leaders use the creation approach to learn about a situation by acting and then observing and analyzing the outcomes of their actions.

The Quilt as Creation Logic

The creation approach illustrated by this experiential exercise is analogous to a form of quilt-making called crazy quilting. Crazy quilting is one of the oldest forms of American patchwork quilting and is defined by combining irregular patches of fabric with little or no regard to pattern or design. This form of quilt-making became popular among Victorian women in the late 1800s. The design, shape, and color of the quilt depended not only on the knowledge and the experience of the quilters but also on the amount and the type of fabric and the creativity they brought to the project.

The quilt-making portion of the exercise highlights the creation component of cognitive ambidexterity. Participants enter the quilt-making room with little information and few resources (six pieces of fabric). They employ a means-focused process in which they begin designing the quilt based on the materials they have. This is very different from creating a quilt design and then going to find the materials that fit it (a prediction-oriented process).

As other participants enter the room, they self-select to join a quilt leader. How they choose a quilt-making team varies. Some participants are attracted by a quilt leader's design and feel they have something to offer. For instance, some may be drawn to a quilt that is unconventional. Other participants connect to those who fit with their knowledge of what a quilt is supposed to be. Still others see that some teams do not have many people, so they join out of perceived need. Regardless of the reason why, each volunteer brings additional resources (fabric), and the quilt design continues to emerge. Sometimes new fabric brought to the team may force the team to go in a different direction. For example, a team may have an emerging design based on hues of blue, and then someone joins the team with red, orange, and green plaid pieces. Should the team accept the resources and go with a different design? The creation approach would argue affirmatively because with each additional set of resources the pool of possibilities expands.

Entrepreneurial leaders use creation logic when the future is highly uncertain and unpredictable and past information is not predictive of future activity. Creation logic is an action-oriented approach based on the notion that new inputs (actions, information, and resources) expand the available opportunities. Furthermore it is an approach in which teams of individuals are co-creating. Individuals bring to the table different knowledge, resources, and networks. They take action and create opportunity by engaging these different forms of capital. The six principles that form the basis of a creation approach are shown in the following sidebar.

Principles of a Creation Approach to Thought and Action

1. If perceived resource needs are beyond your control, start to create something with what you have.

2. When the future is unpredictable, create the future by shaping opportunities.

3. When operating with limited information, take action in the real world to acquire information but expect and leverage surprises or failures.

4. Optimal decision-making is never possible in highly uncertain environments. By starting something with current available means, you are "satisficing" to take swift action.

5. Determine what you are willing to lose (money, time, and social capital) to engage in the activity. Once you know what you are willing to lose, risk is no longer an inhibitor of entrepreneurial action.

6. Outside organizations, customers, and self-selected stakeholders are co-creators and not competitors.

Adapted from Dew et al. 2008; Greenberg et al. 2009; and Sarasvathy 2008.

The creation approach is central to cognitive ambidexterity, as human behavior is never entirely predictable and globalization and technological changes produce novel and complex situations. It is not always possible to gather the appropriate data or to use historical trends to apply a prediction approach.

The application of the creation approach can be seen in the example of Chris Cranston, a small-business owner who founded FlowDog in Waltham, Massachusetts. FlowDog is a canine aquatic and physical rehabilitation center. Prior to starting FlowDog, Cranston was a physical therapist practicing sports medicine. Wanting a change and having a strong desire to work with animals, she learned about a new program at the University of Tennessee that offered certification in canine physical therapy. In 2004 she was among the first 100 graduates of the program. Upon graduating she wanted to open her own facility but realized that few people knew that physical therapy was an option for dogs. There were no data on market size, growth potential, or acceptance by dog owners to using physical therapy. At the time few facilities existed in the country.

Personally, Cranston had limited financial resources and no startup experience. She had no connections in the veterinarian community, and Massachusetts law made it impossible to practice physical therapy on animals without a referral from a veterinarian. Using prediction logic a traditional data analysis would suggest that this was a risky opportunity to pursue, not unlike Clorox's launch into the natural cleaning products market.

Cranston had a car, however, as well as some equipment and her experience and education, which provided her with both knowledge and a network. She started a mobile canine physical therapy practice in 2005. After making a few connections with area vets, she started to get referrals and the business grew by word of mouth. This early market test encouraged her to go a step further, and in 2009 she opened FlowDog—a 3,500-square-foot facility with a 3,000-gallon pool, physical therapy rooms, and a retail store.

The FlowDog example is one in which a creation approach is being used to transform the unknowability of a new situation by

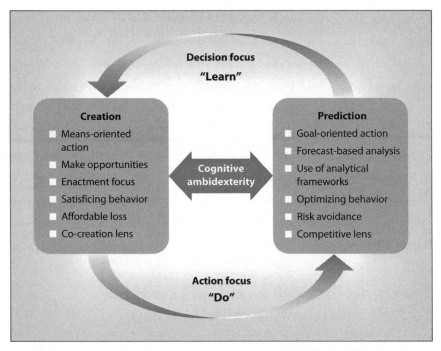

Exhibit 1.2 Cognitive ambidexterity: the complementary logics of entrepreneurial leadership

taking action that enables one to further learn and assess the problems and the opportunities and to select the next course of action. This process of acting, observing, reflecting, and learning is dynamic and assumes that the future is created, not predicted, and is based on an entrepreneurial leader's access to resources and interactions with partners. Without taking small actions and applying learning from every action, FlowDog would not exist today.

Cognitive ambidexterity represents a continuous cycle of applying the creation and prediction approaches (see exhibit 1.2). Stable environments associated with prediction allow one to analyze and then act. Uncertain and even unknowable environments align better with creation thinking that requires action and then analysis. The world, however, is not easily interpreted as either stable or unknowable; therefore the ambidextrous approach of our mental model is necessary.

Greg Treverton (2007), director of the RAND Center for Global Risk and Security, says we cannot solve mysteries with the same mindset with which we solve puzzles. He states, "Puzzles may be more satisfying, but the world increasingly offers us mysteries. Treating them as puzzles is like trying to solve the unsolvable—an impossible challenge. But approaching them as mysteries makes us more comfortable with the uncertainties of our age." Entrepreneurial leaders need to solve both puzzles and mysteries. To be cognitively ambidextrous, they must be alert to changes in the environment and able to select a creation or prediction approach based on what they know about the current and future environments.

Teaching Entrepreneurial Leaders to Be Cognitively Ambidextrous

Teaching entrepreneurial leaders to develop a cognitively ambidextrous approach to decision-making is comparable to teaching people to work with either hand. Most people have a dominant hand they prefer to use to throw a ball, open the door, and sign their name. Each time a task is performed, one unconsciously uses the dominant hand. While ambidexterity is extremely rare, it can be learned with practice and patience.

In a similar way, most individuals prefer a certain approach to thinking—prediction or creation in this case—and select this dominant approach. In the same way that most people are right-handed, most managers are, we believe, more competent with prediction logic. This may have developed because management educators have been more focused on teaching prediction logic, much like teachers historically encouraged all children to use their right hands. Through a change in our management education approach, however, we can introduce and support those leaders who are more oriented to creation logic. More importantly, with a different management education paradigm, we can encourage entrepreneurial leaders to become cognitively ambidextrous as they learn to cycle between the two approaches as the environment demands.

Management education's process orientation presents another challenge to our ability to teach entrepreneurial leaders to be cognitively ambidextrous. With a process-driven pedagogy, students learn to employ frameworks and models in sequential steps. While a process orientation works well under the prediction model, its effectiveness is reduced when used with the creation approach. To teach creation and prediction logics as complementary, educators need to teach a *method* of entrepreneurial leadership (Neck and Greene 2011). This goes beyond understanding, knowing, and talking and demands using, applying, and acting. Most importantly, a method requires practice and experimentation. In an ever-changing—and often unknowable—world, we need to teach methods that stand the test of dramatic changes in content and context.

With a process approach, by comparison, there is an assumption of known inputs and known outputs, as in a manufacturing process. A process also implies that there is a correct result once you decide on the right inputs. Obviously, a process approach limits one's ability to teach entrepreneurial leaders to navigate in unknowable environments. A method approach, by comparison, requires creative and nimble thinking based on a body of skills and techniques. This thinking leads to a heightened level of experimentation, where subsequent iterations represent stages of learning rather than a series of successes and failures. The concept of method requires consistent practice so that knowledge and expertise can be continuously developed and applied to future endeavors.

In the following section, we introduce some unique methods for helping students become cognitively ambidextrous as they engage both creation and prediction approaches. Central to teaching these methods of cognitive ambidexterity is the development of a pedagogical portfolio (Neck and Greene 2011). Finkelstein, Seal, and Schuster

(1998) reported that out of 172,000 faculty in the United States, 76 percent still list lecturing as their primary teaching method. We need to try more-diverse methodologies that enable students to *practice* management or, more importantly, entrepreneurial leadership.

FME: An Experiential Course in Being an Entrepreneurial Leader

One course we have developed to teach students to be cognitively ambidextrous is Foundations of Management and Entrepreneurship (FME). By starting and running a mock new-business venture, course participants learn the tenets of entrepreneurial leadership. The focus of FME is on opportunity recognition, resource parsimony, team development, holistic thinking, and value creation through harvest. The vehicle of learning is a limited-duration business startup steeped in entrepreneurial leadership and a basic understanding of all functions of business. Specific course objectives include:

- Identify, develop, and assess opportunities that create social and economic value

- Practice entrepreneurial leadership

- Identify when and how to use creation and prediction logics

- Understand the nature of an integrated business enterprise

Because FME is a required course, all first-year undergraduates experience the entire cycle of entrepreneurship and learn general management tools through a blend of theory and practice.

FME is a two-semester course. The fall semester is separated into phases in which a method is used to identify 20 business ideas, develop and assess those ideas, and then select two business opportunities that will be pursued in each 60-person FME section. Students align themselves with one of the two opportunities and create a business organization of self-selected stakeholders. The spring semester is reserved for implementing, managing, and harvesting those business ventures.

Specific business topics, often grounded in prediction logic, are covered throughout the two-semester course in addition to the method of FME business creation. The process of developing, launching, managing, and harvesting a business creates a real-world context in which students can practice the basics of business, including accounting, marketing, sales, operations, human resources, information technology, and general management. Instructors introduce these basics in a specific sequence that maps to the startup process, exposing students to topics on an as-needed basis so that they are prepared for each stage of the startup experience. In this way course participants are introduced to traditional prediction logic as they develop their skills and confidence with creation logic.

An example helps illustrate the relevance of both prediction and creation logics in this course. One student group proposed a business idea where they intended to purchase and sell hand sanitizers and refills to large businesses in local communities. The opportunity was based on a predictive analysis that included research into the health benefits of using hand sanitizers and the emergence of wall-mounted dispensers in public spaces. During the spring semester, the team ran into a number of obstacles. One of these obstacles occurred when they encountered challenges in selling to large local businesses. After many failed sales calls, it became clear that many purchasing decisions were made at the corporate level and that purchases were made from pre-approved, established organizations. The team reassessed their target market and used their own networks (parents, professors, and fellow students) to shape the market. Through these relationships, a new opportunity was created. The business began targeting small businesses, organizations that needed to make onetime purchases, and health-conscious friends who wanted units for their dorm rooms. By learning from their initial failure, engaging a variety of stakeholders, and taking action to learn more about the market, the team reshaped the opportunity. Through instruction and experience with both the creation and prediction approaches, students learn the principles behind cognitive ambidexterity.

Additional Pedagogies for Teaching Cognitive Ambidexterity

Beyond a highly experiential course such as FME, there are other pedagogical approaches that can be easily adapted to teach cognitive ambidexterity. Here we briefly highlight three of these approaches: design thinking, serious games and simulations, and reflective practice.

Design thinking   Simon (1996) argued that applied disciplines couldn't be taught under the auspices of the traditional scientific method. Businesses are designed by humans interacting with one another to create something of value. Courses should be designed to help students solve real-world customer and social problems and apply ethnography, data visualization, divergent and convergent thinking, and iterative problem-solving techniques to design new products and services. The learning objectives of these courses can be easily tailored to focus on teaching creation and prediction logics.

Serious games and simulations   Whether games are played on a laptop, game console, or mobile device, evidence is mounting that the combination of gaming and learning as a valuable pedagogy is growing. Edery and Mollick (2009) write about how companies of all types are using games to interact with various stakeholders, including customers (through "advergames") and employees (through training games). They state, "Games are compelling because, at their best, they represent the very essence of what drives people to think, to cooperate, and to create" (4). A colleague, Patricia Greene, has used off-the-shelf games—such as *The Sims* with expansion pack *Open for Business*—to teach students about organization design and how to consciously build company culture as a source of competitive advantage. Through the use of these games, students experience firsthand how and when to engage creation and prediction logics.

Reflective practice　As students work with creation and prediction logics, they will develop their own capabilities further if they have the opportunity to reflect on their own thinking. Journaling, blogging, deep-dive reflection on one incident, and reflective essays—all provide opportunities for students to critically reflect on their own cognitive ambidexterity and to create a plan for their continued development. The key to doing this well is to make reflection an integrated activity across the curriculum so that the responsibility for making connections lies with not only faculty but also students.

Conclusion

In this chapter we emphasize the role of hands-on exercises, repeated practice and experimentation, and continuous learning in teaching entrepreneurial leaders to develop their cognitive ambidexterity. Management education programs need to teach students to become adept with both prediction and creation approaches. When we teach this method, we enable participants to develop a mental model for entrepreneurial leadership. This model includes a toolkit that can be adapted to meet the needs of an ever-changing environment and can be used for solving the known and unknowable social, environmental, and economic problems that we will face in the future. We can no longer teach students *what* to think; we must teach them *how* to think. Giving equal attention to creation and prediction within the mental model of cognitive ambidexterity represents a significant change in management education. Yet we believe that this change is a necessity if management educators are to fulfill our obligation to management students and society as a whole.

References

BigBelly Solar. 2010. "Company History." Accessed March 3, 2011, http://big bellysolar.com/about/history.

Dew, N., S. Read, S. D. Sarasvathy, and R. Wiltbank. 2008. "Outlines of a Behavioral Theory of the Entrepreneurial Firm." *Journal of Economic Behavior and Organization* 66 (1): 37–59.

Edery, D., and E. Mollick. 2009. *Changing the Game: How Video Games Are Transforming the Future of Business.* Upper Saddle River, NJ: Pearson.

Finkelstein, M. J., R. K. Seal, and J. H. Schuster. 1998. *The New Academic Generation: A Profession in Transformation.* Baltimore: John Hopkins University Press.

Greenberg, D., K. McKone-Sweet, J. DeCastro, S. Deets, M. Gentile, L. Krigman, D. Pachamanova, A. Roggeveen, J. Yellin, D. Chase, and E. Crosina. 2009. *Themes for Educating the Next Generation of Babson Students: Self and Contextual Awareness, SEERS, and Complementary Analytical Approaches to Thought and Action.* Babson working paper.

Neck, H. M., and P. G. Greene. 2011. "Entrepreneurship Education: Known Worlds and New Frontiers." *Journal of Small Business Management* 49 (1): 55–70.

Sarasvathy, S. D. 2008. *Effectuation: Elements of Entrepreneurial Expertise.* Cheltenham: Edward Elgar.

Simon, H. A. 1996. *The Sciences of the Artificial.* Cambridge, MA: MIT Press.

Simpson, N. 2007. "Beefing Up the BigBelly Business." *GateHouse News Service,* August 2. http://www.wickedlocal.com/needham/news/x225114365.

Treverton, G. F. 2007. "Risks and Riddles: The Soviet Union Was a Puzzle. Al Qaeda Is a Mystery. Why We Need to Know the Difference." *Smithsonian,* June. http://www.smithsonianmag.com/people-places/10024526.html.

Wang, J. 2010. "Patagonia from the Ground Up." *Entrepreneur,* June. http://www .entrepreneur.com/magazine/entrepreneur/2010/june/206536.html.

Xing, Z. 2007. "Interview: Jim Poss, Inventor of the BigBelly." *Sine English,* January 23. http://english.sina.com/technology/1/2007/0123/101651.html.

CHAPTER 2

Creation Logic in Innovation: From Action Learning to Expertise

Sebastian K. Fixson and Jay Rao

> Most people view product as the one aspect of a business over which they have absolute control—unlike capital, say, or employees. But most products I have seen develop a life of their own, beyond anyone's power to control. Just look at this innocent little snack called Smartfood, which has managed to reroute the lives of everyone drawn into its orbit (Kahn 1988).

SMARTFOOD, A SNACK FOOD MADE FROM PREMIUM-QUALITY WHITE popcorn sprinkled with aged white cheddar cheese, was first introduced to the New England market in 1985 and quickly became America's leading snack food, with sales going from $500,000 in 1985 to $18 million in 1988. What is most interesting about this product innovation is that in many ways it was a by-product of the innovation the entrepreneurial leaders were seeking.

Ken Meyer and Andrew Martin were working on the Tug-N-Tie resealable bag. At the time they were looking to create a resealable bag for the snack food industry that was cheap to produce and easily adaptable to the current technology. They had spent two years developing the Tug-N-Tie bag only to find that snack food companies weren't interested in buying it. They decided to make Smartfood to show the industry that the bag worked. The irony is that when Smartfood was launched in 1984, it was never sold in the Tug-N-Tie bag (Kahn 1988).

Innovation is one of the critical quests of many entrepreneurial leaders. While every generation claims that in its own time business competition reached unprecedented levels, today's entrepreneurial leaders face a unique set of challenges to predictably innovate and compete. The perfect storm has been created by globalization, economic and technological changes, and an increased emphasis on environmental and social impact. In almost all markets, this storm has caused product variety to dramatically increase, most product life cycles to shorten, and the number of competitors to substantially increase. As a consequence any competitive advantage that an organization might have today is short-lived and will likely need to be continually re-created. As such, an organization's ability to repeatedly and reliably generate new products and services is essential. To innovate is the best choice, and perhaps the only one, to ensure the growth of new organizations and the long-term survival of existing ones.

While innovation may be important, it is also very difficult. Recent surveys demonstrate that many executives rate their current innovation efforts as unsatisfactory. For example, a recent McKinsey study shows that more than 70 percent of participating executives indicate that innovation is among the top three drivers of their companies' growth, but only one-third of the executives are confident in their ability to actually stimulate innovation (Barsh, Capozzi, and Davidson 2008). Similarly, another recent study shows that only 55 percent of the surveyed company leaders are satisfied with their companies' financial returns on their innovation investments (Andrew et al. 2010).

The lack of innovation that these executives point to may connect to how we currently conceptualize innovation. In popular myth innovation is often portrayed as an idea occurring to a genius in a flash; as something that happens only to individuals with exceptional skills, genes, or luck; or as a product of circumstances that border on the mystical. In contrast to this myth, we believe that innovation is a method that can be learned, practiced, and improved; that involves multiple people; and that is predicated on passion and hard work.

Furthermore, as innovation work is done in an unknowable environment, it demands that an entrepreneurial leader engage a cognitively ambidextrous mindset in which one cycles between a creation approach of acting and a prediction approach of learning from the data that are created during the action. Innovation occurs as entrepreneurial leaders start small with the resources at hand and rapidly create prototypes to generate new data and new ideas. They are able to minimize risk by failing fast and cheaply, learning quickly, and rapidly changing directions when reality does not match assumptions. Using their cognitively ambidextrous mindset, entrepreneurial leaders experiment, succeed, fail, and learn.

The challenge is how to teach future entrepreneurial leaders to be cognitively ambidextrous in their method of innovation. Stemming from the aforementioned myths of innovation, some people suggest that individuals can't be taught to be innovative. By highlighting superstar innovators such as Steve Jobs of Apple, Bill Gates of Microsoft, and Mark Zuckerberg of Facebook—all of whom have incomplete formal educations—it is sometimes implied that formal education may be detrimental to developing innovative capacities. Not surprisingly, we don't follow this argument. Instead the challenge may be that too many formal education approaches teach students in traditional ways that rely on lecturing about the innovation process rather than *experiencing* it.

To develop entrepreneurial leaders, we as educators need to create learning experiences that are based on a context and enable leaders to practice the innovation method of the real world. We need to consider moving away from a pedagogy focused on lecturing about a prediction approach and pursue a pedagogy that enables students to *experience* both the prediction and creation approaches embedded in all innovation.

In this chapter we describe courses we have developed to teach entrepreneurial leaders to be cognitively ambidextrous in their approach to innovation. We provide examples from diverse contexts so that the reader can explore how these ideas can be taught to undergraduates or to experienced managers who are trying to build a culture of innovation and entrepreneurial leadership. Although these examples come from different realms of management education, they are similar in that they rely on an experientially based pedagogy to develop cognitive ambidexterity.

Defining Key Innovation Activities

Moset experts agree that despite differences in labeling, innovation projects tend to involve three broad sets of nonsequential activities:

- Recognizing an opportunity

- Creating alternative options

- Selecting and refining options

By focusing on these activities, one can recraft the teaching of innovation to apply the principles of both creation and prediction logics. In so doing entrepreneurial leaders are able to develop a more accurate frame of cognitive ambidexterity that is needed to test and shape innovative opportunities.

Recognizing an opportunity requires a serious effort to fully understand the problem for which a solution is sought, including the problem's context and the stakeholders' interests. It is important to note that the focus of this activity is on understanding the problem and not on creating the solution. The design community labels this approach as developing deep empathy for the user and other relevant stakeholders (Leonard and Rayport 1997).

Entrepreneurial leaders will need to rely on their passion and their discipline to explore the experience of users with an open mind, as they will likely travel down many winding paths to develop deep empathy.

As the Smartfood example shows, Meyer and Martin's passion propelled them to create their Tug-N-Tie bag; at the same time, their passion and open minds enabled them to be open to pursuing the Smartfood opportunity. In addition, developing this deep empathy requires individuals to engage in a co-creation process as the relevant stakeholders share their perspectives. Because empathy goes beyond factual knowledge, the best—and perhaps only—path to its success-ful development requires entrepreneurial leaders to directly encoun-ter and try out the experiences of their customers. In the Smartfood case, Meyer and Martin used their networks to consider diverse stake-holders' interests. It was out of one of these conversations that the ideas materialized to focus on the popcorn and not the bag. Through this co-creation process, entrepreneurial leaders learn to understand the problem from multiple perspectives, a key issue that is discussed in more detail later in this book.

The second key set of innovative activities is *creating alternative options*. This involves the iterative application of creation and predic-tion logics to arrive at a large number of potential solutions to increase the probability of finding a good one (Terwiesch and Ulrich 2009). Each idea generated is essentially an action that provides access to new ideas and new information that may have not been considered before. By learning from each idea, entrepreneurial leaders drive an iterative process that reveals new options. As this description suggests, innova-tive opportunities seldom arise through a prediction approach alone in which entrepreneurial leaders weigh the costs and the benefits of each option to select an optimal solution. Rather entrepreneurial leaders take action, learn from the action, and use this knowledge to guide the next choice. By cycling between creation logic and prediction logic, entrepreneurial leaders generate alternative solutions to a problem.

Meyer and Martin certainly used this approach as they developed the Smartfood product. After deciding to focus on Smartfood, they encountered numerous problems related to manufacturing and distribution. For example, an early manufacturing problem arose when the coating of each popcorn kernel with oil and cheese was inconsistent, which affected the taste (Kahn 1988). To solve this problem, these entrepreneurial leaders experimented with the manufacturing process. With each change they made, they learned from their action until they eventually arrived at a new, improved manufacturing process that yielded a more consistent cheese coating and taste. While technology played a supporting role, learning from experience was central to the solution (Kahn 1988).

The final set of activities of innovation involves *selecting and refining options.* This begins with generating information about the options. Prototyping—the early and rough testing of ideas and their feasibility—is a preferred way to generate this information. The goal of prototyping in early-stage development is not confirmation but exploration. In other words ideas are tested until they break so that one can learn about the ideas' potential and limits. Prototyping is essentially creating experiments, taking action, and learning from the action to guide future action. The results from early prototypes provide new information about both the problem itself and the various options in the associated solution space. Similar to empathy development, this learning is best fostered through active experimentation. Prototyping is the vehicle with which to test and assess the opportunities that the creation logic helped generate.

The three sets of activities that underlie innovation parallel the central elements of the creation approach of cognitive ambidexterity. As we've designed courses in innovation, we have strengthened our pedagogy for teaching entrepreneurial leaders to apply a creation approach to innovation. In the following section, we provide examples from both undergraduate and executive education courses to highlight how we help entrepreneurial leaders develop their capacity to engage in a creation approach to innovation.

Teaching a Creation Approach to Innovation

We have found that experiential learning, and the active engagement of the student in the learning experience, is the most-effective method for enabling students to connect creation logic and innovation. There are two major dimensions to consider in building experiential learning in innovation. First, the *team* assigned to any innovation learning activity is critical. Many modern technologies require participants with different multidisciplinary competencies. In addition to skill diversity, trust and psychological safety are essential if team members are to embrace open experimentation, including the possibility of failure (Edmondson and Nembhard 2009). Second, the choices of type, scope, and context of the learning project are important. The innovation *project* should stretch the team to explore unconsidered possibilities, but at the same time it should not represent an impossible goal. In line with an appropriate project scope choice, the project context should support the project and the team but not remove all constraints—which are sometimes the source of innovative ideas.

The following discussion highlights how we manage these aspects of experiential learning in our innovation courses.

Creation Logic in Undergraduate Product Design and Development Course

One of the novel ways that we introduce a creation orientation to innovation is in an interdisciplinary undergraduate course in Product

Design and Development. This one-semester course combines students and faculty across three different disciplines and three separate schools: business (Babson College), engineering (Olin College of Engineering), and industrial design (Rhode Island School of Design). Working in interdisciplinary teams, students experience the process of product development, from opportunity recognition to prototype construction to economic and environmental analyses of the proposed solution.

With action and experience as major learning modes of the course, teams work on semester-long projects, learning about users and markets, creating novel ideas, and developing and refining prototypes. The course unfolds as the faculty introduce tools and methods in brief lectures, in-class exercises and discussions, and studio-style work. Throughout the course, testing, experimentation, and learning from failure are experienced as key pieces of the product development cycle. Using $500 maximum seed money, past student project teams have developed a wide variety of innovative products, including new public water fountains, intelligent energy-saving power extension cords, innovative travel luggage, and solutions to prevent road accidents involving pedestrians and automobiles.

One of the ways we highlight a creation orientation to innovation is by teaching students to work within the team and with other stakeholders. The complexity of today's unknowable problems requires a multidisciplinary perspective. The impact on learning from working in multidisciplinary teams can be significant (Hey et al. 2007). At the same time, collaboration across disciplines can be difficult, as each participant has developed his or her own language, values, and incentives. The socialization of professional occupations is remarkably strong, even for students in institutions of higher learning (Ettlie 2002, 2007). Thus having students from different disciplines (such as business, engineering, and industrial design) working together on a project introduces them to the challenges of co-creating with stakeholders who have differing perspectives. The type of team composition is similar to the real-world innovation teams that students will experience when they graduate.

One of the interesting ways in which students experience the dynamics of collaboration when using a creation approach arises from how the teams assign tasks to different individuals. Some teams decide early on that team members will work on problems best suited to their skill sets. Other teams choose the opposite approach, where team members volunteer for tasks to develop a new skill. In the latter cases, students tend to teach and share their specialized knowledge, and overall these teams approach their projects more holistically. Although our data set is small, it appears that the latter approach leads to better project outcomes and higher levels of satisfaction among the team members. Students from teams in which peer-to-peer teaching was largely absent tended to voice disappointment in debriefing sessions about the unwillingness of some of their teammates to share their knowledge.

Such interdisciplinary teams enable students to learn about a number of elements of collaborative creation. First, course participants are alerted to the different approach to selecting team members when engaging a creation orientation to innovation. Rather than selecting team members for specific roles, members are chosen based on their knowledge and skill set; and if smart choices are made, roles will emerge out of these skill sets. By not committing individuals to particular roles, teams achieve greater knowledge cross-pollination, which supports a creation approach. Second, students come to understand the importance of treating all individuals as co-creators rather than as competitors, which is consistent with a creation orientation in innovation. Through this collaborative approach to creation, entrepreneurial leaders are able to more widely leverage others' knowledge and skills to guide action.

Encouraging collaborative creation and mutual teaching within teams is one of the major elements we are developing. We emphasize the importance of trust in building relationships. For example, the very first assignment we introduce is an exercise that has nothing to do with the project directly: students on the same team are assigned to learn about one another. We have found that this approach not only highlights the importance of interpersonal trust on teams but actually begins to build it. In addition, we have integrated a brief lecture and an associated exercise on team dynamics early in the course. We find it important to provide ongoing coaching to monitor the team's internal dynamics and to build students' understanding of partnerships. While this approach is resource intensive, it is worthwhile because it improves participants' learning of this central element of the creation approach.

With regard to project and team formation, a core theme is that passion helps inform the creation approach, although passion can emerge in different ways. For example, in our first year of teaching this course, we had each student submit 10 ideas to the teaching team and describe his or her best idea to the class in a one-minute presentation. We then used student preferences as the main factor to simultaneously select projects and assign students into teams. We were following the rationale that intrinsic motivation is a key element for effort, creativity, and ultimately high performance (Amabile 1997). In addition, we wanted students to feel some passion for their innovation so that we could explore the importance of passion to the creation approach.

We found, however, that students' preference patterns tended to differ by school association. To create multidisciplinary teams, fewer students got their preferred project choice. The constraint of creating multidisciplinary teams superseded our ability to connect each student with his or her passion. The following year we flipped the sequence of problem presentation and team formation; that is, we first created interdisciplinary teams and then had students identify and develop opportunities. Most teams developed substantial passion for their own project. With this method we were able to demonstrate how one student's passion, like most positive emotions, is contagious and can get others more engaged with a project. In addition, we can demonstrate to students how different levels of passion can affect the action taken. As such we too have learned from our action.

For the semester project, we engage participants in three sets of innovation activities—recognizing an opportunity, creating alternative options, and selecting and refining options—and ask them to practice prediction and creation logics throughout, thus developing their cognitive ambidexterity.

For example, in introducing the activities associated with recognizing an opportunity, we both enable students to learn from action and instruct them in the tools and the techniques they need to successfully navigate the product design and development process. The faculty might introduce user-oriented techniques such as ethnography, and the teams then redefine their paths based on what they find during their ethnographic research. Through the application of both creation and prediction logics, a team takes action, planning and generating its next steps. For instance, one team followed this process as they focused on water fountain construction. Through discussions with consumers on how they approach alternative water sources such as bottled water, as well as observational research, including video analysis, this team developed insights regarding water fountains. A substantial portion of their learning came through extensive interactions with key stakeholders. These stakeholders co-created the team's definition of the opportunity. As the team developed their deep understanding of how individuals used water fountains, they recognized the opportunities for improvements relative to existing water fountains, in terms of both functionality and appearance.

Creation logic orientation also occurs as participants create alternative options. In connecting creation logic to activities associated with generating options, we discuss extensively the importance of experimentation and learning from your actions. While we highlight that learning from failure is part of this, we find that true understanding comes only from experience.

For example, a team that focused on preventing road accidents involving pedestrians and automobiles was initially exploring ways to prevent pedestrians from stepping into traffic by installing barriers. Following creation logic, this team met with pedestrians, drivers, city planners, and police to examine the feasibility of their idea. They learned that barriers, even visually attractive ones, are not appropriate for many situations. When the team recognized the problems with their idea, they initially reacted to the experience as a failure. Through discussions and problem reframing, however, we helped the students understand the importance of experimenting and learning from their action. This learning, even about the problems of their initial idea, led to the subsequent design of a device that did not constrain pedestrians' movements but rather increased their awareness of potential danger from approaching vehicles.

In the third set of activities, selecting and refining options, we have found prototyping to be an ideal means of introducing the principles of creation logic. When prototyping, students often need to consider the range of skills and knowledge within their team and identify prototyping options that are feasible given the available skills and resources. This discussion highlights how different options are available based on the combination of individuals on each team.

For example, course participants often need access to workshops to build models and prototypes. Because most university workshops have strict rules limiting the use of the space and the machinery to their own students, and usually only to students who have extra training, different students may have access to different resources. This experience facilitates learning about heterogeneous access to resources, a common challenge for innovation teams. Course participants learn how to assemble the skills available to the team into something larger than the sum of its parts and to enlist key stakeholders to supplement the team's skills. In this way students learn the function of self- and social awareness—of *who I am* and *whom I know*—when employing creation logic.

Course participants also learn the Smartfood lesson of how action leads to solutions that could not be predicted in a class discussion. For example, during the process of building a functional water fountain prototype that allowed the team to vary water pressure, the team noticed that they could create a water arc that made refilling water bottles significantly easier. By experimenting and learning from their actions and being open to new possibilities, this team solved the more challenging problem of creating water fountains that can be used to refill water bottles as well as to provide sips of water.

In sum we view our Product Design and Development course—an experiential approach to teaching how to innovate—as an innovation project itself. Through this experiential course, participants develop their confidence with engaging creation and prediction logics. From the start (recognizing an opportunity) to the end (prototyping) participants learn about the value of taking action that is rooted in an understanding of who you are, whom you know and have access to, and the general context. Participants learn that action gives them access to new data and new stakeholders and that this information enables further refinement of actions to arrive at an innovative opportunity.

With its focus on developing entrepreneurial leaders' cognitive ambidexterity, this course is itself a prototype that we continue to experiment with to find better solutions to the various challenges. That said, the course has established itself as a successful, interdisciplinary method of developing entrepreneurial leaders' cognitive ambidexterity (Fixson 2009).

A Creation Orientation to Innovation in Executive Education

Today's Fortune 1000 executives and managers are very comfortable with and adept at managing complicated problems with a good deal of uncertainty. Using their business school training as well as their work experience, managers tend to approach the future through traditional strategic planning techniques—such as SWOT (strengths, weaknesses, opportunities, and threats), STEP (social, technological, economic, and political), and value chain analyses—that tap existing knowledge to take action. Executives approach the future by performing environmental scanning and analysis, followed by setting a strategy. Next they put in place a project plan to execute the strategy, using milestones, trend lines, and key performance indicators to allocate budgets. When performance does not meet projections, executives spend money and energy to get performance back to the trend line.

Innovation is often about dealing with "unknown unknowns," however, and existing knowledge can be grossly inadequate in such situations, leading to faulty predictions of the future. In unknowable contexts a firm has to learn through "experience," uncovering the salient variables through creation logic. Such experiential learning can take several forms.

As children we learn by imitating others and by playing and experimenting: *what will happen if I do this?* Most importantly, because children are not afraid to fail, they are able to acquire several skills much faster than adults, such as learning a language. On our way through adolescence, most of us stop playing to avoid embarrassment when failure occurs. In the workplace we instead imitate our leaders, peers, and competitors. Thus to teach entrepreneurial leaders to deal with unknown unknowns, we have to find a good substitute for childhood play. As managers and leaders, we learn when we have an unforgettable experience—a surprise success, an unexpected failure, a provocation, or a jolt to our day-to-day existence.

Yet applying creation logic to innovation projects within firms is only now becoming mainstream. In a recent Babson Executive Education survey sample of global executives, 51 percent said that experimentation is now their organization's preferred approach to understanding and acting on potential opportunity (Wilson and Desouza 2010). Although scientists and engineers have been much more comfortable with this logic and practice, most business majors, managers, and executives are either unaware of this approach or apprehensive about it. As discussed, the predominant focus of management training and the prevalence of yearly strategic planning exercises have marginalized creation logic, especially within large enterprises.

At Babson Executive Education, when we deliver innovation programs for firms, we deliberately teach a creation approach through the use of games, experiments, simulations, and action-learning projects. Some of the following innovative experiential pedagogies were developed by our colleagues at Babson:

- **TechMark.** In this simulation, developed by Robert Eng, participants face unexpected internal and market variables that affect the overall performance of an organization. The game is played in several rounds, requiring participants to reflect on their decisions and make changes dynamically.

- **Mount Everest.** This is a game in which participants learn to act with a limited amount of information while also managing new and unexpected variables appearing in the environment.

- **The Spaghetti Game.** Participant teams navigate high levels of uncertainty with either a creation or a prediction approach. Teams that pursue a creation approach, for instance through rapid prototyping, usually win; whereas those that pursue predictive planning for a longer period of time usually fail. The game illustrates how taking action before analysis (rapid prototyping) can uncover unknown obstacles and opportunities much faster.

■ **First Service.** This exercise helps participants test innovation decisions in business environments defined by high levels of service complexity.

These simulations and classroom games do involve some analysis and predictive logic. Yet the predominant focus is on the experiential process and action-based learning. The goals here are threefold:

■ To educate the executives about the existence of the creation logic concept

■ To expose them to the lingua franca—the concepts of tools—of creation logic and innovation

■ To get them to use creation logic in their own firm's innovation projects

A few key elements of these program designs are central to teaching executives how to engage cognitive ambidexterity.

First, executives usually participate in our innovation programs in teams. By design the teams tend to be hierarchy-neutral and skill-neutral, putting all members on a level playing field that may not exist in their regular work environment. Such parity introduces unseen dynamics within the team, including new forms of collaboration and decision-making, especially when teams compete against one another.

Second, by putting teams into unique and novel situations, we force them to break out of their traditional thinking patterns and be exposed to a different set of skills. As a consequence participants find themselves in unfamiliar situations, which jolts them into a state of alertness and openness to learning. In addition these simulations and games involve the task of uncovering hidden variables through experimentation, rapid prototyping, and making mistakes. Thus participants develop the key skills of being able to reflect on what, why, and how failures occur.

Third, most of the simulations and games are played in several rounds, creating opportunity to pause after each round for reflection on consequences of decisions and actions. Hence participants enter into subsequent rounds with new knowledge and new data to inform future actions.

Well-designed simulations and games—those that have unknown unknowns—help participants practice both creation and prediction logics in alternating fashion and identify and exploit innate and otherwise dormant entrepreneurial traits and leadership skills. The ultimate goal in our approach to executive education is to help entrepreneurial leaders more effectively lead innovation projects within their organizations. Hence we integrate real projects from the organization into our educational programs.

The most effective organizations apply these lessons to start several small projects with the resources they have on hand. They establish proof of concept via quick feedback loops between the voice of demand (customer) and the voice of supply (technology). They minimize risk by failing fast and cheaply and learning quickly. They acquire resources and assets to scale only when some success materializes or a proof of concept is established. This is creation logic in action.

Conclusion

This chapter shows how the opportunity for teaching entrepreneurial leaders to facilitate innovation lies in developing cognitive ambidexterity. Through employing both creation and prediction logics, entrepreneurial leaders have a greater ability to successfully lead the innovations that their organizations need to survive. Creation logic and prediction logic are intertwined approaches that shape opportunity through action that generates data, predictive analysis of the data, and further action.

In introducing cognitive ambidexterity in the context of innovation, faculty must rely on experiential methods in which students have the opportunity to engage in the innovation method. Through these types of exercises, they develop their own skills with using a cognitively ambidextrous approach.

References

Amabile, T. M. 1997. "Motivating Creativity in Organizations: On Doing What You Love and Loving What You Do." *California Management Review* 40 (1), 39–58.

Andrew, J. P., J. Manget, D. C. Michael, A. Taylor, and H. Zablit. 2010. *Innovation 2010: A Return to Prominence—and the Emergence of a New World Order.* Boston: Boston Consulting Group.

Barsh, J., M. M. Capozzi, and J. Davidson. 2008. "Leadership and Innovation." *McKinsey Quarterly* 1: 37–47.

Edmondson, A. C., and I. M. Nembhard. 2009. "Product Development and Learning in Project Teams: The Challenges Are the Benefits." *Journal of Product Innovation Management* 26 (2): 123–38.

Ettlie, J. E. 2002. "Research-Based Pedagogy for New Product Development: MBA's versus Engineers in Different Countries." *Journal of Product Innovation Management* 19 (1): 46–53.

Ettlie, J. E. 2007. "Empirical Generalization and the Role of Culture in New Product Development." *Journal of Product Innovation Management* 24 (2): 180–83.

Fixson, S. K. 2009. "Teaching Innovation through Interdisciplinary Courses and Programmes in Product Design and Development: An Analysis at Sixteen US Schools." *Creativity and Innovation Management* 18 (3): 199–208.

Hey, J., A. Van Pelt, A. Agogino, and S. Beckman. 2007. "Self-Reflection: Lessons Learned in a New Product Development Class." *Journal of Mechanical Design* 129 (7): 668–76.

Kahn, J. P. 1988. "The Snack Food That's Eating America: A Portrait of the Marketing Strategy, Research, and Development of Smartfood Popcorn." *Inc.*, Aug 1. http://www.inc.com/magazine/19880801/5918.html.

Leonard, D., and J. F. Rayport. 1997. "Sparking Innovation through Empathic Design." *Harvard Business Review*, November/December, 102–13.

Terwiesch, C., and K. T. Ulrich. 2009. *Innovation Tournaments: Creating and Selecting Exceptional Opportunities.* Boston: Harvard Business School.

Wilson, J. H. and K. Desouza. 2010. "Finally: A Majority of Executives Embrace Experimentation." HBR blogpost. http://blogs.hbr.org/research/2010/12/while-he-was-at-amazon.html.

CHAPTER **3**

Prediction Logic: Analytics for Entrepreneurial Thinking

Tom Davenport and Julian Lange

C *REATIVITY* AND *ACTION,* TWO CONCEPTS DETAILED IN THE FIRST two chapters, are more frequently associated with entrepreneurial leadership than are terms like *prediction, analytical,* and *quantitative.* As discussed in chapter 2, the popular myth assumes that entrepreneurs have a vision for a new product or service and are determined to carry it out despite any obstacles. The image of an intrepid entrepreneurial leader in a garage seldom includes printouts of regression models or chi square statistics.

Such myths do have some logical underpinnings. Analytical and data-based approaches were often not available to founders of startups. First, startups did not have the history of operations that is required to accumulate sufficient data for analysis. In addition, entrepreneurs in early-stage firms may have lacked the financial, technological, and human resources to perform extensive quantitative analyses. Analytical hardware and software and skilled people may well have been too expensive to acquire outside of large organizations. In the past analytics clearly weren't easy for small new firms to engage. These impressions have some support in academic research (see Sarasvathy 2001).

However, we argue that similar to the misconceptions about entrepreneurs discussed in the previous chapters, neither popular conceptions nor limited academic research is sufficient to conclude that analytical thinking has no place in entrepreneurial leadership. As implied by the focus on cognitive ambidexterity in chapter 1, the prediction approach suggests that analytical and quantitative practices should be in every entrepreneurial leader's toolkit and that entrepreneurial leaders should be confident in using them. In short we believe that prediction logic, analytics, causal logic, and the scientific method have strong roles in the creation of social and economic opportunity.

Numerous points support the growing importance of prediction logic to entrepreneurial leaders. First, many real-world leaders counter the popular stereotype of non-analytical entrepreneurial leaders. For example, a recent *New Yorker* article by Malcolm Gladwell (2010) argues that many entrepreneurs employ rigorous analysis to minimize the risk of their entrepreneurial ventures. In addition, many successful entrepreneurial leaders engage analytics as a core capability of their startups; these include Sergey Brin and Larry Page of Google, Jeff Bezos of Amazon.com, Michael Bloomberg of Bloomberg LP, and Reed Hastings of Netflix. Like many analytically oriented entrepreneurial leaders, these individuals see the potential in using analytics not only to differentiate their business models but also to create innovations for customers.

Second, there are many data-intensive industries, including financial services, retail, and online commerce, in which success would be difficult for any entrepreneurial leader unable to analyze data and make quantitatively based decisions. Finally, we believe that the barriers to the use of analytical tools by entrepreneurial leaders have decreased dramatically over the past several years. We discuss each of these factors in greater detail in this chapter.

These factors further support our perspective that entrepreneurial leaders in startups and smaller firms must use not only creation logic but also prediction logic as they pursue growth. And indeed many seem to be doing so already. For example, in a recent Babson

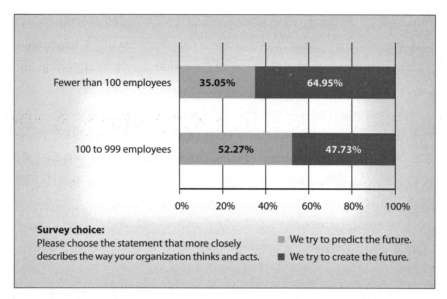

Exhibit 3.1   Predictive orientation versus creation orientation as related to firm size

Executive Education analysis of 622 companies, we found that more than 35 percent of small ventures (with fewer than 100 employees) have a predictive orientation. That percentage grows to more than 52 percent in firms with 100 to 999 employees, many of which are led by their founders (see exhibit 3.1).

The Logic of Analytics and Entrepreneurial Leadership

While not all analytical approaches are appropriate at all times for entrepreneurial leaders, there are some approaches that fit. For example, randomized testing, which we sometimes refer to as *reactive analytics* (to contrast with the *predictive* type), involves testing various ideas to see which work better in practice. This analytical approach involves rigorous statistical comparison of randomly assigned test and control groups. It is commonly used in testing the value of marketing promotions, changes to stores and branches, alternative web page designs, and a variety of other business improvements. Without the rigor involved in randomized testing, it is impossible to know whether an intervention actually produces the desired change or whether random variations are occurring.

These methods are particularly useful in conjunction with creation logic. After an entrepreneurial leader has taken action, he or she can employ these prediction-oriented techniques to evaluate actions and guide future decisions. This continuous cycle of doing and learning defines entrepreneurial leadership. Here's how Joshua Herzig-Marx, a recent MBA graduate and an entrepreneur of a data-oriented business, describes his approach:

> Testing and learning requires two things we determined early on. One is that it has to be easy enough that we can run a lot of tests. The second thing is that it has to be easy enough that you can learn quickly about what is working and what isn't. Testing and learning is really about the ability to turn dials quickly and create an ability to see what happened. We use a random control group for directional measurement. In everything we do, in every promotion we run, we try to design a hypothesis-driven test.

Entrepreneurial leaders need to consider when in the entrepreneurial life cycle is it most conducive to use analytics and when is it not. The earliest stages of product and service development—sometimes referred to as the "fuzzy front end" of the process—typically do not yield much data and are more appropriate for engaging creation logic. At this stage potential customers of new products may be of limited value in specifying what they need. As business conditions become more unknowable, entrepreneurial leaders may have to rely more on creation logic, expertise within their personal and professional networks, and small-scale testing to calibrate demand. Once action is taken and some data are gathered, a prediction approach based on employing analytics can be useful for assessing the action and using this new data to guide future actions.

For example, Alessi, a well-known Italian design studio, develops new product designs by first conceptualizing the product using creative and intuitive design logic and then testing it using an analytical approach. Alberto Alessi, the head of this family business, notes:

> We have a very helpful tool that we call, ironically, "the formula." It's a mathematical model that we use once we have a well-done prototype. Not the first or the second prototype, but from the third one on. The purpose of the formula is to understand what the reaction of our final customers could be toward this new product and what the product's life could be should we decide to start production (Capozzi and Simpson 2009).

The quantitative formula, which was derived from an analysis of 300 design projects at Alessi, assesses such factors as sensory appeal, ease of use by customers, function, and price. Alberto Alessi states that the formula is an excellent predictor of sales for familiar product categories but that it must be "tuned" for new categories.

Learning from Analytical Industries

In some industries entrepreneurial leaders are almost compelled to use analytics to make decisions. These industries tend to involve large numbers of consumers, large volumes of transactions, and hence large amounts of data. The only way to know customer preferences and behaviors, determine the success of new products, and monitor operations is to use and analyze data.

In financial services, for example, data are usually plentiful; and because money is generally an undifferentiated product, analytics is a good way to select assets, forecast values, and make automated and semi-automated decisions. Many recent financial entrepreneurial leaders established hedge funds in the past couple of decades because of the relative freedom from regulation and the potential outsized returns. Hedge funds often employ quantitative strategies for asset management and trading. For example, one of the most successful hedge funds ever, Paulson and Co. (founded by John Paulson), based many of its gains on an initial intuition that housing prices might decline, which would offer opportunities for shorting investment assets linked to housing prices and mortgage repayments. A quotation from a book about the firm and its activities describes the analytical approach:

> They crunched the numbers, tinkered with logarithms and logistic functions, and ran different scenarios, trying to figure out what would happen if housing prices stopped rising. Their findings seemed surprising: Even if prices just flatlined, homeowners would feel so much financial pressure that it would result in losses of 7 percent of the value of a typical pool of subprime mortgages. And if home prices fell 5 percent, it would lead to losses as high as 17 percent (Zuckerman 2010).

Other industries are similarly data-rich and analysis-intensive. For example, we recently surveyed analytical applications and trends in the retail industry (Davenport 2009). The results indicate 18 well-established trends in retail analytics, including analytical applications, organizational trends, and strategic initiatives. Some of the analytical applications include assortment optimization, customer-driven marketing, fraud detection, integrated forecasting, and localization. In addition, we found five more emerging analytical trends, such as real-time offers and video analytics. Given so many options, the greatest difficulty for analytics in retail is often deciding which capability to build first.

Although the most aggressive users of retail analytics are large chain retailers, it would be difficult for entrepreneurial leaders in this industry to compete without some level of prediction logic and analytical capability. Small emerging retailers have, for example, made effective use of loyalty cards and the data derived from them. Leveraging analytics and prediction logic also provides emerging firms with a way to help larger retailers and product vendors solve problems for which they previously had no data. For example, Joshua Herzig-Marx's company, Incentive Targeting, has used analytics to gather new and unusual data on retail grocery customers. Herzig-Marx's firm is able to provide clients and product vendors with data-driven answers to questions about customers and innovation:

> We get asked all the time, "What else do people who buy my product buy?" Or, "If a customer bought my product last month, how many of them are going to buy again next month?" Another sort of question companies ask about is whether they should extend a product category like "organic." For instance, a common type of question is "Are new parents who buy a lot of organic products more likely to respond to an offer for organic diapers?"

Online retailers and e-commerce sites have even more data available to them than do brick-and-mortar stores. Each visit to a website generates a large amount of data on the number of unique visitors, time spent on the site, click-throughs, and conversion rates. By leveraging prediction logic to analyze these data, entrepreneurial leaders can design their sites, test changes, and present customized offers to customers based on previous behavior. Through the use of these different types of analytics, entrepreneurial leaders can use prediction logic to analyze data and create opportunity.

Decreasing Barriers to Analytics for Entrepreneurial Leaders

Beyond the growing business value of analytics, the other advantage is that entrepreneurial leaders can more easily embrace analytical approaches as the barriers to their use steadily erode. Analytics used to require large information technology (IT) organizations, massive data warehouses full of proprietary transaction data, costly software and hardware, and expensive PhD analysts. Most, if not all, of these barriers, however, are now smaller or nonexistent.

Data, for example, are available from a variety of public sources (sometimes for free), and it's very easy to generate and capture online data no matter how small the organization or department. Analysis tools are also more readily available. Just as many students learn analytics in part through spreadsheets, the same technology sits on every entrepreneurial leader's computer. Microsoft Excel is still the most common analytical tool, and the latest version can handle more than a million rows of data while generating a variety of statistical and optimization analyses. For analyses of web data, the most common web analytics tool, Google Analytics, is free. More-powerful analytical software is increasingly available on a software-as-a-service basis, where you can buy software "by the drink" rather than acquire an entire package. Even developing one's own analytical tools is becoming cheaper with open-source software and rapid application prototyping approaches.

Analytical services are rarely free, but the options for acquiring them are proliferating and costs are declining. Individuals with MBAs can perform detailed analyses, and even those with PhDs in statistics are available on an outsourcing basis from low-cost India-based firms. There is no reason why entrepreneurial leaders cannot make use of analytics.

Teaching Entrepreneurial Leaders to Engage Analytics

Because cognitive ambidexterity requires entrepreneurial leaders to be proficient with both creation and prediction logics, we require all of our business programs to include substantial analytical coursework. In our degree programs, all students have required prediction logic courses and are able to take many other prediction logic elective courses. The pedagogy that underlies these courses helps students develop prediction logic and demonstrates the connection between the prediction and creation approaches.

At the most basic level, in introducing students to prediction logic we teach them a range of quantitative tools. We also teach students about the importance of in-context interpretation and communicating results. Students learn to select analytical tools and the implications these choices have for future action based on creation logic. In this way students learn how they can build from prediction logic and analytical understanding to communicate with and generate interest in others who may be involved in subsequent actions. For more-experienced students, particularly at the graduate level, our pedagogy regarding prediction logic is based on cross-functional integration. Analytical courses are taught as integrated modules with other business functions and skills. Students learn how analytics are fundamentally linked to the decisions they make as they pursue social and economic opportunity.

As discussed in chapter 2, we rely heavily on experiential learning to teach prediction logic. Experiential learning enables students to see and feel the impact that different analytical tools have on the actions they take and how gathering different data can lead to different outcomes. The following examples show how students are introduced to the use of analytics in courses that are focused on starting and growing companies, rather than in courses designed to teach the analytical tools themselves. In this way, through learning by doing, students observe firsthand the power of combining an analytical (prediction) approach and a creation approach to pursue opportunities.

Prediction Logic in a Venture Growth Strategies Program

One of our core entrepreneurship courses is Venture Growth Strategies. It is offered in two separate versions, one for undergraduates and one for MBA students; each section is appropriate to the skills and the needs of the student cohort. This course focuses on the opportunities and the challenges of managing growth in entrepreneurial settings, either in an individual company or as a part of a larger corporation. Growth is the ultimate resource constrainer, stretching all systems in a company to the limit and often beyond. Consequently, the course emphasizes management "at the limit" of what students may have already learned in other functional courses. Budding entrepreneurial leaders are introduced to a series of frameworks, analytical skills and techniques, and decision-making tools that they can use in growing entrepreneurial businesses.

To teach prediction logic, we rely on non-traditional, experiential learning methods as well as more-traditional case-based methods. Some classroom meetings include discussions of traditional cases and readings describing growth-related issues. Guest speakers, including entrepreneurial leaders in high-growth firms, provide additional perspective.

What makes the course different from more-traditional courses is that a central module revolves around a sophisticated international simulation exercise in which student teams build and grow virtual businesses and compete with one another in a high-growth environment. The teams start with a clean slate in planning their strategies, and, equally important, the simulation is extremely responsive to the different strategies undertaken by the participating teams. This provides students with a dynamic learning experience that reflects real-world conditions and outcomes.

During the simulation each student team is asked to manage the growth of a multiproduct company, with products ranging from a single, undifferentiated, imported product to a portfolio of highly differentiated products. Management decisions involve strategy, marketing, finance, production, technology, R&D, and other functional areas. The course thus provides students with an opportunity to apply functional skills they have learned in other courses to build a growing company in a highly competitive, rapidly changing environment.

A key learning component of the simulation is the use of analytics to support decision-making. The simulation software provides students with data on market share, pricing, profitability, fixed and variable costs, return on investment (ROI), and other important performance measures. Students use these data as a component of their decision-making and observe the results of their decisions. They are also able to purchase additional market research data on competitors' results. In this way students are introduced to the use of analytics in making and adjusting decisions and strategies over time.

Learning is further reinforced by having students prepare a term paper on a high-growth company facing a growth crisis. Students apply course concepts and tools learned in the simulation to the analysis of the growth crisis, the generation of alternative courses of action, and the selection and the justification of their recommendation for how the company should proceed.

The traditional cases in this course also illustrate the use of analytics by entrepreneurs who are building companies. As mentioned earlier, while some companies and industries lend themselves to the use of analytics, we believe that all companies can benefit from a prediction/analytical approach in conjunction with a creation approach. Two of the cases used in the Venture Growth Strategies course illustrate this principle: *Patio Rooms of America* (Bygrave 1999) and *Matt Coffin* (Bygrave 2006). These cases describe the distinctive methods used by two management degree recipients in building their companies, and in both cases analytics are a key component of success.

Patio Rooms of America illustrates MBA graduate John Esler's use of both prediction analytics and creation to build a new organization. The case outlines the process Esler follows in starting and growing a company that constructs patio room additions to existing houses in the New England area. *Patio Rooms* describes Esler's handling of a variety of issues facing the company, including marketing, sales, operations, finance, and planning. The particular applicability of the *Patio Rooms* case stems from its illustration of Esler's use of analytics in sales, marketing, and operations. Despite the fact that Esler's business is at a very early stage, he insists on the development and the use of metrics. He devises systems to collect and analyze data relating to lead generation, closing sales, pricing, capacity utilization, efficiency, cash flow, profitability, and employee performance. He continuously monitors the business's success factors and adjusts his strategy and tactics based on the actual results.

The *Matt Coffin* case describes the creation of a highly successful Internet-based business. The case traces serial entrepreneur Matt Coffin's journey from Babson's undergraduate program through a variety of entrepreneurial ventures to the ultimate creation of his company Lowermybills.com. The case illustrates the interaction among Coffin's engagement of creation logic, his desire to create social opportunity by helping people lower their monthly bills, and his use of analytics in areas ranging from website design to advertising placement to employee motivation.

A key lesson from the juxtaposition of the two cases is that the use of analytics can be a crucial component in the success of traditional bricks-and-mortar businesses that don't easily lend themselves to the collection and the analysis of data as well as in the success of Internet-based businesses, which generate large amounts of readily available real-time data.

Prediction Logic in an Entrepreneurship Track

A second example of an entrepreneurship course that uses experiential learning and analytics is the Entrepreneurship Intensity Track. This is an elective course for graduate students who intend to start an entrepreneurial endeavor directly after graduation. To apply for the course, students must have a complete business plan and must successfully navigate through two screenings. The first consists of interviews with entrepreneurship faculty members; the second entails a presentation that attracts an experienced mentor who is willing to work with the student throughout the semester. The class is structured such that participants spend the majority of their time in the field, meeting with potential customers, developing their network of individuals who will help create the opportunity, obtaining product prototypes, and building their entrepreneurial teams.

What is unique about this course is that at this stage of the entrepreneurial process, students are more likely to apply creation logic in their approach. The course focuses students' attention on the importance of engaging prediction logic even at this early stage of a startup venture. Students use analytics in varying degrees of sophistication, depending on the nature of the particular business. Some businesses such as Internet-based enterprises lend themselves more readily to analytics. The design of websites, the analysis of customer behaviors and reactions to alternative offerings related to pricing, product presentation, and, as mentioned earlier, the availability of reasonably priced (or even free) analytical tools—all make it easy for students to understand the use of analytics in their decision-making.

Increasingly, students are also recognizing the importance of analytics and prediction logic in more-traditional startup contexts. For example, Internet-based market survey tools make it possible for entrepreneurial leaders to obtain useful data to assess and guide intuitive hypotheses concerning customers and product offerings. The analysis of such data can guide their future actions and creation approach as they connect with customers to build a robust market entry strategy. Similar data can be obtained regarding supply-chain actors and other crucial elements in building a new venture. Perhaps the most important learning is seeing firsthand the interplay of creation and prediction logics though hypothesis formulation, conducting small-scale tests that allow for analysis of market feedback, and more-effective action.

Students are encouraged to develop and use two unique analytical tools: planning timelines and dashboard techniques. At the outset of the course, students create timelines that detail and prioritize the important milestones that they intend to achieve during the semester, leading to the establishment of their businesses. Additionally, instructors call upon all students to make individual dashboard presentations enumerating the metrics and the data that they have chosen to inform their decisions about midcourse corrections. Depending on the particular business, data may be more or less difficult to obtain. Nonetheless all course participants are aware of the necessity of choosing factors they must measure, determining how they will obtain the data, and anticipating how they will use the data to make decisions and adjust their strategies.

These courses and techniques represent a work in progress. They provide examples of some ways in which students can gain insight into how to combine prediction and creation approaches in the development and the implementation of entrepreneurial thought and action.

Conclusion

In this chapter we highlight the importance that analytics, a mode of prediction logic, plays as a complement to creation logic for entrepreneurial leaders of startup endeavors. For these leaders, building social networks for funding and expertise, building opportunities based on whom you know, and selective risk-taking—all affect the success of a new venture. As our entire society becomes more reliant on data and analysis, however, entrepreneurial leaders also need to do the same. Indeed it is difficult to imagine that an entrepreneurial leader could ultimately succeed in several data-intensive industries without an analytical orientation from the outset. Through a number of examples of prediction logic courses, we have illustrated how management educators can frame courses that enable entrepreneurial leaders to develop cognitive ambidexterity.

References

Bygrave, W. 1999. *Patio Rooms of America*. Babson Park, MA: Babson College Case Collection.

Bygrave, W. 2006. *Matt Coffin*. Babson Park, MA: Babson College Case Collection.

Capozzi, M. M., and J. Simpson. 2009. "Cultivating Innovation: An Interview with the CEO of a Leading Italian Design Firm." *McKinsey Quarterly*, February. http://www.mckinseyquarterly.com/Cultivating_innovation_an_interview_with_the_CEO_of_a_leading_Italian_design_firm_2299.

Davenport, T. H. 2009. *Realizing the Potential of Retail Analytics: Plenty of Food for Those with the Appetite*. Babson Park, MA: Babson Working Knowledge Research Center Report.

Gladwell, M. 2010. "The Sure Thing: How Entrepreneurs Really Succeed." *New Yorker*, January 18. http://www.newyorker.com/reporting/2010/01/18/100118fa_fact_gladwell.

Sarasvathy, S. D. 2001. "Causation and Effectuation: Toward a Theoretical Shift from Economic Inevitability to Entrepreneurial Contingency." *Academy of Management Review* 26 (2): 243–64.

Zuckerman, G. 2010. *The Greatest Trade Ever: The Behind-the-Scenes Story of How John Paulson Defied Wall Street and Made Financial History*. New York: Crown Business.

A New Worldview: Social, Environmental, and Economic Responsibility and Sustainability

CHAPTER 4

SEERS: Defining Social, Environmental, and Economic Responsibility and Sustainability

IN 2003 ROBERT CHATWANI, A MARKETING EXECUTIVE AT EBAY, was traveling to India with his family. As he visited open-air markets, he kept hearing from local craftspeople that they wanted to find ways to access more shoppers and bigger markets. With more buyers, these artisans could create more opportunity for themselves, their families, and their communities (Kiser 2010). When he returned home, Chatwani experimented with selling artisan products from India on eBay. He sourced $700 worth of Indian jewelry, which he then sold on eBay for $1,200. After his experiment Chatwani went to then-CEO Meg Whitman, eBay founder Pierre Omidyar, and other key players to secure their support to engage the eBay platform to help craftspeople in developing countries reach buyers in developed countries. With their cooperation, he started gathering data to understand the market and the opportunity.

Chatwani's big break came in 2005, when a mutual friend introduced him to Priya Haji, a social entrepreneur who had founded an organization called World of Good, which was bringing fair-trade and ethically sourced products to market (Kamenetz 2008). Chatwani and Haji created a strategic partnership between eBay and World of Good and launched the new business WorldofGood.com. Their passion, skilled relationship building, and cognitive ambidexterity helped them create what is now the world's largest multiseller marketplace for socially and environmentally responsible products (Kiser 2010).

In propelling eBay into this new social and economic opportunity, Chatwani was clearly using a different approach to decision-making. Using creation logic, he relied on his understanding of himself and his networks, in and outside of eBay, to create the opportunity. He also relied on an understanding of the context and of eBay's culture to support his efforts. Omidyar had built eBay on the principle that individuals throughout the world are connected by their fundamental desire to pursue opportunities and that those opportunities can be a force for good (Root 2009). While eBay had empowered millions of people to become entrepreneurs, it hadn't yet expanded the model to developing countries. Starting WorldofGood.com was simply an extension of eBay's culture and value proposition.

Using prediction logic, Chatwani also drew upon analytical tools to ascertain how to tailor eBay's core business to the needs of artisans and how to capitalize on the growing consumer market that was starting to align personal values with purchasing decisions (Kiser 2010). As Haji said, if fair trade was going to pull people out of poverty, it must connect with "Joe American, who does shop at Wal-Mart, who has never traveled internationally, but who is a thoughtful, kind person, and would like to think about things he buys differently" (Kamenetz 2008).

Underlying Chatwani's use of cognitive ambidexterity was his fundamentally different *rationale* for business based on his passion for the social, environmental, and economic opportunity of his endeavor. This passion drove him to convince eBay executives to support him and opened the door to the partnership with Haji. WorldofGood.com emerged from Chatwani and Haji's creativity, strong sense of social responsibility and human compassion, and fundamental belief that they could create a profitable business that would have a strong social impact.

In this chapter we begin the exploration of the fundamentally different worldview that is the basis for Chatwani's, as well as other entrepreneurial leaders', endeavors. This worldview is based on understanding and valuing social, environmental, and economic responsibility and sustainability.

The Mandate for SEERS

A decade ago organizations were asking whether they should consider social and environmental issues in conjunction with profitability. Today the discussion has shifted from a question of *whether* to a question of *how:* How can an organization consider social, environmental, and economic value creation? A recent study by Accenture shows that 96 percent of global CEOs believe that sustainability issues need to be fully integrated into their strategies and operations if their organizations are to be successful (Grayson 2010). While this shift in perspective may be partly driven by changes in worldview, it is also driven by pressures from external stakeholders, including the government, the media, and activist groups as well as investors, consumers, and employees.

Nike, for example, has been widely criticized for its many human rights violations. In 1996 Nike was decried when a *Life* magazine story showed a young Pakistani boy sewing a Nike soccer ball. The following year Nike was rebuked when it was revealed that workers in one of its Vietnamese contract factories were being exposed to toxic fumes that were 177 times the legal limit (Connor 2001). While Nike has made some efforts in social sustainability, it continues to be criticized for poor worker conditions. Yet, on the environmental front, Nike was ranked among *Newsweek*'s top 10 green companies in 2010 and was recognized for its programs to evaluate and improve the environmental footprint of its suppliers (Newsweek's Green Rankings 2010).

These two evaluations seem to be in stark contrast. How is it possible that Nike is a leader in environmental sustainability yet lags behind with management practices that are not socially responsible? Can this difference be attributed to the complexity of managing a network of suppliers around the world? Can it be attributed to the tensions that exist among social, environmental, and economic value creation? Whatever the reason, Nike has learned that public shaming and consumer perceptions of its social and environmental responsibilities can have a huge impact on its brand image and that it must creatively and responsibly manage both the environmental and the social footprint of its supply chain. Nike is learning that it must adopt a more systematic and holistic view of all SEERS components. As Nike's experience shows, a piecemeal approach can be a zero-sum game, generating as many negatives as positives.

Other organizations are responding to similar pressures as they change how they source materials. According to a survey of 188 procurement professionals, more than half of companies have policies on "greening" their supply chain, and companies are nearly unanimous in their belief that green supply chains will continue to grow (Allen 2010). Industrywide certification programs have been developed to ensure that suppliers maintain certain environmental and social standards. For example, ICTI Care Process (ICP), the toy industry's ethical manufacturing certification program, was developed in an effort to ensure safe and humane workplace environments for toy factory workers worldwide. Factories work with ICP to earn certification, and buyers sign on to source their materials only from certified factories. These programs encourage entrepreneurial leaders to think more broadly about their responsibilities for their supply chain.

Organizations are also changing their approach to SEERS in response to the changing cultural values of today's younger workforce. The Cone 2006 Millennial Cause Study indicated that 61 percent of millennials—individuals born between 1979 and 2001—feel personally responsible for making a difference in the world. These feelings of responsibility translate to how and where these young people want to engage their financial and human capital. For example, nine out of 10 millennials surveyed said they were likely or very likely to switch from one brand to another if the second brand was associated with a good cause. Eight out of 10 millennials want to work for a company that cares about its relationship with society and the environment, and half would refuse to work for an irresponsible corporation (Cone Millennial Cause Study 2006).

These changing attitudes of the millennial generation are also translating to changes among MBA students. The Aspen Institute found that MBA students are expressing increased interest in finding work that offers the potential to make a contribution to society (26 percent of respondents in 2007 compared with 15 percent in 2002) (Aspen Institute 2008). If entrepreneurial leaders want to tap in to the intellect and the spending power of this rising generation, they are going to need a SEERS worldview. Similarly, business schools need to better prepare students to lead organizations with this perspective.

To support organizations and encourage a SEERS worldview, in July 2000 the United Nations launched the UN Global Compact, which encourages businesses worldwide to adopt socially and environmentally responsible policies and to report on their implementation. As a leadership initiative endorsed by chief executives, it seeks to align business operations and strategies with 10 principles related to human rights, labor, the environment, and anti-corruption. Within the world of management education, these principles have been translated into the Principles for Responsible Management Education (PRME), as shown in the following sidebar.

The Principles for Responsible Management Education

As institutions of higher education involved in the development of current and future managers, we declare our willingness to progress in the implementation, within our institution, of the following principles, starting with those that are more relevant to our capacities and mission. We will report on progress to all our stakeholders and exchange effective practices related to these principles with other academic institutions.

Principle 1: Purpose. We will develop the capabilities of students to be future generators of sustainable value for business and society at large and to work for an inclusive and sustainable global economy.

Principle 2: Values. We will incorporate into our academic activities and curricula the values of global social responsibility as portrayed in international initiatives such as the United Nations Global Compact.

Principle 3: Method. We will create educational frameworks, materials, processes, and environments that enable effective learning experiences for responsible leadership.

Principle 4: Research. We will engage in conceptual and empirical research that advances our understanding about the role, dynamics, and impact of corporations in the creation of sustainable social, environmental, and economic value.

Principle 5: Partnership. We will interact with managers of business corporations to extend our knowledge of their challenges in meeting social and environmental responsibilities and to explore jointly effective approaches to meeting these challenges.

Principle 6: Dialogue. We will facilitate and support dialogue and debate among educators, students, business, government, consumers, media, civil society organizations, and other interested groups and stakeholders on critical issues related to global social responsibility and sustainability.

We understand that our own organizational practices should serve as an example of the values and the attitudes we convey to our students.

Source: *Principles for Responsible Management Education website. Retrieved March 21, 2011.* http://www.unprme.org/the-6-principles/index.php.

The Principles for Responsible Management Education were designed to provide guidance to management educators on developing curricula that are focused on social and environmental responsibility. While PRME has helped usher these concepts into management education, SEERS has not yet become embedded into management curricula. Business schools have been surprisingly slow to consider social and environmental responsibility and sustainability and the challenges and the opportunities this creates for managers. While there are almost 10,000 business schools worldwide, fewer than 350 have signed on to the UN PRME (Grayson 2010). Management educators may believe in the principles of social, environmental, and economic responsibility and sustainability, yet they are struggling with how to engage these ideas in their curricula and institutions.

The following section highlights the unique approach that we have taken across our curriculum to instill in all entrepreneurial leaders the importance of a SEERS worldview.

Rooting a SEERS Worldview in Entrepreneurial Leaders

To engage a SEERS worldview, entrepreneurial leaders must both understand and operationalize it in their decision-making. To help develop their SEERS worldview, we show entrepreneurial leaders how to think about SEERS in a way that avoids false dichotomies that arise when we discuss "social impacts" as opposed to "environmental impacts" as opposed to "economic impacts." To do this we explore some of the dichotomies that prevent a holistic viewpoint from developing. For example, we discuss the following issues:

- The distinction between shareholders and stakeholders

- The separation between business and society/community

■ The distinction between industrial resources and environmental resources

■ The interdependence between industrialized countries and developing countries

Through these discussions entrepreneurial leaders recognize the interdependencies among all these categories and the need to avoid such dichotomies to apply a holistic SEERS worldview.

As entrepreneurial leaders come to understand business and organizations with a SEERS worldview, they also need to explore how they can use this worldview in their actions and decision-making. There are interdependencies and mutual impacts among society, environment, and economics even when those impacts are not actually identified, quantified, or incorporated into our thinking and decision-making. To understand these impacts and to take actions embedded in the SEERS worldview, entrepreneurial leaders need to consider four elements: purpose, multiple stakeholders, metrics, and implementation.

Purpose

Entrepreneurial leaders use discussions of purpose by explicitly naming and critically examining the purpose of the issue, decision, or process under consideration in terms that are broad enough to include social, environmental, and economic impacts. This might mean asking whether a new pharmaceutical drug's only purpose is to increase the firm's bottom line or whether it also encompasses other purposes. If the drug offers a meaningful step forward in supporting health, a follow-up question could be about health for whom; HIV drugs, for example, have long been the focus of debates over cost and accessibility, particularly by individuals in poor counties. If the purpose discussion also includes ecological impacts, it will likely turn to questions about disposal of the drug or how it breaks down because some drug compounds eventually end up in lakes and rivers. If the conversation is framed in light of social entrepreneurship, the discussion may start with the question of a new drug's purpose and then consider regulatory implications, trade policy, intellectual property rights, and the drug's availability to those who need it most. In social entrepreneurship it is equally important to consider economic viability in conjunction with social and environmental responsibility and sustainability. These are deeply complicated issues, and each individual's values and disciplinary perspectives may influence how and which aspects are emphasized. Through these discussions of purpose, entrepreneurial leaders begin to understand how to look at social, environmental, and economic issues simultaneously rather than sequentially.

Expanding this discussion of purpose also enables entrepreneurial leaders to examine financial calculations without being constrained by them. While financial viability and sustainability remain central to any organizational decision, entrepreneurial leaders also recognize that this is but one of many types of input for decision-making. By considering the purpose in *both* societal and business terms, entrepreneurial leaders scrutinize the common assumption that maximizing shareholder wealth will maximize value for the society at large over time. By juxtaposing short-term economic impact against long-term and wider societal, environmental, and economic impacts, actions that are technically defensible from a narrowly constructed economic standpoint can be challenged. Focusing on purpose enables entrepreneurial leaders to consider different types of value creation as they explore social and economic opportunity.

Multiple Stakeholders

Consideration of purpose leads naturally to consideration of multiple stakeholders. As entrepreneurial leaders engage a deeper understanding of purpose, they consider the perspectives of, the impacts on, and the rights and responsibilities of multiple stakeholders. They also need to consider how to prioritize different stakeholders' responsibilities, rights, and power.

In some cases, the costs of a business strategy are borne by stakeholders who have little voice or power in the decisions. The costs of the collapse of Bear Stearns and Enron, for example, reverberated far outside the walls of the companies, and those costs could be discussed in relationship to economics, politics, and globalization. Considering multiple perspectives also forces entrepreneurial leaders to examine how the SEERS worldview may vary depending on the type of organization in which they are situated (for example, a multinational corporation, a family-run business, an NGO, or a nonprofit).

Metrics

Metrics, the third core element of SEERS, considers whether a discussion explicitly names and critically examines what is being measured and what is not being measured in the performance metrics applied to the opportunity under consideration. Do the metrics examine performance across different time frames—long term, midterm, as well as short term? Do they seek to measure so-called externalities—the impact of action outside the organization? In an increasingly interconnected world, one organization's externality is likely another organization's direct cost, raising questions of how, and by whom, they should count as liabilities and costs as well as who is responsible for what effects. Thus the role of metrics is central to how entrepreneurial leaders approach SEERS through the accounting and finance disciplines, which are discussed in chapters 6 and 7.

Implementation

The final element to acting from a SEERS worldview is implementation. Do we ask *how* to achieve a sustainable solution to a particular challenge or simply *whether* we can do so? By asking *whether,* we set up a situation in which the choice is either/or—whether or not to do something. Asking *how* unleashes creativity and demands cognitive ambidexterity.

To teach this approach to implementation, we can engage implementation-scripting cases from the Giving Voice to Values curriculum (see chapter 11 for details on this pedagogical approach). By teaching entrepreneurial leaders the content and the skills that make the SEERS worldview a genuine option, we instill in them the confidence that they can find truly creative SEERS-based options to what have historically been seen as zero-sum choices.

Designing Courses to Instill in Students a SEERS Worldview

There are two different approaches to helping budding entrepreneurial leaders develop a SEERS worldview. In some courses, case materials can be woven into existing courses to highlight the connection between the SEERS perspective and the course content. In the following sidebar we provide a brief description of the Maine Lobster Industry case to illustrate how this approach was taken in a strategy course. In other instances it is most appropriate to design an entire course around the SEERS worldview; the following section describes an innovative course that does just that.

The Maine Lobster Industry Case

In an unusual case on the Maine lobster industry designed for a strategy course, entrepreneurial leaders explore how to integrate concepts of cognitive ambidexterity and SEERS to respond to complex business problems (Rangan, Hariharan, and Wylie 2010). This is a two-part case in which the (A) case provides a historical perspective of the lobster industry and identifies the key stakeholders and the (B) case describes the crisis faced by the Maine lobster fishing industry from 2006 to 2009 in terms of low demand, low prices, and escalating costs, leading to severe survival pressures on lobster harvesters. The case series discusses the threats to the sustainability of lobsters, the livelihood of the communities of lobster harvesters, the resulting tensions that arose, and, in particular, how these tensions escalated into violent confrontations among harvesters in 2009.

Through class discussion participants are able to assess the *purpose* and the perspectives of the *stakeholders* (lobster harvesters, processors, environmentalists, and public policymakers) and to critique the ways that stakeholders have dealt with or, in some cases, taken advantage of the turmoil in the industry. *Metrics* are used to assess both environmental and economic impacts on the industry stakeholders.

Finally, the case discussion asks students to engage creation and prediction logics to put their SEERS worldview into *action*. The case discussion allows for a realistic assessment of the difficulties and the challenges of creating positive social and environmental change.

Solving Big Problems

Professor Gaurab Bhardwaj developed the Solving Big Problems course to help students define and solve "big problems" that cross business and society. Bhardwaj defines *big problems* as those that, if solved even partly, will transform industries, change the way we live, and greatly better people's lives. Engaging a strategic perspective, students first learn about identifying big problems and then developing strategies to address them. Students begin by focusing on discerning what matters to them, what they are passionate about, and how their skills and capabilities can enable them to address certain problems. Essentially, participants discover what *they* believe are the big problems and recognize that their choice of problems is based on their values and sense of purpose. Through a deeper understanding of themselves, their passions, and the world around them, participants are able to identify and take ownership of big problems.

As you might expect, there is no textbook that provides a framework for solving big problems. The material used in this innovative course includes websites, videos, articles, and books. The course starts by defining the nature of big problems, identifying their character-istics, explaining why they exist, and assessing why they have not been solved. Class participants study entrepreneurial leaders (Nelson Mandela and Norman Borlaug, for example) and organizations (such as the UN World Food Programme) that have solved big problems. Through analyses of such people and organizations, students identify why and how they were able to solve those problems. Similarly, they consider why good solutions are often not adopted.

For example, the class considers one of the leading causes of death of women and small children—inhaling smoke from open cook-ing fires in poorly ventilated homes, which according to the United Nations accounts for 1.9 million deaths per year. Although clean stoves have been developed at low cost and offered for free, widespread adop-tion has not occurred (Bunting 2010). Some issues of adoption may include how the stoves are distributed and the cultural and systematic barriers to adopting the new technology.

Guest speakers and site visits provide students with additional examples of how individuals and organizations have solved or are working on big problems. As the course progresses, participants come to understand and believe that they, as entrepreneurial leaders, can take action. Suddenly, the big problems do not seem quite so abstract or overwhelming.

Throughout the course Bhardwaj repeatedly comes back to a central strategy and SEERS question that critically names and exam-ines the purpose of the issues being discussed. He continually asks students to consider *For whom am I solving this problem?* He also asks participants how the solution affects multiple stakeholders: *Whose problems am I not addressing? What is the effect of the solution on other stakeholders?* and *How can we engage stakeholders in the solution?* It is critical to teach students to examine problems and solutions from a new angle—taking the focus away from oneself and shifting it to other stakeholders. Similar discussions arise regarding metrics as students consider the effects of the solution and how different measurements and definitions of success might affect the action taken.

The course, as noted in its title, focuses on discovering how solutions can be successfully implemented. Among the assignments are two written papers. The first is retrospective in nature and asks participants to consider a big problem that has been solved. The goal of this assignment is to have students use strategic analysis and predictive logic to learn how to solve big problems by analyzing past problems and their solutions. Participants must explain why the problem existed, evaluate the solution, and develop principles of strategic problem solving from the solution. Big problems that students have chosen to study include the GI Bill, the Manhattan Project, the development of penicillin, the abolition of slavery, and international climate agreements.

The second assignment is forward thinking and asks participants to discuss the problem that they think is most important today, why they think it is important, and whose problems they are addressing. Based on the strategic principles reviewed in class, students are asked to develop a solution that specifies who needs to be involved, what technologies or products can address the issues, and what cultural, political, or social issues they need to consider. Some of the problems students have addressed include how to reduce oil-based pollution, how to address gender inequality in Afghanistan, how to eradicate diseases such as malaria in developing countries, and how to alleviate food and water shortages. Developing solutions requires students to apply their SEERS worldview to guide their actions.

Through this course students learn to apply strategic problem solving to the complexity of today's social, environmental, and economic problems. As a result, they develop both their cognitive ambidexterity and a SEERS-based view of business. Through this learning students develop the confidence that they can make a difference. These skills are critical to preparing entrepreneurial leaders to create social and economic opportunity in response to the problems that face business and society jointly.

Conclusion

In a BSR/GlobeScan State of Sustainability Poll (2010), workers' rights, human rights, and climate change were identified as the most urgent priorities for businesses' sustainability efforts over the next year. These sustainability issues bring strategic, operational, regulatory, marketing, and financial challenges to all businesses. Entrepreneurial leaders must be aware of and responsive to the social, environmental, economic, and ethical factors that affect their core business strategies. Rather than seeing these issues as peripheral or nice to address, entrepreneurial leaders understand that business and society are fundamentally linked and that societal issues are business issues. By introducing students to SEERS—a new worldview—engaging them in an assessment of purpose, multiple perspectives, stakeholder power and influence, and performance metrics and teaching them to take action based on this view, we can better prepare entrepreneurial leaders to create social and economic opportunity.

References

Allen, C., ed. 2010. "Green Supply Chain Procurement Study Results." Accessed March 2, 2011, http://www.californiagreensolutions.com/cgi-bin/gt/tpl .h,content=791.

Aspen Institute Center for Business Education. 2008. "Where Will They Lead? MBA Student Attitudes about Business and Society." Accessed March 2, 2011, http://www.aspencbe.org/documents/ExecutiveSum maryMBAStudentAttitudesReport2008.pdf.

BSR/GlobeScan State of Sustainability Poll 2010. 2010. Accessed March 2, 2011, http://www.bsr.org/en/our-insights/report-view/bsr-globescan -state-of-sustainable-business-poll-2010.

Bunting, M. 2010. "How Hillary Clinton's Clean Stoves Will Help African Women." *Guardian.co.uk,* September 21. http://www.guardian.co.uk/commentisfree/cifamerica/2010/sep/21/hillary-clinton-clean-stove-initiative-africa.

Cone Millennial Cause Study. 2006. Accessed April 21, 2011, http://www.coneinc.com/stuff/contentmgr/files/0/b45715685e62ca5c6ceb3e5a09f25bba/files/2006_cone_millennial_cause_study_white_paper.pdf.

Connor, T. 2001. *Still Waiting for Nike to Do It.* San Francisco: Global Exchange. http://www.globalexchange.org/campaigns/sweatshops/nike/NikeReport.pdf.

Grayson, D. 2010. "Schools Ignore Sustainability Revolution." *Financial Times,* October 3. http://www.ft.com/cms/s/2/63cf95b0-cd5f-11df-ab20-00144feab49a.html#axzz18opztxny.

Kamenetz, A. 2008. eBay's Fair-Trade MarketPlace. *Fast Company,* October 1. http://www.fastcompany.com/magazine/129/trade-goods.html.

Kiser, C. 2010. "Leadership at eBay: Corporate Social Responsibility through Entrepreneurial Thought and Action." *Babson Insight.* Accessed March 2, 2011, http://execed.babson.edu/thought-leadership/leadership-at-ebay.aspx.

Newsweek's Green Rankings 2010. 2010. Accessed March 2, 2011, http://www.newsweek.Com/feature/2010/green-rankings.html.

Rangan, S., S. Hariharan, and D. Wylie. 2010. *Lobster (A) and Lobster (B): The Maine Lobstering Industry in 2006.* Babson Park, MA: Babson College Case Collection.

Root, J. 2009. "Meet Robert Chatwani, Founder of eBay's WorldofGood.com." *Planet Green,* September 3. http://planetgreen.discovery.com/work-connect/robert-chatwani-ebay-worldofgood.html.

CHAPTER **5**

Beyond Green: Encouraging Students to Create a Simultaneity of Positive SEERS Outcomes

Toni Lester and Vikki L. Rodgers

THE SLOW RESPONSE OF BRITISH PETROLEUM (BP) TO ADOPT A quick and comprehensive approach to the 2010 *Deepwater Horizon* oil rig explosion and spill (Isikoff and Hirsh 2010) reinforces the stereotype that business has little concern and competency to address major environmental challenges. Furthermore business schools have been slow to address ways in which education can be used for shaping the attitudes of future business leaders through socially and environmentally responsible curricula. These topics may be covered in one or two electives, but for the most part an across-the-curriculum approach to teaching these issues is rare. The *Princeton Review* didn't start ranking business schools based on their coverage of environmental issues until 1997 (Green Colleges 2010), and *Newsweek* didn't start its green business rankings until 2009 (McGinn 2009). No doubt this is because, beyond the activities of a few well-known programs and businesses, there was not much to report.

This dynamic is changing rapidly in response to an increased demand from a new generation of environmentally conscious students.* Today management faculty are exploring ways to engage in the kind of interdisciplinary approach to curriculum development that is needed to shape how future entrepreneurial leaders act in relation to this topic. Similarly, business leaders are beginning to measure the extent to which their activities have a negative and positive impact on the environment, and leadership conferences are placing environmental issues at the top of their agendas.

This chapter provides a historical context for the relationship between business and environmentalism and discusses how business schools, particularly our own, are tackling this issue. We also examine how co-curricular activities that inspire students to explore their own impact on the environment are used in conjunction with curricular changes.

The Historical Context for Business and Environmental Sustainability

When the first Earth Day celebrations took place in the United States more than 40 years ago, the business community often positioned itself in direct opposition to environmental concerns. President Ronald Reagan, perhaps the greatest champion for business and deregulation, was famous for dismissing the problem of global warming by stating that trees caused more carbon emissions than industrial pollution. He even appointed conservative attorney Ann Gorsuch Burford to head the Environmental Protection Agency, and she made it her

---

*For instance, the *Princeton Review* gives 703 colleges "Green Ratings" in the 2011 editions of its annual college guides. It says that in a recent survey of 12,000 college applicants and parents, "64 percent of respondents said they would value having information about a college's commitment to the environment. Within that cohort, 23 percent said such information would 'very much' impact their decision to apply to or attend a school."

mission to minimize the enforcement of environmental regulations (Shabecoff 1989).

In the ensuing years, the relationship between the business world and environmental protection groups remained fraught with conflict. One well-known megalawsuit brought by the victims of the *Exxon Valdez* oil spill typifies this. Exxon repeatedly resisted fulfilling its promise to make spill victims "whole," by engaging in a 20-year effort to reduce the $5 billion punitive award rendered against it down to $507 million. By the time of the final damage award ruling against Exxon, "more than 6,000 claimants had died without any closure, and untold numbers had reached the brink of bankruptcy" (Ott 2008).

Still it would be a gross exaggeration to categorize *all* for-profit leadership as anti-environment because many of the strongest advocates for the environment have come from the business world. Many companies have pushed for the adoption of market-based approaches, such as the current 20-year-old system that allows companies to trade pollution credits so that they can "cheaply reduce emissions at one plant, and not reduce pollution and perhaps even increase it at another plant, but overall across the country reduce emissions" (Mieszkowski 2004). While admittedly controversial because it still allows for the production of problematic pollution, this scheme has produced reductions in overall pollution levels nationwide. Similar approaches are used internationally to enable countries to reach their emissions targets by allowing them to "buy carbon credits from other nations, which either have no emissions targets . . . or have reduced their emissions below their agreed target" (Laurance 2007).

Today some companies are partnering with activists to create solutions to environmental problems. For example, Greenpeace historically staged high-profile actions to draw attention to corporate practices that harm the environment. In 2004, however, it began working with the electronics industry to help make supply chains greener, remove toxic chemicals, address climate change, and take responsibility for e-waste. "Through toxic chemical testing, exposure of illegal e-waste transfers, and promotion of greener alternatives, Greenpeace has catalyzed improvements to the environmental and health performance of companies like Apple, HP, Sony, Nokia, Philips, and others" (Herrera 2010). Similarly, McDonald's partnered with the Environmental Defense Fund in the 1990s to reduce the environmental impact of its packaging (Environmental Defense Fund 1999).

What Is Happening at Business Schools Today?

Environmental Leadership, a Component of Entrepreneurial Leadership

Both in and out of the classroom, business schools are demonstrating leadership around environmental sustainability issues. In so doing they are modeling for students how to manage these issues when they become entrepreneurial leaders. First, many schools have signed the American College and University Presidents' Climate Commitment (ACUPCC), "a high-visibility effort to address global climate disruption undertaken by a network of colleges and universities that have made institutional commitments to eliminate net greenhouse gas emissions from specified campus operations, and to promote the research and educational efforts of higher education to equip society to re-stabilize the earth's climate" (ACUPCC 2011). After Babson signed on to the ACUPCC in 2009, we reduced energy consumption by 6 percent in one year.

Second, some schools are demonstrating their SEERS perspective by encouraging students to create *personal* solutions to the kinds of environmental problems that the ACUPCC seeks to solve. For instance, our undergraduates can choose to live in a special-interest dormitory, called the Green Tower, where they can connect with others who share similar values, generate ideas about how to make the campus more environmentally sustainable, and brainstorm about the creation of earth-friendly entrepreneurial projects. One of the innovations that came from the Green Tower was a bike-share program to help reduce auto emissions on campus. The Green Tower also hosts a "dark dorm" competition to inspire other students to reduce their energy use in the dormitories.

In our graduate program, a student club hosts one of the largest annual conferences on green technology in the country—the Babson Energy and Environmental Conference. The conference exposes participants to "emerging business strategies, innovative companies, and clean technologies that are driving this sector forward" (Babson Energy 2010). Following creation logic, the club connected with the Green Tower and together they persuaded the college to install a wind turbine that contributes to the reduced use of nonrenewable energy sources on campus.

Finally, universities can partner with one of the new entrepreneurial ventures that have emerged to help colleges reduce their carbon footprints and mentor students in the process. One such venture, Greener U, has an Eco-Rep Program in which student representatives are chosen to be "environmental change agents" and are taught "practical skills in communication, social marketing, and green event planning." Student reps are encouraged to pick an issue that is important to them and develop a plan of action to educate their classmates about the issue, with the ultimate goal of convincing them to live in a more environmentally conscious manner (Babson Energy 2010). We have been working with Greener U since 2009, and the relationship has given rise to new environmental and economic opportunities that students are pursuing. Hopefully, these experiences will prepare students to follow in the footsteps of Jim Poss (see chapter 1) and find economic opportunity embedded in environmental issues.

Co-curricular activities provide students with opportunities to become part of the solution to environmental problems and to experiment with new ideas. Through co-curricular experiences around SEERS, students are able to employ both creation and prediction logics to explore and pursue social and environmental opportunities. Through action experiments in which they build new relationships and gather new data, students develop the skills to create social and economic opportunity.

Businesses can adopt similar programs by allowing employees to attend conferences, work with others who are passionate about environmental issues, and experiment with actions that will solve the environmental problems in their organizations. This approach mirrors the action experiments that Robert Chatwani took at eBay before launching WorldofGood.com (see chapter 4).

Programs in Environmental Sustainability

Business schools are adopting different approaches to building curricula that cover the relationship between environmental and economic responsibility and sustainability. Several schools are creating curricula that leverage the strengths of different disciplines and even different programs. For instance, the Yale School of Management offers a joint MBA/master's of environmental management in partnership with its School of Forestry and Environmental Studies (University of Wisconsin 2010). The University of New Hampshire launched a new EcoGastronomy double major that enables students to integrate "sustainable agriculture, hospitality management, and nutrition through a selection of courses relating to climate change science and policy, marine sciences, sustainable engineering, environmental sociology, as well as a sustainable living minor" (Green Honor Roll 2010).

Another innovative partnership between Babson College, the Olin College of Engineering, and Wellesley College launches in fall 2011. Called Innovation, Design, Entrepreneurship, Arts, and Sciences (IDEAS), this program will be undertaken "alongside any degree program. Students can choose among a common set of courses that will emphasize a liberal arts (science, social science, and humanities) understanding of environmental issues, the role of business and entrepreneurial leadership in solving environmental problems, and an appreciation of how the practice and process of engineering and design can contribute as well" (Babson, Wellesley, and Olin Colleges 2009). Introductory and capstone courses will help students integrate the themes and the issues that arise across disciplines and campuses to develop new and insightful ways of addressing some of the world's major environmental challenges.

These types of programs bring a diverse set of students together and provide a wide variety of courses of study, creating an understanding of multiple perspectives and deepening future entrepreneurial leaders' awareness of the complexity of solutions to environmental concerns.

Teaching the SEERS Worldview: Business School Curricula

At Babson, faculty are developing and delivering environmentally focused electives ranging from business courses, such as Financing Green Ventures and Marketing Green Products, to liberal arts and science courses, such as Economic Botany; Climate Change, Business, and Society; and Eco-tourism, Biodiversity, and Conservation Policy in Costa Rica. Aside from stand-alone electives such as these, faculty are also integrating materials about sustainability into core courses to encourage students to focus on what Babson president Leonard Schlesinger calls a "simultaneity of positive outcomes," meaning building profitable businesses that are responsive to the needs of the environment and of humanity (Schlesinger 2010).

It is critical that a cross-disciplinary approach to sustainability is taken so that future leaders will recognize multiple perspectives and roles related to environmental sustainability efforts. To provide more-concrete examples of how to focus on the environmental component of

SEERS, we describe a science course that is designed to teach business students the core concepts and applications of environmental science. We then provide details for a teaching case developed for a business law course on the regulatory and ethical climate for businesses. The course and the case that follow illustrate the cross-disciplinary contextual analysis that is needed to help entrepreneurial leaders cultivate a SEERS worldview.

A Course in Environmental Sustainability Designed Specifically for Business Students

To be effective and innovative business leaders, students must understand and appreciate the environmental issues facing our world today. With this in mind, we teach a course that exposes students to the scientific causes of environmental problems, the impacts of those problems on both natural ecosystems and society, and the role that businesses unavoidably and intricately play. Our course in Environmental Technology was originally developed and delivered in fall 2003 and has undergone significant revisions every year to incorporate the latest developments in new technologies.

The course provides a holistic approach to SEERS education. The goal is for students to gain a scientific understanding of why we need to consider environmental sustainability in all aspects of future economic development. We specifically designed this course to teach future corporate leaders how environmental problems influence business innovation and how to recognize the resulting entrepreneurial opportunities.

The course is split into three modules. The first covers the world's energy issues, focusing on fossil-fuel limits, pollution by-products, resulting climate change, renewable-energy options, and infrastructure restrictions. Many students are particularly interested in investing in or using renewable-energy forms, so we discuss the specific technology and the tradeoffs of various forms of "clean" power.

In the second module, we look at specific types of air, water, and solid-waste pollution, how this pollution is produced, what the impacts are for both human health and natural ecosystems, and how technology can be used to mitigate pollution. The third course module focuses on the over-exploitation of our limited resources, including water, soil, forests, and biodiversity.

Various case studies are used throughout the course to bring in specific examples of how businesses are involved in issues of environmental responsibility. Students are challenged to lead class discussions on relevant economic and ethical considerations.

One case study example that works well in this course is the Cape Wind Project, America's first offshore wind farm. Energy Management Inc. has recently been approved to build 130 wind turbines in Nantucket Sound to "produce up to 420 megawatts of clean and renewable energy" (eCape Inc. 2010). Although many see this project as a positive direction for sustainable energy initiatives, a number of groups, including the Alliance to Protect Nantucket Sound, oppose the installment of the turbines. Among the environmental reasons for opposition are noise pollution; threats to federally protected birds, seals, fish, turtles, and mammals; and even an increased possibility of oil spill incidents. Beyond just the environmental concerns, there are also potential economic losses, such as declines in property values, reduction in tourism, negative impacts on the local fishing industry, job losses, and increased energy costs (Alliance to Protect Nantucket Sound 2010).

This case is particularly interesting because it clearly demonstrates the complexity of environmental issues by showing not only environmental versus economic tradeoffs but also the differing interests of groups that all consider themselves to be "environmentally friendly."

During this course students are tasked with considering the impact of their own personal lives on the natural environment. One way they must consider this is by researching and writing a product impact statement for one simple product they use in their everyday lives. Plastic bottles, pens, paper, silverware, and printed silicone wristbands are just some examples of products that have been selected in the past. In doing this exercise, students research the environmental impacts involved in the manufacture, use, and breakdown of their chosen product. Many students are surprised to learn exactly how raw materials are obtained and how long it takes for various materials to decompose in landfills. This exercise along with the resulting class discussion encourages students to grasp the global impact of their own actions and consider alternative choices.

This course also has a semester-long capstone project that gives students the opportunity to be virtual entrepreneurs within the field of environmental technology. Working in small groups, students must invent and design a new environmental product or application that they believe is both scientifically feasible and commercially viable. They must then compile a written portfolio that includes details on the product design; the technology needed for the product to work; governmental regulations that may affect product production, use, or end-of-life disposal; target audiences; marketing slogans; cost predictions; timelines; and any ethical issues that may arise. In addition they must calculate the overall environmental impacts of their new product, both positive and negative. This project culminates in students pitching their new product ideas at an evening forum, where both professors and peers evaluate the potential of their unique products.

This capstone project allows students to see how environmental science, technology applications, ethical considerations, and business opportunities intersect to produce viable solutions to current environmental problems. We also see the effects of teaching students how to think as they engage creation logic to develop social and economic opportunity.

It is often assumed that business leaders must choose between environmental sustainability and profits, but this is far from true. In today's world, society's problems are business problems. Within this course we emphasize what has been recently reported in the *Harvard Business Review*: "becoming environment-friendly lowers costs because companies end up reducing the inputs they use. In addition, the process generates additional revenues from better products or enables companies to create new businesses" (Nidumolu, Prahalad, and Rangaswami 2009). Developing entrepreneurial leaders who understand the need for and the benefit of environmentally sustainable thinking and innovation is integral to society's future progress, especially during economically difficult times. The case study of Bisphenol A (BPA) in plastic baby bottles also drives home this point.

An Interdisciplinary Case Study of BPA in Baby Bottles

This case was first taught in a business law course on product liability issues and ethics. When the case was first introduced in 2009, there was still a debate in the scientific community about the negative effects of BPA on humans, and the regulatory climate was not yet fixed. The case thus offered an excellent opportunity to teach students how to cultivate entrepreneurial leadership in the face of uncertainty.

BPA makes plastic containers shatter and heat resistant (Hopp and Kurfirst 2008). Because BPA acts like the hormone estrogen, many scientists point out the risk to children three years old and younger who use baby bottles and sippy cups made with BPA because these critical years shape the hormonal life of children (BPA Plastic Baby Bottles 2009). Not surprisingly, parents of young children have expressed the most concern about BPA, especially in relation to one of the most popular baby bottles on the market—Dr. Browns, made by Handicraft. Handicraft's reaction was to dismiss consumers' concerns and downplay the risks of BPA. During class discussion, we consider the cost of this kind of business reaction relative to the possible investments in finding alternative materials for products.

Despite concerns raised by parents, and an independent panel of scientific advisers about BPA's health risks, the US Food and Drug Administration, the regulatory body charged with investigating and regulating such products, decided not to ban the manufacture of BPA for the uses described above (BPA Plastic Baby Bottles 2009). Without a federal law regulating bottle sales nationwide, consumers who believed that their children sustained health injuries because of BPA bottles use had to rely on negligence lawsuits to obtain some form of redress.

To win a negligence suit in most states, the claimant has to show the following:

- A harm occurred.

- There was a foreseeable risk that the harm would occur.

- The defendant's failure to prevent the risk caused the harm.

A company could defend against this claim by arguing that the risk was not foreseeable or that it took reasonable precautions to prevent it. One such claim against Handicraft was filed in the state of Ohio by a group of parents. They argued that BPA leeched into their children's drinks and that Handicraft was "aware of the risks of BPA but intentionally and negligently misrepresented their products as safe and intended for use by infants and children in their advertising, packaging, labeling and public statements" (Ohio Residents File Class Action 2008).

To understand the complexity of taking action around these issues, students use this information to prepare for a mock-trial debate in which they are asked to represent either the bottle seller or the parents in a similar lawsuit. Here are questions student teams must consider:

- Given the debate about BPA's health risks, could they successfully argue before a judge that the company had serious reason
  to foresee those risks when it sold the bottles to parents?

- Could other things have caused the children's illnesses, such as
  exposure to other toxins?

If the answer to these questions is no, most likely the company
would prevail in the suit.

The mock-trial assignment provides students with a useful analytical framework for thinking about how they as future entrepreneurial leaders could adopt interventions that both keep them out of
court and are responsive to customer needs. Some of the interventions
students have envisioned include having the company switch to glass
bottles and giving more-conspicuous warnings on the labels of bottles
made with BPA. All of these interventions could fulfill the "reasonable
precaution" requirement in negligence law and enable the organization to employ a SEERS worldview.

Law, as we teach it, is a floor, not a ceiling. We therefore also
encourage students to consider if creative *ethical* solutions can also
satisfy the open-ended legal context. We assign an article on ethics that
summarizes the views of various philosophers, such as John Rawls and
Immanuel Kant (Oppenheimer and Mercuro 2005, 308–47). Students
are asked to consider how Rawls's difference principle—which permits
a redistribution of goods held by well-off members of society to help
the worst-off members of society—might be used. Such analysis helps
students think about how to get Handicraft to shift its focus from its
bottom line to developing a safer baby bottle that would benefit (or
at least not harm) the infants using it. We also pay attention to Kant's
categorical imperative, a concept that encourages students to imagine
themselves as one of those affected by BPA.

To help students grasp this issue from other perspectives, we
encourage them to ask their friends and family about their awareness

of BPA's risks and, in particular, to get the views of mothers they know on the pros and cons of these kinds of bottles as well as the pros and cons of breastfeeding. Students learn that mothers report a variety of responses, including that they preferred plastic bottles because plastic is lighter than glass and thus easier to carry if you are going out with a child. With respect to breastfeeding, some of the mothers who worked outside the home opted not to breastfeed because they felt it was too cumbersome and that baby bottles afforded them more freedom. Moreover, not being able to breastfeed while at work was a concern. Quickly the discussion of environmental issues turns to social issues.

Indeed, borrowing from feminist theory and cultural studies, we introduce how contemporary activists are trying to "reposition breast-feeding as a valued part of women's reproductive rights and lives . . . [so that] "women's decisions to breastfeed . . . [do] not result in the loss of their economic security or any rights or privileges to which they are otherwise entitled" (Labbok, Smith, and Taylor 2008). By asking students to talk to mothers, we help them see the multidimensional nature of a SEERS worldview.

It is also important that students consider their own values and identity with their SEERS worldview, so part of the conversation focuses on their own personal preferences—to understand who they are and where they stand. We ask students to consider how they would want their own children to be fed. The majority of the class often decide that they personally would prefer not to use BPA baby bottles, which introduces the question of how they can transfer their personal values to business decision-making.

Finally, to connect the importance of creation logic and action, we ask students to develop business solutions to the concerns about BPA. Because entrepreneurial leadership can take the form of a new venture or occur inside an existing organization (Neyer, Neck, and Meeks 2000), students are encouraged to envision new entities or innovative changes in internal organizational policies that would speak to the legal, cultural, ethical, and environmental dimensions of the case. This approach also reflects the SEERS worldview, which avoids privileging economic value creation over social and environmental sustainability. Instead social and environmental sustainability become front and center when considering the various approaches for action.

The class developed a wide range of solutions. One team suggested that established organizations switch to a newly designed glass bottle with a plastic cover to reduce the risk of breakage. Another team suggested that there needed to be greater organizational leadership in existing workplaces to make them friendlier to new mothers by setting up private breast-pumping rooms and daycare for infants. Using a SEERS worldview, these teams created a social, environmental, and economic opportunity out of an unknowable and uncertain situation.

Conclusion

Environmental sustainability must be a key area of study in business schools today. This can be achieved using a number of different approaches. One popular option is for business schools to create specialty programs, such as IDEAS, devoted to SEERS topics. In addition, specific core courses can focus on environmental understanding and incorporate business applications. Our course in Environmental Technology is one example of how to do this successfully.

It is also important that schools show that environmental sustainability is relevant to *all* areas of study. Faculty can do this by incorporating examples similar to the case study on BPA, which looks at a particular business problem from a cross-disciplinary analytical perspective and guides students in developing critical and action-oriented thinking that produces safer, healthier, and more innovative and environmentally friendly products and organizational policies. By teaching environmental sustainability, business schools can help counter the negative impression left by companies like BP and Exxon and demonstrate that it is possible to create environmentally friendly and financially viable business and management models about which they can be proud.

Further, while this chapter shows how questions relating to environmental sustainability can be taught at the university level, most of these recommendations can be transferred to management development programs as well.

First, top leadership needs to model environmental stewardship by communicating throughout the organization that this critical issue is directly tied to overall business performance. Whether it is recycling programs, energy-efficient buildings, more fuel-efficient logistics, or new product design efforts, these programs enable entrepreneurial leaders to see the opportunities that are embedded in unknowable environmental problems.

Second, environmental sustainability must be built into everyone's job. In a campus environment, this means that students, faculty, and staff are given the opportunity to participate in a variety of programs designed to cultivate greater awareness about environmental issues and promote a creation-oriented approach to addressing them. In other organizations it may mean that all frontline and back-office employees, from the bottom to the top of the organization, are involved.

Third, similar to the university training described in the BPA case, corporate training can occur in management development programs, encouraging employees to attend sustainability conferences or to get involved in new partnerships with NGOs.

Finally, responsibility for the implementation of environmental sustainability should not be relegated to just one person or group in an organization; it needs to be built into the whole business model.

References

ACUPCC [American College and University Presidents' Climate Commitment] website. 2011. Accessed March 22, 2011, http://www.presidents climatecommitment.org/about/mission-history.

Alliance to Protect Nantucket Sound. 2010. Accessed March 2, 2011, http://www.saveoursound.org.

Babson Energy and Environmental Conference 2010. 2010. Accessed March 2, 2011, http://babsonenergy.com/?page_id=128.

Babson, Wellesley, and Olin Colleges Launch New Partnership [news release]. August 24, 2009. http://www3.babson.edu/newsroom/releases/babson olinwellesleypartnership.cfm.

"BPA Plastic Baby Bottles Banned in Chicago." 2009. *AboutLawsuits.com,* May 14. http://www.aboutlawsuits.com/bpa-plastic-baby-bottles-ban ned-in-chicago-3919.

eCape Inc. 2010. "Cape Wind: America's First Offshore Wind Farm on Nantucket Sound." Accessed March 2, 2011, http://capewind.org.

Environmental Defense Fund. 1999. "Better Packaging with McDonald's." Accessed March 2, 2011, http://business.edf.org/casestudies/better-pack aging-mcdonalds.

"Green Colleges." 2010. *Princeton Review.* Accessed March 2, 2011, http://www.princetonreview.com/green.aspx.

"Green Honor Roll." 2010. *Princeton Review.* Accessed March 2, 2011, http://www.princetonreview.com/green-honor-roll.aspx (last viewed on June 1, 2010).

Herrera, T. 2010. "How NGO Partnerships Have Changed over 20 Earth Days." *GreenBiz.com,* April 22. http://www.greenbiz.com/blog/2010/04/22/how-ngo-partnerships-changed-over-20-earth-days?page=0%2C1.

Hopp, A. G., and L. S. Kurfirst. 2008. "Plastic Additive Bisphenol-A: Product Liability Class Actions on the Rise." *Client Bulletin,* May 15. http://www.wildman.com/bulletin/05152008.

Isikoff, M., and M. Hirsh. 2010. "Slick Operator: How British Oil Giant BP Used All the Political Muscle Money Can Buy to Fend Off Regulators and Influence Investigations into Corporate Neglect." *Newsweek,* May 7. http://www.newsweek.com/2010/05/07/slick-operator.html.

Labbok, M. H., P. H. Smith, and E. C. Taylor. 2008. "Breastfeeding and Feminism: A Focus on Reproductive Health, Rights and Justice."

International Breast Feeding Journal 3 (8). http://www.international breastfeedingjournal.com/content/3/1/8.

Laurance, W. F. 2007. "A New Initiative to Use Carbon Trading for Tropical Forest Conservation." *Biotropica* 39 (1): 20–24. http://www.global canopy.org/themedia/NewCarbonTrading.pdf.

McGinn, D. 2009. "The Greenest Big Companies in America." *Newsweek,* September 21. http://www.newsweek.com/2009/09/20/the-greenest -big-companies-in-america.html.

Mieszkowski, K. 2004. A-pillaging We Will Go." *Salon.com,* June 30. http:// www.salon.com/technology/feature/2004/06/30/bush_vs_the_envi ronment/index.html.

Neyer, G. D., H. M. Neck, and M. E. Meeks. 2000. "The Entrepreneurship: Strategic Management Interface," in *Strategic Entrepreneurship: Creating a Mindset,* ed. M. Hitt and R. D. Ireland. Oxford: Blackwell Press.

Nidumolu, R., C. K. Prahalad, and M. R. Rangaswami. 2009. "Why Sustainability Is Now the Key Driver of Innovation." *Harvard Business Review* 87 (9), 56–64. http://hbr.org/2009/09/why-sustainability-is -now-the-key-driver-of-innovation/es.

"Ohio Residents File Class Action Complaint against Makers of Baby Bottles with BPA." 2008. *InsureReinsure.com,* July 29. http://www.insure reinsure.com/BlogHome.aspx?entry=844.

Oppenheimer, M., and N. Mercuro. 2005. "Efficient but Not Equitable: The Problem with Using the Law and Economics Paradigm to Interpret Sexual Harassment in the Workplace," in *Law and Economics: Alternative Approaches to Legal and Regulatory Issues,* ed. M. Oppenheimer and N. Mercuro. Armonk, NY: M. E. Sharpe.

Ott, R. 2008. *Not One Drop: Betrayal and Courage in the Wake of the Exxon Valdez Oil Spill.* White River Junction, VT: Chelsea Green.

Schlesinger, L. 2010. Presidential strategy document. Accessed March 2, 2011, http://president.babson.edu/strategy.aspx.

Shabecoff, P. 1989. "Reagan and the Environment: To Many, a Stalemate." *New York Times,* January 2. http://www.nytimes.com/1989/01/02/us/reagan -and-environment-to-many-a-stalemate.html.

The Princeton Review Gives 703 Colleges Green Ratings in New 2011 Editions of Its Annual College Guides and Website Profiles of Schools [news release]. August 2, 2010. http://www.princetonreview.com/green/press-release.aspx.

University of Wisconsin School of Business. 2010. "MBA Programs with a Sustainability Focus." Accessed March 2, 2011, http://www.bus.wisc.edu/sustainability/resources/universityprograms.

CHAPTER **6**

Sustainability Metrics: Has the Time Arrived for Accountants to Embrace SEERS Reporting?

Janice Bell, Virginia Soybel, and Robert Turner

I N THE 1990S, WHEN MANAGERS AT HEWLETT-PACKARD (HP) recognized that the soldering lead used in the company's manufacturing process was toxic, they voluntarily initiated R&D projects to develop nontoxic, non-tarnishing, non-oxidizing alternatives. In 2006, when the European Union passed the Restriction of Hazardous Substances Directive, HP was in compliance; this earned goodwill from regulators that resulted in a voice in future regulation of the industry, and it opened European markets for new services from HP (Nidumolu, Prahalad, Rangaswami 2009).

Here's another real-world example: In 2004 Costco Wholesale beat Wall Street's expectations, posting a 25 percent profit and 14 percent sales growth. The market responded with a 4 percent decline in Costco's stock price because analysts were concerned about Costco's strategy of paying high wages relative to its competitor, Wal-Mart. Costco paid its workers well and achieved lower employee turnover, higher sales per square foot, and lower wages per dollar of sales than Wal-Mart did, yet Wall Street didn't appreciate Costco's human resource strategy and failed to reward it for its socially and economically responsible approach to employee compensation (Holmes and Zellner 2004).

In chapters 4 and 5 we introduced SEERS and the importance of developing entrepreneurial leaders who have a distinct worldview that connects social, environmental, and economic responsibility and sustainability. Whereas those chapters centered on the social and environmental aspects of a SEERS worldview, this and the following chapter focus on the economic aspect of SEERS and the need to combine social and environmental data with financial data regarding economic performance.

The two real-world examples at the start of this chapter highlight the complexity that arises when organizations and entrepreneurial leaders manage in a way that integrates social, environmental, and economic value creation. Why did these companies, both of which embarked on voluntary social and environmental activities, experience different reactions to their laudable efforts? It is because the links among these three components are not always direct. Social and environmental sustainability may yield economic sustainability, but there is no straight line connecting social and environmental efforts to cost savings, higher profitability, or favorable stock market responses, as the Costco story illustrates. Entrepreneurial leaders need to understand the tensions and the synergies among the three principles of SEERS. Furthermore they need to understand how to marshal internal and external accounting practices to support their SEERS perspective.

This chapter explores the issue of engaging accounting methods and reports to develop a comprehensive SEERS perspective. We discuss the importance of accounting standards to the development of SEERS and explore some challenges and opportunities in developing these standards. We then introduce unique ways in which we can educate future entrepreneurial leaders to engage accounting standards to support a SEERS worldview.

The Demand for SEERS Information

Stakeholder Demand (External Users)

Many individuals in their various roles as consumers, employees, investors, community advocates, or voters have demanded that organizations attend to social and environmental issues similar to those HP and Costco addressed. These stakeholders want to welcome to their community, buy products from, and work for or invest in organizations that are socially and environmentally responsible. They also want such organizations to be economically viable. As a result, these stakeholders must rely on information from annual reports, rating agencies, news releases, magazine articles, websites, blogs, and corporate social reports to gain information about an organization's SEERS performance. For example, Johnson and Johnson started voluntary reporting of its sustainability efforts in 1993 as a result of information requested by customers, employees, the community, and shareholders (Borkowski, Welsh, and Wentzel 2010).

Organizational Demand (Internal Users)

Most organizations have a long history of attending to economic performance; for many of them, however, attending to broader issues of sustainability is still in its infancy. The Institute of Management Accountants noted that "while some organizations . . . are leading the way, many are either ignoring the issues, have not yet made a start, or are trying to figure out what to do, how to do it, and how to take action in a way that adds value" (Institute of Management 2008).

To embed social and environmental considerations into organizational decisions regarding international expansion, product and process design, marketing approach, and investments, relevant social and environmental metrics must exist. These metrics must be systematically collected and easily accessed so that they can be considered with traditional economic information in internal decision-making.

Sodexo is a multinational company in the food service and facilities management industry that has committed to embedding social and environmental issues into internal decision-making around product offerings, materials sourcing, and logistics. Although the company has spent almost two years developing metrics and training line personnel about sustainability best practices, it has not yet developed a system that routinely reports sustainability data to inform decision-making, nor has it linked sustainability metrics to the formal incentive system. It is safe to say that in spite of making real progress, Sodexo has yet to imbed sustainability issues deeply into its decision-making processes; decisions are still made primarily on economic considerations (Bell, Erzurumlu, and Fowler, forthcoming).

SEERS Reporting Requirements

To communicate the importance of and their commitment to social and environmental issues, many companies publish stand-alone reports, collectively referred to as *corporate social responsibility* reports (CSR). CSR reports are now required in Australia, Canada, South Africa, the United Kingdom, and parts of Europe. And though not required in the United States, they have gained wider acceptance and are issued by many US-based multinational organizations.

CSR reports are intended to provide information on an entity's environmental, social, and economic performance and its initiatives for improving performance in these three areas. Because of these requirements surrounding CSR reporting beyond North America, the reports tend to be more comprehensive than those of Canadian and US companies. These reports include sustainability objectives (as well as measures of performance against those objectives), stakeholder discussions, and a process for determining materiality and assurance (Craib and PricewaterhouseCoopers 2010).

Metrics and verbal descriptions of social and environmental impact are found in diverse sources, including articles, news releases, blogs, corporate websites, CSR special reports, and rankings and ratings by NGOs. Because such descriptions and metrics are rarely comprehensively available in traditional financial reports, external stakeholders who are inclined to consider social and environmental performance as well as financial performance must search multiple sources to locate and analyze pertinent information.

For example, an investor interested in Exxon's donations to groups that deny climate change would find this information in newspapers, websites, and blogs (Piltz 2007); information about Exxon's failure to disclose strategies to provide diversified clean energy sources would be discovered through journal articles (Haldis 2009); while information about worldwide environmental expenditures, greenhouse gas emissions, and efforts to improve communities in which they are located is in the company's corporate citizenship reports. Combining this information with financial statements and related footnote disclosures places a heavy information-processing burden on decision-makers that may inhibit them from making informed decisions. Thus, while many people may want to develop a SEERS worldview, they often do not have available or credible information with which to analyze sustainability decisions.

Even when we consider nonprofit organizations that are focused on environmental and social issues, it is difficult to assess their contributions due to a lack of consistent outcome measures. If a SEERS-based decision-making worldview is to emerge, users must have established, recognized metrics and data in a single report to support their endeavors (Eccles and Krzus 2010). Availability of recognized metrics also enables entrepreneurial leaders to more systematically direct the internal organization to engage a SEERS approach and to articulate to external stakeholders the advantages of this approach.

Voluntary Reporting on Corporate Social Responsibility

Research shows that there are two primary reasons why organizations voluntarily provide information about their social and environmental performance to external stakeholders and attempt to use such information in their internal operations: ethics and economics (Borkowski, Welsh, and Wentzel 2010).

Some leaders feel strongly that it is their ethical duty to be socially and environmentally responsible in how they run their organizations. For them it is simply the right thing to do. They feel the need to be transparent with external stakeholders and to share information on actions and outcomes. Other organizations feel that attending to social and environmental issues will lead to a better corporate reputation that will ultimately lead to higher shareholder value. These organizations expect higher sales, lower costs, reduced risk of negative campaigns, lower cost of capital, and better stock performance. These leaders believe that voluntary sustainability disclosures provide useful information to investors making investment decisions. The economic reason for reporting has research support, with stronger results observed for countries in which stakeholders matter more than shareholders (Dhaliwal, Radhakrishnan, and Tsang 2010).

Five Problems with Voluntarily Supplied SEERS Data

Lack of agreed-upon metrics   Despite a voluntary, widely applied corporate sustainability framework—the Global Reporting Initiative (2006)—social and environmental metrics that integrate with existing corporate initiatives, cut across industry settings, and contain leading indicators for the specific company are nonexistent (Searcy 2009). In lieu of standard metrics, organizations offer multiple metrics or simply use verbal descriptions of social and environmental activities, which are often confusing and difficult to decipher. Within an organization the metrics reported may change over time as external forces influence content. For example, Johnson and Johnson started reporting new metrics because they were either being reported by competitors or being requested by the Dow Jones Sustainability Index, even though Johnson and Johnson felt that they were not important for its operations (Borkowski, Welsh, and Wentzel 2010).

Lack of systems to routinely collect and validate data   While many reports follow the guidelines of the Global Reporting Initiative, typically the data that form the basis of these reports are collected haphazardly without the benefit of a corporate sustainability performance system (Bell, Erzurumlu, and Fowler, forthcoming; Borkowski, Welsh, and Wentzel 2010; Searcy 2009). Further research has shown that CSR reports contained image-enhancing information, had weak stakeholder engagement, and lacked a systematic and robust data collection process (Adams 2002, 2008). Most importantly, many of these reports failed to include independent assurance on the data reported (Mock, Strohm, and Swartz 2007). Without a means to ensure the credibility of such reports, they can be nothing more than marketing pieces for the company, in essence a "greenwash."*

Lack of focus on economic sustainability of NGO and nonprofit organizations   While NGO and nonprofit sustainability reporting may include data on economic performance, contrary to the belief of many users these reports do not focus on whether the entity will exist in the future. Instead the focus of the economic performance data is on the economic impact that the organization has on specific groups or society as a whole. This difference is most important to those who rely on NGOs and nonprofits to continue to provide services. Companies

---

*Websites such as EthicalShopping.com, Inhabitat.com, and TreeHugger .com list companies, products, and claims that they consider greenwash.

can have important missions and perform well on them but not be able to continue due to the lack of a proper business model.

Consider, for example, the case of Seedco's Community Childcare Assistance program, started in 2000 and closed in 2004 (Seedco Policy Center 2007). Seedco, a national nonprofit organization, outlined on its website its mission and economic impact on specific groups in society. Yet its Community Childcare Assistance program, designed to provide on-demand childcare for participants in welfare-to-work programs, suffered a major economic failure when revenues fell short of costs, despite having a positive economic impact on the participants and their employers.

To continue providing social or environmental benefits, an NGO or nonprofit must be economically viable. This is why SEERS is based on social, environmental, and economic responsibility and sustainability: the three components must be interconnected if an organization is going to survive and thrive.

Lack of integration into decision-making routines and performance management systems   SEERS reporting and leadership are not much more accurate inside the organization, in part because sustainability metrics are either nonexistent or, when they do exist, the metrics are complex, difficult to locate, and often suspect. Entrepreneurial leaders who engage a SEERS worldview often discover that sustainability metrics and verbal descriptions of corporate citizenship are not included in performance measurement and management systems. As a result, employees rarely use sustainability information in routine decision-making.

Consider the Flügger Group, one of Scandinavia's leading manufacturers and sellers of paint and home décor. In the 1990s despite management's belief that the company was taking environmental issues seriously, the company leaked organic solvents into the Soran River and was criticized by the media for irresponsible behavior.

In response management decided to extend the performance management system for quality to include external dimensions of the environment. As a result, the company went from 628 adverse environmental events between 1995 and 1999 to none at all from 2000 to 2004 (Sebhatu 2008).

Lack of integration with formal incentive systems Because most organizations and individuals operate based on the principles of "you get what you measure" and "you cannot control what you do not measure," sustainability metrics and goals must be available, clearly stated, tracked, and evaluated if entrepreneurial leaders are to build organizations that are focused on SEERS. Metrics, both at the organizational level and at other levels of the organization, must be developed, measured on an ongoing basis, and used in the assessment and the evaluation of responsible parties and tied to their incentive system. Without established metrics it is difficult to focus the various divisions, departments, and individuals within the organization on responsibility and sustainability.

The Role of the Accounting Profession in SEERS

Traditionally, society (investors, creditors, unions, government agencies, and other stakeholders) relied on external accounting reports to provide financial information about profit-seeking organizations' return to investors and lenders and their stewardship of entrusted assets. External financial statements are considered key to the existence of financial markets, as they help ensure that capital flows to the most efficient and effective firms (Financial Accounting Standards Board 2010; International Financial Reporting Standards 2010). Nonprofits and NGOs, which pursue a social mission through their operations, also rely on traditional financial statements to discharge their fiduciary responsibilities to stakeholders.

With the push for greater corporate accountability, many external organizations are asking for sustainability data to be included in a single report, preferably with audited financial statements included in the annual report (Eccles and Krzus 2010). Some organizations have begun experimenting with "full-cost accounting" and "triple-bottom-line reporting."

When sustainability data are included in accounting documents, external auditors are responsible for their evaluation if the data conflict with knowledge they have gained during the audit process. The use of external auditors is presumed to lend some credibility to the sustainability data and their collection, although often external auditors do not have the technical expertise to do so.

In response to the push for sustainability, some external groups are developing metrics and certification methods (such as Leadership in Energy and Environmental Design [LEED], organic food standards, B corporations, and the Dow Jones Sustainability Indices) that are applied to companies in an industry or across industries. Unfortunately, the verification of these metrics is usually limited to a review of the data-gathering method and does not extend to the content of the specific metrics reported. There are obviously numerous challenges and inconsistencies with engaging in triple-bottom-line reporting.

Why Is the Accounting Profession Hesitant to Engage a SEERS Approach?

The accounting profession's conceptual framework establishes *decision usefulness* as the central criterion for accounting information. To have decision usefulness, data are to be both *relevant* (providing timely predictive or feedback value) and *reliable* (meaning the information can be verified, has representational faithfulness to what it purports to measure, and is neutral) (Financial Accounting Standards Board 2010; International Financial Reporting Standards 2010).

For the accounting profession to engage SEERS metrics, the data must likewise be both relevant and reliable; yet because there is no agreement on the metrics regarding SEERS, the relevance of the data is questionable. Moreover, because the data that organizations provide are often suspect, the reliability is also questionable.

For accountants to incorporate SEERS and sustainability metrics into a predictive model of analysis and reporting, a number of industrywide issues must be resolved. First, the accounting profession must develop suitable criteria to support practitioners' evaluation of SEERS data. Practitioners need these criteria to ensure that the data are measurable, complete, and free from bias. Second, and perhaps more importantly, accountants and entrepreneurial leaders must gain knowledge of SEERS and its associated financial and nonfinancial issues. They must also be knowledgeable about how to leverage the data to compile an informed, credible SEERS report. With this knowledge entrepreneurial leaders will lead the way in building sustainability reporting that supports SEERS.

Outside the United States, some accounting professionals are examining how to combine sustainability metrics with existing financial data to improve reporting. Some improvements have been made to establish unbiased methods for systematically collecting, reporting, and ensuring the reliability of sustainability metrics and for developing external reports that explain how sustainability links to the organization's strategy and goals. In other instances, sustainability performance metrics are tracked to specific roles and responsibilities and are included in the organization's internal performance management systems.

To help meet external reporting challenges, in December 2010 the International Accounting Standards Board issued a nonbinding practice statement that allows management to provide a historical and prospective commentary on its financial statements that adds context.

The practice statement *did not preclude* the reporting of nonfinancial metrics (such as sustainability and environmental data) in the commentary but required management's statements to abide by the International Financial Reporting Standards conceptual framework (IFRS 2010).

Although the accounting profession may be making some progress on considering sustainability, it is not moving quickly. As educators we are focused on how to use our current understanding of accounting practices to develop entrepreneurial leaders who are considering these complex accounting issues and are using their knowledge to act their way into feasible solutions that provide relevant and reliable data. If we are able to develop accountants and entrepreneurial leaders who have this worldview, in their privileged position as information providers these individuals will be better positioned to lead their organizations to define, measure, and assess SEERS efforts.

Toward an Accounting Curriculum That Supports SEERS

In both our undergraduate and graduate programs, we have developed the accounting curriculum around two critical themes that enable our students to make connections between accounting practices and SEERS-based decision-making.

First, in our discussion of traditional management and financial accounting topics, we focus on the implications of management discretion in reporting to both internal and external decision-makers. Students develop a comprehensive understanding of the limitations of generally accepted accounting principles (GAAP) in external reporting and of traditional management accounting metrics in internal reporting. Second, we depend heavily on our integration with other disciplines so that we provide the rich context needed to think broadly about how both internal and external accounting data are and could be used in decision-making. We continue to develop new course materials to support these themes and to reflect ever-changing conditions and practices.

The Implications of Management Discretion in Reporting

Financial accounting   In introductory financial accounting courses, faculty are focused primarily on preparing students to be informed users of financial statements prepared using GAAP. While we cover fundamental concepts—such as the accrual basis and the framework of the financial statements; mechanics of methods, such as inventory cost flow assumptions; and traditional ratio analysis techniques— we discuss earnings management, both its implications for financial statements and its roots in management incentive structures. We use current events to highlight these financial reporting results. For example, we recently discussed the BP oil disaster as an illustration of the GAAP requirement to estimate its cost and associated liability and of the limitations of the footnote disclosure.

In our graduate introductory financial accounting course, we discuss earnings management extensively in the context of every topic, from revenue recognition and receivables to operating leases. Every year we update course materials to use the most recent annual reports available, and we require students to analyze footnotes. Through this hands-on approach, students see the information that is reported and, just as significantly, the information that is *not* reported. These discussions of accounting practices enable us to introduce students to the truths that are often hidden behind the financial statements.

Entrepreneurial leaders must first understand the challenges and the limitations of current accounting practices before they can imagine more-comprehensive approaches that will support a SEERS worldview. This discussion inevitably leads to a conversation about how accounting practices affect the prioritization of social, environmental, and economic values and how these practices would need to be done differently to take responsibility for both business and society.

Students learn to view events from a multistakeholder perspective and develop a healthy respect for both the usefulness and the limitations of financial data to various social and environmental stakeholders. This case discussion is eye-opening for many course participants, who come to understand the need for more-comprehensive accounting practices that consider social, environmental, and economic value.

Managerial accounting   Our introductory management accounting courses develop strategic cost analysis tools, often in the context of social and environmental responsibility. One innovative scenario that we use in the undergraduate course addresses the tradeoffs managers make in a job-costing case: a project manager gives incorrect instructions to subordinates writing code for a video game and causes the project to materially exceed its budgeted costs.

Students calculate the cost of the job, charging the incorrect work directly to the job as labor. We then discuss which stakeholders may be affected by this accounting decision and explore the implications for the various groups. Most students conclude that the wasted hours need to be written off as losses or put into overhead (quality control failures), but they then must address how they would convince the project manager and, failing that, what alternatives they might use to resolve the issue. The discussion highlights that management's accounting decision regarding allocation of the wasted hours is critical to the subsequent decisions made.

In covering the use of accounting metrics in performance evaluation, we have found that the balanced scorecard is also useful for teaching entrepreneurial leaders to build an accounting framework that can be expanded beyond finances to include environmental and social sustainability metrics, as well. In introducing the balance scorecard, we focus on its behavioral implications and accounting practices. We consider how a performance measurement system can be used to encourage ethically and socially responsible behavior. We also ask entrepreneurial leaders to consider how to use the balanced scorecard to develop more-comprehensive measures of performance that consider social, environmental, and economic metrics. This discussion helps students recognize the importance of engaging accounting measurement to direct behavior and opens them up to the possibility of using accounting to focus themselves and their organizations on SEERS.

Integration across Disciplines

In all of our programs, we teach introductory financial accounting in the rich context of an integrated curriculum. For freshmen there is a yearlong course, Foundations of Management and Entrepreneurship (see chapter 1), in which student groups start and run a business. Our introductory financial accounting course connects with this experience, particularly in our coverage of historical ratio analysis and building projected financial statements.

In the graduate program, the introductory financial accounting course connects both with finance, through building projected financial statements and forecasting cash flows, and with strategy, through a joint class introducing basic concepts of financial footprints of industry characteristics and strategic choices. Students must use accounting information in the context of rigorous prediction logic to see both its value in assessing economic sustainability and its limitations in assessing environmental and social responsibility.

Ethics is a recurring theme in financial accounting courses, raised repeatedly in discussions of earnings management and specifically in a joint session with law focused on accounting fraud; most recently this involved an analysis of the WorldCom case.

We discuss the Sarbanes-Oxley legislation and the challenges of its requirement that CEOs and CFOs (chief financial officers) certify the accuracy of their companies' financial reports. We focus specifically on how managers can incorporate an ethical framework that considers multiple stakeholders in developing internal controls and reporting practices that strengthen the organization.

Management accounting courses also integrate ethics in discussions of management uses of accounting information in performance evaluation and cost allocations. Referring again to the discretionary nature of accounting, we also discuss CSR reporting and the challenges it poses to developing standard practices around social and environmental reporting. We use case discussions to encourage students to consider how they would address this challenge and create practices and metrics that are supportive of SEERS.

Our management accounting courses also connect directly with core courses in operations and organizational behavior. In the undergraduate course, for example, we have tailored a product design exercise, which is taught jointly by the accounting and operations management faculty, to include environmental and economic trade-offs. Working in small teams, students are given specific roles and are instructed to design a payload lander that meets the following criteria:

- It successfully lands.

- It is artistic, stackable, and green.

- It yields a profit.

One member of each team is assigned a role that is focused on the use of reusable, recyclable parts and obtaining a LEED certification for the product. Other team members have roles in which they focus on the client's needs, the creativity of the design, or the budget management and profitability. Students learn about the potential incompatibilities and tensions between environmental and economic value. They must work together and integrate concepts from multiple disciplines to develop an integrated economic and environmental solution.

Creating New Materials to Develop
SEERS Accounting Practices

As we teach entrepreneurial leaders how accounting practices can be leveraged to support SEERS, we also highlight how corporate sustainability reports must be developed to support this integration.

For example, when we conduct an industry analysis of the US carpet manufacturing industry, we focus on social, environmental, and economic issues. In this analysis we highlight the company Interface Inc., which since 1997 has articulated the goal of ecological sustainability by 2020. Interface's website includes multiple environmental metrics (such as landfill waste volume, energy use, greenhouse gas emissions, and water intake), but its Form 10-K reports only traditional financial metrics. We use financial statement analysis to assess the financial impact of Interface's strategic choices, and we discuss how environmental sustainability metrics might be combined with financial metrics to better capture the firm's position. Through these discussions, entrepreneurial leaders learn the inherent value of developing an integrated SEERS worldview in which they examine the financial consequences of corporate choices to include social and environmental sustainability and responsibility as components of the strategic mission.

The Interface example highlights how we focus student attention on integrating environmental reporting into economic reporting. On the flip side we highlight the importance of economic sustainability to social and environment sustainability. We consider nonprofits and NGOs, which are unable to deliver on their strategic missions if they are not economically viable. Managers of both types of organizations rely on accounting reports for information to make long-term strategic decisions and everyday operating decisions.

From an economic standpoint, entrepreneurial leaders must understand the business model of an organization and how it generates profits and cash. We train students to forecast financial information to assess if an entity is capable of existing economically, that is, if it provides the required return to its equity providers while maintaining adequate cash flow to continue to operate and grow.

We also stress the importance of economic stewardship to the long-term survival of organizations that have a social or environmental mission. In the graduate management accounting course, for example, we discuss an organic-farming case to demonstrate that, even with its social and environmental mission, for the entity to remain viable it must make decisions about product lines and sales channels based on their profitability.

A current challenge to teaching budding entrepreneurial leaders to connect accounting practices to a SEERS worldview stems from the lack of available material to support this educational approach. We have had to develop our own teaching materials that demonstrate how for-profit organizations and individuals are engaging a SEERS worldview.

One such case focuses on the strategic deployment of sustainability at Sodexo. Beginning with a discussion of the history and the drivers of Sodexo's sustainability efforts, the case focuses on the management and structural gaps that sometimes derail sustainability efforts, the conflicts that arise between supply-chain management strategies for profitability and the sustainability group's strategies, and the challenges in developing and tracking sustainability metrics and in embedding them in the organization's performance management. This case series enables students to learn from an organization that is engaging a SEERS worldview and to explore the emerging accounting practices that integrate social, environmental, and economic measures.

As future entrepreneurial leaders consider how to connect accounting practices to support SEERS, they need to explore the added complexity of how to manage various components of the supply chain. We developed that opportunity in another case—Eastern Tire—which is based loosely on Ford Motor Company's experience with the separation of tread and the catastrophic failure of tires purchased from a Chinese manufacturer. With the Eastern Tire case, we explore a focal organization's responsibility for the actions of its value-chain members as well as its approach to managing the incident.

Conclusion

In management programs around the world, students are more engaged with issues of social and environmental sustainability. They often make decisions to attend a particular program based on its rankings by the Aspen Institute or in recent *Businessweek* reports on sustainability in management curricula. We have determined a few critical factors that management programs—and business organizations—must consider as they focus on developing entrepreneurial leaders who possess a SEERS worldview.

First, sustainability must be taught from a multidisciplinary approach across an entire curriculum so that students understand how all aspects of the organization support their ability to develop and engage this new worldview of business. Many management programs were unsuccessful in their teaching of ethics because they taught it in a compartmentalized manner or relegated it to the efforts of the organizational behavior faculty. We suspect that the development of a SEERS worldview in entrepreneurial leaders will fail if approached in the same way.

To fully embrace SEERS, students must learn the strategic implications of their decisions and a detailed approach to implementation that is based in cognitive ambidexterity. Through an integrated teaching approach, management students can ask and answer some of the challenging issues associated with exploring the synergies and the tensions of social, environmental, and economic responsibility and sustainability.

Second, students must be introduced to the subjective elements of objective concepts so that they develop a more nuanced understanding of SEERS. When we introduce accounting methods and principles, students must learn how management decisions influence the outcomes on both internal and external financial statements. They must also understand the limitations of accounting data in terms of capturing sustainability efforts. With this understanding, we prepare entrepreneurial leaders who will create new reliable and relevant ways of engaging accounting practices to support SEERS. With this knowledge these leaders will be able to take a different approach to decision-making, using a fundamentally different worldview.

References

Adams, C. 2002. "Internal Organizational Factors Influencing Corporate Social and Ethical Reporting: Beyond Current Theorizing." *Accounting, Auditing, and Accountability* 15 (2): 223–50.

Adams, C. 2008. "A Commentary On: Corporate Social Responsibility Reporting and Reputation Risk Management." *Accounting, Auditing, and Accountability* 21 (3): 365–70.

Bell, J, S. Erzurumlu, and H. Fowler. Forthcoming. *Sodexo: Establishing a Sustainable Supply Chain.* Working paper.

Borkowski, S, M. J. Welsh, and K. Wentzel. 2010. "Johnson & Johnson: A Model for Sustainability Reporting." *Strategic Finance,* September, 28–37. http://www.imanet.org/PDFs/Public/SF/2010_09/09_2010_bor kowski.pdf.

Craib and PricewaterhouseCoopers. 2010. *CSR Trends 2010: Stacking up the Results.* Toronto: Craib Design and Communications. http://www.pwc .com/ca/en/sustainability/publications/csr-trends-2010-09.pdf.

Dhaliwal, D., S. Radhakrishnan, and A. Tsang. 2010. *Nonfinancial Disclosure and Analyst Forecast Accuracy: International Evidence on Corporate Social Responsibility Disclosure.* Working paper, Singapore Management University. http://papers.ssrn.com/sol3/papers.cfm?abstract_id= 1596458.

Eccles, R. G., and M. P. Krzus. 2010. *One Report: Integrated Reporting for a Sustainable Strategy.* Hoboken, NJ: John Wiley and Sons.

Financial Accounting Standards Board. 2010. *Conceptual Framework: Statement of Financial Accounting Concepts No. 8*. September. http://www .fasb.org/cs/BlobServer?blobcol=urldata&blobtable=MungoBlobs& blobkey=id&blobwhere=1175821997186&blobheader=application/pdf.

Global Reporting Initiative. 2006. *Sustainability Reporting Guidelines: Version 3.0*. http://www.globalreporting.org/NR/rdonlyres/ED9E9B36-AB54-4 DE1-BFF2-5F735235CA44/0/G3_GuidelinesENU.pdf.

Haldis, P. 2009. "ExxonMobil, Chevron, GM among Companies on Climate Watch List." *Global Refining and Fuels Report* 13 (4): 9. http:// business.highbeam.com/61528/article-1G1-194532830/exxonmobil -chevron-gm-among-companies-climate-watch.

Holmes, S., and W. Zellner. 2004. "The Costco Way." *Businessweek*, April 12. http://www.businessweek.com/magazine/content/04_15/b3878084_ mz021.htm.

IFRS Foundation. 2010. "IASB Publishes IFRS Practice Statement on Management Commentary." December 8. http://www.ifrs.org/News/ Press+Releases/Management+Commentary+Practice+Statement.htm.

Institute of Management. 2008. *The Evolution of Accountability—Sustainability Reporting for Accountants*. Montvale, NJ: IMA. http://www.nick shepherd.ca/pdf/SMA_Sustainability_063008.pdf.

International Financial Reporting Standards. 2010. *Conceptual Framework for Financial Reporting: Project Summary and Feedback Statement*. September. http://www.ifrs.org/NR/rdonlyres/6A6ABF86-D554-4A77-9A4A -E415E09726B6/0/CFFeedbackStmt.pdf Accessed 2/02/2011.

Mock, T. J., C. Strohm, and K. M. Swartz. 2007. "An Examination of Worldwide Assured Sustainability Reporting." *Australian Accounting Review* 17 (1): 67–77.

Nidumolu, R., C. K. Prahalad, and M. R. Rangaswami. 2009. "Why Sustainability Is Now the Key Driver of Innovation." *Harvard Business Review* 87 (9): 56–64. http://hbr.org/2009/09/why-sustainability-is -now-the-key-driver-of-innovation/es.

Piltz, R. 2007. "House Science Investigations Chairman Calls on Exxon to Account for Global Warming Denial Funding." Climate Science Watch.

May 21. http://www.climatesciencewatch.org/2007/05/21/house-science -investigations-chairman-calls-on-exxon-to-account-for-global -warming-denial-funding.

Searcy, C. 2009. "Setting a Course in Corporate Sustainability Performance Measurement." *Measuring Business Excellence* 13 (3): 49–57.

Sebhatu, S. P. 2008. *Sustainability Performance Measurement for Sustainable Organizations: Beyond Compliance and Reporting.* Karlstad, Sweden: Service Research Centre, Karlstad University. Accessed March 3, 2011, http://www.ep.liu.se/ecp/033/005/ecp0803305.pdf.

Seedco Policy Center. 2007. *The Limits of Social Enterprise: A Field Study and Case Analysis.* http://www.seedco.org/publications.

CHAPTER 7

The Financial Challenge: Reconciling Social and Environmental Value with Shareholder Value

Richard Bliss

I N THE FINANCE COMMUNITY, SHAREHOLDER VALUE HAS LONG BEEN the performance metric of choice for academics and professionals. Along with increasing profits, the maximization of shareholder value is viewed by many as the primary objective of corporate managers and is a pillar of most finance courses. As we introduce the importance of SEERS, the immediate question arises regarding how social and environmental sustainability, financial performance, and shareholder value are related. Can these concepts not only coexist but be taught in a cohesive, effective pedagogy? As the importance of developing a SEERS worldview becomes more central for both organizations and entrepreneurial leaders, we have an obligation to try. The task of incorporating SEERS into a finance perspective based on predictive logic, however, can be formidable. To illustrate this challenge, we begin with what appear to be simple questions about sustainability and corporate social responsibility, activities resulting from a SEERS worldview.

The first question relates to the ranking of companies in terms of corporate social responsibility, or CSR.* Each rating approach evaluates a different aspect of sustainability and responsibilities and, for many, the top-rated company can be on the list one year and off the next.

Take Monsanto for example. In 2010 the company was ranked 31 in *Corporate Responsibility Magazine*'s "best corporate citizen" ranking and was also one of the "least ethical companies" in the Covalence rankings (Cause Integration 2010). There was also a major change in the top 100 "best corporate citizens" from 2009 to 2010: 44 companies from *Corporate Responsibility Magazine*'s 2009 "best corporate citizen" ranking disappeared from the 2010 ranking, including CSR darlings Agilent (recognized by RiskMetrics Group's 2010 Global ESG 100, *Newsweek*'s 2009 Green Rankings, and Corporate Knights' Global 100) and General Electric (recognized by *Ethisphere* magazine as among the 2009 Most Ethical Companies, *Newsweek*'s 2009 Green Rankings, and 2010 Corporate Knights Global 100) (Ravich 2010).

The second question refers to exhibit 7.1, which shows two-year stock returns for four companies: Whole Foods Market Inc., Timberland Co., Exxon Mobil Corporation, and Huntsman Corporation (*Fortune* magazine's *least*-admired American company in 2007 based on social responsibility). Which companies do you think have the positive and negative returns? The two companies with positive stock returns are Exxon Mobil and Huntsman, and the two companies that lost about 40 percent of their value are Timberland and Whole Foods.

---

*In this chapter we use the term *CSR* somewhat interchangeably with *SEERS* because it is a common term in finance for a firm's social and environmental responsibility. The goal of CSR is for a company to share its actions, take responsibility for them, and encourage a positive impact through its activities on the environment, consumers, employees, communities, and other stakeholders. As noted in chapter 6, however, the concepts of CSR and SEERS are not the same, as SEERS argues for a more holistic approach to social, environmental, and economic value creation.

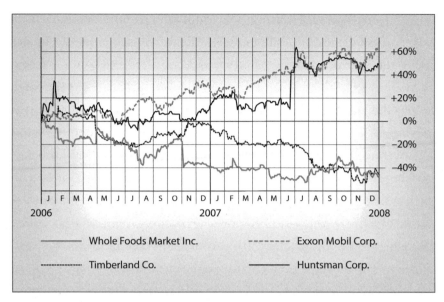

Exhibit 7.1 Two-year stock returns for Whole Foods, Timberland, Exxon, and Huntsman

These examples—while admittedly unscientific—highlight two of the impediments to a rigorous reconciliation of SEERS and shareholder value. The first is that there are many ways to define CSR, but there is no single, established method that allows us to quantitatively evaluate and rank companies. In contrast, there are financial standards—GAAP, International Accounting Standards (IAS), and Sarbanes-Oxley—that permit an "apples-to-apples" comparison of corporate financial performance and regulatory compliance across industries and countries (see chapter 6).

The second impediment is that, despite hundreds of empirical studies, there is no clear or consistent evidence that CSR activities produce superior financial returns to shareholders. This lack of an obvious link between social and environmental responsibility and shareholder value creates conflict for investors and corporate managers who must balance their legal and fiduciary responsibilities with the mounting pressure to embrace SEERS.

Finance educators and professionals who rely on predictive logic based in reams of data and economic theory face a quandary. On one hand, the lack of standardized data and the inconclusive connection between CSR and financial performance make it tempting to dismiss SEERS as just another management fad. On the other hand, some managers believe that social and environmental responsibility matter but are unsure how it connects to profitability and shareholder value. As educators, we face heightened student awareness and interest in social and environmental responsibility and evolving questions about the role and the responsibilities of corporations. The combination of these factors is why we should strive to better understand the topic and educate our students—the world's future entrepreneurial leaders—in how to engage a SEERS worldview from a finance perspective.

Rather than try to justify social and environmental sustainability on philosophical or moral grounds—as some advocates do—the finance perspective contends that SEERS needs to be considered and evaluated within the shareholder value framework. Certain social and environmental activities are not at odds with increasing shareholder value. Indeed, focusing on these value-creating activities allows us to avoid throwing the baby out with the bathwater. We hope to convince the reader and our finance colleagues that by evaluating SEERS activities with financial analytical rigor embedded in prediction logic, we can focus on those practices that are aligned with shareholder value and at the same time improve both the content and the effectiveness of our teaching.

Financial Framing of SEERS

We begin by highlighting some of the challenges to incorporating social and environmental value creation into the world of finance. It may also help explain why both finance academics and industry professionals have often viewed social and environmental responsibility skeptically. We believe that the difficulties of reconciling CSR with shareholder value creation fall into three broad areas: defining CSR, measuring and evaluating CSR, and assessing the relationship between CSR and financial performance.

Defining Corporate Social Responsibility

The definition of socially responsible corporate behavior is not clearly developed.* The possible behavioral activities range from obeying environmental laws to reducing the carbon footprint of the supply chain, from obeying local labor laws to providing health insurance, and from making charitable donations to producing antiracism public service announcements. It is therefore difficult to classify companies as having "good" or "bad" CSR.

For example, is McDonald's a responsible corporate citizen for using recyclable packaging materials when its products are nutritionally suspect and its suppliers practice large-scale corporate agriculture? Are Monsanto's genetically modified seeds the answer to global famine or a threat to biodiversity? Should Archer Daniels Midland be praised for its role in expanding ethanol production or pilloried for the fact that corn-based ethanol may actually contribute more to the problem of climate change than comparable amounts of fossil fuels? Should these companies be praised for certain activities and criticized for others? Is there a way to evaluate a company's net contribution to society? And how do the shareholders react to these different types of activities?

---

*The academic literature uses both *CSR* and *corporate social performance* (*CSP*), although the distinction is not always clear. CSR is the socially responsible behavior the firm undertakes, whereas CSP represents how stakeholders assess the quality and the impact of those behaviors. Luo and Bhattacharya (2009, 201) summarize the distinction as follows: "While firms invest in CSR initiatives, CSP, as the measure of firms' aggregated historical social performance relative to competition, is what stakeholders reward the firms for and, therefore, what is potentially linked to firm financial performance."

Measuring and Evaluating CSR

Chapter 6 discusses the challenges associated with CSR reporting and the lack of consistent standards to guide it. There are a variety of reporting guidelines and standards for CSR, and each measures something different. In addition, there are many rankings and lists that purport to provide evidence on a company's CSR or sustainability activities, yet the methodologies behind some rankings are subjective at best. A similar problem is the lack of a mandatory disclosure requirement for companies to provide information about their social and environmental activities, and when they choose to report there are few consistent standards.

Contrast this with the financial data available to investors, corporate managers, and academics wishing to evaluate corporate performance. Every public company is subject to mandatory quarterly financial disclosure requirements. The content and the format of those disclosures are clearly defined and subject to Securities and Exchange Commission requirements and the rules of GAAP or IAS accounting standards. These issues are similar to the challenge of providing reliable and relevant data (see chapter 6). There is no question that the information available for assessing financial performance is more clearly defined and readily available than data on social and environmental performance. For those leaders who are used to making decisions based on reliable and relevant measures of future financial implications, it is challenging to incorporate social and environmental activities, which can be more difficult to measure.

Another challenge for finance is the focus on *shareholder* value creation. A focus on social and environmental value means broadening the managerial focus to include other *stakeholders,* such as employees, suppliers, customers, and the local community. When this happens, the objective becomes maximizing aggregate stakeholder welfare rather than simply share price. The problem is that stakeholder theory, at least in its current state of development, does not clearly define aggregate welfare or explain how to quantify the tradeoffs among competing stakeholders.

Therefore even when companies assess and report their social and environmental activities, there is no effective way to compare the information across companies. It is therefore not surprising that many companies fail to report their activities in any quantitative way or that their CSR reports have limited information. Companies may choose to present only the positive outcomes for stakeholders rather than the tradeoffs that were made. The CSR report can become more of a means of improving the company reputation and brand image than an accurate assessment of its actual performance.

The Disconnect between CSR and Financial Performance

Perhaps the biggest challenge in reconciling corporate social responsibility with a financial model is that there is inconsistent evidence that CSR produces better financial performance for a firm. We can evaluate this issue from two perspectives. The first reviews the link between CSR and individual firm financial performance, and the second looks at the returns from socially responsible investing (SRI). While there is some evidence of a relationship between CSR and corporate financial performance, it is neither consistent nor conclusive.

Orlitzky et al. (2003) used meta-analysis to review 52 academic studies of the link between CSR and corporate financial performance (CFP), concluding that corporate social performance (CSP) is positively associated with CFP. The researchers found little evidence of causality, however, concluding, "The relationship seems to be bidirectional and simultaneous." In other words, companies with high CFP also have high CSP. Does good financial performance permit companies to do good, or does doing good lead to better financial performance? We do not know.

Margolis and Walsh (2003) examined 127 published studies of CSR and CFP between 1972 and 2002. The majority (109 studies, or 86 percent) model CSR as the independent variable predicting CFP. Of these, 54 report a positive relationship, 7 a negative relationship, and 48 no relationship or mixed results. For the 22 studies that modeled CFP as the predictor of CSR, 16 (73 percent) found a positive relationship—that is, good financial performance led to more CSR. It is difficult to draw definitive conclusions, however, because the remaining 109 studies measure CFP in 70 different ways and assess CSR based on 27 different data sources. Margolis and Walsh concluded, "A definite link between CSP and CFP may turn out to be more illusory than the body of results suggests." How can we determine a link between social responsibility and financial performance when CSR is not well defined or measured?

Another way to assess the link between corporate social responsibility and financial performance is to consider the performance of socially responsible investing funds. SRI has grown dramatically in the United States and around the world. In 1995 there were 55 SRI mutual funds managing $12 billion and total SRI assets of $639 billion. By 2010 those numbers had grown to 493 funds and $569 billion, and total SRI assets were $3.07 trillion, or 11 percent of the $25.2 trillion under professional management (Social Investment Forum Foundation 2010).

In Europe between 1995 and 2005, the number of SRI mutual funds increased from 54 to 375, with $30 billion of assets under management (Renneboog, Ter Horst, and Zhang 2008, 1726). Total European SRI assets increased from €2.7 trillion to €5 trillion from 2007 to the end of 2009 (Eurosif 2010). Clearly, there is increased demand for SRI funds, and investors may be looking for ways to evaluate the CSR practices of firms so that they may invest in those firms.

While we know that the popularity of SRI funds has increased, we need to consider whether SRI funds outperform other funds. Renneboog, Ter Horst, and Zhang (2008) provide a comprehensive review of the academic research on SRI investing. Their empirical evidence shows little difference in SRI performance in the United States, the United Kingdom, Canada, and Australia and underperformance by SRI funds in continental Europe and the Asia-Pacific region. Exhibit 7.2 shows the recent performance of two popular CSR indices—the Dow Jones Sustainability World Index and the FTSE4Good Index, compared with the MSCI World Index. The data add support to the claim of no consistent, superior performance by companies with better SRI/CSR metrics.

The lack of a consistent, discernible link between CSR activity and financial performance in this research does not mean that specific CSR activities cannot benefit individual companies. It means that the financial impact of a firm's social and environmental sustainability activities needs to be critically assessed, just as its other activities and investments must be assessed. In this context the challenge becomes defining the CSR activities most likely to enhance shareholder value. This is the goal of the next section.

Period ended 3/31/2010	CSR indices		
	DJSWI[1]	FTSE4Good[2]	MSCI[3]
1-year	39.5%	56.2%	37.7%
3-year	−18.8%	−15.7%	−17.6%
5-year	21.4%	15.3%	21.1%

1. Dow Jones Sustainability World Index:
   http://www.sustainability-index.com

2. FTSE4Good Index:
   http://www.ftse.com/Indices/FTSE4Good_Index_Series/index.jsp

3. MSCI World Index:
   http://www.mscibarra.com/products/indices/international_equity_indices/gimi/stdindex/performance.html

Exhibit 7.2 Performance of corporate social responsibility indices

Analyzing SEERS from a Finance Perspective

Because the social and environmental components of SEERS are currently ill defined, lacking in objective measure, and not yet clearly linked to financial performance, can SEERS still be reconciled with shareholder value? From a financial vantage point, we believe that the answer is a qualified yes. In this section we present an approach that incorporates components of SEERS into financial analysis and education. By focusing on those elements of SEERS with a clear connection to financial performance, we can maintain shareholder value without sacrificing analytical rigor. We believe that such an approach is not only defensible but also reflective of the way social and environmental responsibility is viewed by leaders in many corporations. As this statement from Matt Kistler, senior vice president of sustainability at Wal-Mart, reiterates, "If this was not financially viable, a company such as ours would not be doing it" (Bhanoo 2010).

How do we teach budding entrepreneurial leaders to consider the financial benefits of SEERS activities? From a finance perspective, we believe that entrepreneurial leaders should focus their resources on the social and environmental activities that they believe will have a positive impact on profitability and shareholder value. Based in predictive logic, finance theory allows us to evaluate the financial impact of these investments and activities just as we would other company investments.

Finance theory defines the current value of any asset as the present value of the cash flows it is expected to generate in the future. There are two variables in this analysis: expected cash flows and a risk-adjusted discount rate. Discounted cash flow techniques—the most widely used tools for evaluating investments and valuing companies—are based on this simple concept. With discounted cash flow, two components can increase the value of a company today: one is an increase in the expected future cash flows (through cost reduction or revenue enhancements); the second is a decrease in the risk of those cash flows as proxied by the discount rate.

Thus for SEERS activities to create shareholder value, they must either increase future cash flows (profits*) or reduce the risk of those cash flows. Some individuals might scoff at the need for such a direct connection, arguing that any socially responsible behavior is beneficial in general. Most finance professionals are more pragmatic, however, and not only would understand but hopefully would endorse SEERS activities with a clear link to incremental cash flow or risk reduction. Engaging the predictive logic of finance, we suggest that SEERS activities should be subject to cost/benefit analyses comparable to those that guide most corporate resource allocation decisions.

To facilitate this predictive analysis, we propose three categories to evaluate SEERS activities: cost savings, revenue enhancement, and risk reduction. Of course, the delineation is not always clear and some SEERS activities may fall across more than one category. Our framework for reconciling SEERS and shareholder value is summarized in exhibit 7.3, which shows the three categories of SEERS activities and ranks them based on the estimated strength of their connection to shareholder value. At of the top of the figure are SEERS activities that clearly increase cash flow and are relatively easy to identify and connect with shareholder value. At the bottom are activities that have a weaker connection to financial performance or that are more difficult to quantify in terms of costs and benefits. Although this exhibit and its categories are somewhat subjective, we believe it's useful for advancing our understanding of how to consider SEERS activities within our current methods of financial analyses. The following discussion describes each type of activity and provides real-life examples.

---

*Although *profits* and *cash flow* are not synonymous, for the sake of simplification we make the reasonable assumption that they are closely correlated.

SEERS and shareholder value	SEERS/CSR activities	Examples
Strong connection ↕ Weak connection	**Cost savings** Direct or indirect	▪ Using lower-cost recycled materials ▪ Reducing packaging materials and shipping costs ▪ Improving human resources policies to increase productivity
	Revenue enhancement Direct or indirect	▪ Charging a premium for socially responsible products ▪ Using cause marketing ▪ Giving to charity and getting involved in the community
	Risk reduction Direct or indirect	▪ Heading off taxes and unfavorable regulation ▪ Protecting the company's reputation ▪ Preventing boycotts and other social ostracism

Exhibit 7.3   SEERS/CSR and shareholder value

Cost Savings

The simplest way to increase profits is to reduce expenses. The link between SEERS and cost reduction can be direct or indirect. If achieved directly, that is, with no additional spending or investment, the benefits are obvious and unambiguous. SEERS activities that fall into this category include a switch to less expensive but more socially responsible production inputs. Examples of direct cost reduction include a newspaper publisher's switching to recycled newsprint priced below virgin paper and a restaurant's purchasing locally grown produce that is cheaper than the offerings of its usual distributor.

In practice most SEERS choices have an impact on multiple cost items and may involve significant investment. The savings in these cases are indirect. A common example of this is efforts to reduce energy used in heating, cooling, and lighting commercial buildings. This can be achieved in many ways, including insulation, smart controls, and compact fluorescent lighting. Each of these changes involves an upfront investment that yields future cost savings in the form of reduced energy consumption. The environmental benefit comes from reduced use of fossil fuels and fewer greenhouse gas emissions. For any of these investments, we can estimate future cost savings, use discounted cash flow techniques to weigh them off against the required investment, and make a decision based on the expected impact on shareholder value.

Another example of indirect cost savings can be found in the way companies package their products. Environmentally friendly packaging design can reduce material requirements, cut shipping and warehousing costs, and encourage recycling. Here are three real-world examples:

- Procter and Gamble's redesign of the Folgers coffee container to reduce plastic consumption by 1 million pounds annually

- Nestlé's use of smaller labels on its Poland Spring and Deer Park bottled water brands, which saved 20 million pounds of paper

- Coca-Cola's change of the Dasani water bottle shape to reduce material usage by 7 percent (Demetrakakes 2007)

Each of these activities reduced cost due to material savings and decreased shipping expenses due to lighter weight and reduced size. There are costs involved in the redesign process, and there may be additional investment in equipment, but, again, we can quantify the costs and the expected benefits using the traditional tools of financial analysis.

There are many examples where SEERS reduces costs and enhances revenues. Wal-Mart attributed more than $100 million of its 2009 revenue to its decision to switch to recyclable cardboard when shipping to its 4,300-plus stores in the United States. Now it sells the cardboard to a recycler rather than pays to ship the waste to a landfill (Bhanoo 2010). In this case, Wal-Mart reduces its disposal costs by switching to recyclable cardboard, which it then sells to generate new revenue. Even if the new cardboard is more expensive, the incremental cost is more than offset by the new revenue and the reduction in disposal costs. Wal-Mart estimated the 2009 environmental benefits as 8,600 fewer tons of cardboard in landfills and 125,000 trees saved (Wal-Mart Stores Inc. 2010, 13).

Another category of cost savings involves the intersection of SEERS and a company's employees. The premise is that more-loyal employees save a company money by reducing turnover and increasing productivity. Lower turnover means reduced costs for hiring and training, while higher productivity improves profit margins. The first link between SEERS and loyalty is based on the idea that employees are less likely to leave socially responsible companies, which share their values, a claim borne out by survey data.*

As an example, Timberland combines both approaches by shutting down one day a year so that all 5,400 employees can participate in company-sponsored philanthropy. It also allows workers one week off with pay each year to work with local charities, and it offers paid six-month sabbaticals for four employees each year to work at a nonprofit.

---

*Companies' CSR practices, especially external ones, have a significant positive influence on employees' organizational commitment (Brammer, Millington, and Rayton 2007); 57 percent of employees say their company's CSR reputation is a factor in retaining them (Towers Perrin Global Workforce Study 2007–2008); 40 percent of MBA graduates rated CSR as an "extremely" or "very" important company reputation measure when job hunting (Hill and Knowlton 2008); and 92 percent of students and entry-level hires seek an environmentally friendly company (Monster.com 2007).

This is not inexpensive; the one-day shutdown alone costs the company $2 million. Timberland management believes that such expenditures help the company attract and keep the best talent, which benefits the bottom line. In the words of President and CEO Jeffrey Swartz, "People like to feel good about where they work and what they do" (Pereira 2003).

Loyalty and productivity may also improve at companies with socially responsible human resource (HR) policies, which might include paying above-market wages; providing discretionary benefits like healthcare and retirement; offering workplace perks like free lunch, on-site gyms, and childcare; and ensuring safe and fair working conditions globally.

Starbucks, for example, realized early on that its employees (called "partners") were critical to creating its competitive advantage, the "customer experience." Being able to attract, train, and retain new employees was also critical to its rapid growth plans. To accomplish this, Starbucks pays above-market wages and offers health and dental benefits, vacation time, a 401(k) plan, and stock options to even part-time employees. The company also provides numerous opportunities for advancement, knowing that its typical hire will want new challenges. Does it work? Turnover of Starbucks baristas is 80 percent annually, whereas the industry average for quick-service restaurants is 200 percent (Weber 2005).

Companies like Timberland and Starbucks believe that their investment in CSR and socially responsible HR practices yields tangible financial benefits by creating a loyal and productive workforce. The question with respect to shareholder value is whether those benefits outweigh their costs.

Revenue Enhancement

For many firms the financial goal of SEERS may be to increase revenue. As with cost reductions, the link between SEERS and revenue can be direct or indirect. The direct link occurs when customers pay a premium for the socially or environmentally responsible characteristics of the company's products. When companies pursue CSR to attract new customers, the connection to revenue is indirect. The indirect approach has a more tenuous connection to profitability and shareholder value.

Consumers pay a premium for socially responsible products for many reasons. In some cases they believe that the products are superior. For example, some consumers believe that organic produce and free-range meats are healthier and taste better, which justifies a higher price. In others cases the products are of equal quality or functionality but have been sourced in a more environmentally friendly manner or provide social or environmental benefits in use. The electricity from a wind turbine is identical to the electricity from a coal plant; however, generating the former does not produce CO_2 or contribute to climate change.

For SEERS-based revenue enhancement to create shareholder value, the additional costs of social responsibility must be offset by the premium customers are willing to pay. Balancing these considerations can be challenging. For example, in 2008 Costco and Sam's Club introduced a newly designed 1-gallon milk jug. The square container carried significant environmental benefits, including easier stacking, storage, and transportation. It also did away with the need for traditional milk crates. The benefits included significant labor savings, less fuel and water consumption, and a lower price to consumers. Consumers initially rejected the new jugs, however, claiming that they were difficult to pour. The jug was subsequently redesigned, and in-store pouring classes were introduced. The point is that consumers will not accept reduced functionality as a tradeoff for improved environmental product characteristics.

Contrast this example with Dutch Boy's 2002 introduction of the Twist & Pour paint container. The new container was completely recyclable and stacked more efficiently for transportation and storage. It also provided tangible benefits to the consumer, including an integral pouring spout, a twist-off lid that better preserved the paint, and an easy-to-grip handle. Even though the container cost $2 more than a traditional metal paint can, sales at Dutch Boy tripled in the first year (Bishop 2008). By improving both performance and environmental characteristics, Dutch Boy was able to increase its total revenues.

Another revenue-enhanced component of SEERS may be the ability to generate additional business from existing customers or to attract new ones. One method of indirect revenue enhancement is *cause marketing,* which Wikipedia (2010) defines as a type of marketing involving the cooperative efforts of a for-profit business and a nonprofit organization for mutual benefit.

An early example of this was the 1983 partnership between American Express and the Statue of Liberty–Ellis Island Foundation. American Express pledged a one-penny donation toward the Statue of Liberty renovation for each transaction made with an American Express card and $1 for each new card application. The campaign included $4 million in advertising and resulted in $1.7 million being donated toward the $62 million renovation. More importantly for the company, use of American Express cards rose by 28 percent in just the first month, compared with the previous year, and new card applications increased by 45 percent (Adkins 2003, 670). In this example, the implications for company profitability and shareholder value could readily be estimated.

Other ways of engaging SEERS to indirectly increase revenue include charitable giving and involvement in the local community. In some cases these activities may be connected to the company's product or service. For example, in 2010 Aéropostale donated 15,000 coats from the previous season to nonprofit Cradles to Crayons, which provides clothing to children in need. The benefits of donating these coats exceeded the incremental revenue that Aéropostale might have made from selling marked-down off-season coats.

In other cases such actions may have no direct connection to the company's products or revenue, but they help build the company's reputation which, over a longer period of time, might help retain existing customers and attract new ones, indirectly increasing revenues. Examples of this type of activity include McDonald's Ronald McDonald House and Goldman Sachs's 2008 pledge of $100 million to "10,000 Women," a global initiative delivering business education to women in developing countries. Cynics might argue that some of these activities are meant to repair rather than build reputations, but the goal is consistent: to enhance the company's image in the eyes of employees, customers, investors, and other stakeholders.

In considering the revenue-enhancement opportunities of SEERS activities, organizations must be cognizant that there is a limit to the premium that customers may pay for socially conscious goods and services. The tradeoffs inherent in such decisions can create conflicts with other stakeholders and other core aspects of a company's strategy.

For example, Wal-Mart complained about the high prices associated with using renewable energy and was concerned that the costs would have to be passed on to consumers, threatening the company's "always low prices" mantra (Ailworth 2010). Merck, which in partnership with the Gates Foundation launched an initiative in 2000 to improve HIV/AIDS treatment in Botswana, had to balance the R&D costs of developing new drugs and the need for patent protection with the very real social crisis HIV and AIDS were causing in Africa.

Risk Reduction

The final financial classification of SEERS initiatives is that of reducing risk. If the volatility of a firm's cash flow decreases, so should its cost of financing (Luo and Bhattacharya 2009). Reducing the discount rate in any discounted cash flow analysis increases the current value of future cash flows. Even if it requires new investment or additional expense, a sufficiently large reduction in risk can increase shareholder value.

The first way SEERS can reduce risk is by heading off potentially expensive regulation and taxation. Consider the American Beverage Association's recent television and print ads showing Coca-Cola, Pepsi, and Dr Pepper employees removing full-calorie soft drinks from school vending machines. The campaign (American Beverage Association, n.d.) touts the collaborative effort among fierce industry rivals and claims, "Together, we've reduced beverage calories in schools by 88 percent." What the ads fail to mention are the recent efforts at both the federal and state levels to impose new taxes on sugar-laden beverages. The taxes would raise revenue that would be used to offset the contribution of these drinks to obesity-related health problems.

Kevin Keane, senior vice president of public affairs at the American Beverage Association, summarized the industry's perspective as follows: "You're always in a far better position to be on offense than on defense all the time, and our companies recognize that and are doing bold things in the public policy arena that others will follow" (Zmuda 2010).

In other cases the risk is not of additional regulation or taxation but to the company's reputation. As mentioned in chapter 4, Nike has had to respond to questions from customers and activists about its social and environmental impacts. When a 1996 *New York Times* column highlighted the conditions under which Indonesian women were producing Nike products, the company found itself at the center of a public relations nightmare (Herbert 1996). Labor groups protested Nike's practices and accused it of hypocrisy, noting that the company was in the midst of an ad campaign that touted sports and exercise as a path to female empowerment. Brewing boycotts of Nike products by consumer groups increased the risk considerably. As a result, later in the year the company created a new department to monitor compliance with labor standards by its supply-chain partners. By 1998 Nike had established SEERS initiatives connected to its core business functions in response to the labor crisis and the potential damage to its reputation (Kytle and Ruggie 2005).

The examples of cost savings, revenue enhancement, and risk reduction in this chapter suggest that organizations can connect SEERS to financial value creation. Yet as entrepreneurial leaders use these models, they need to be cautious to avoid value-destroying behavior that occurs when they unilaterally pursue social initiatives that competitors eschew. This type of activity can put an organization in a vulnerable position in either the product or capital markets.

Coining the term *supercapitalism*, Robert Reich (2008, 10) argues, "Competition is so intense that most corporations cannot accomplish social ends at a cost to their consumers or investors, who will otherwise seek and find better deals elsewhere." Reich cites numerous examples of companies whose SEERS activities had to be scaled back in the face of declining financial performance. These include Levi Strauss, which almost went bankrupt due to its commitment to domestic manufacturing, and Marks & Spencer, a perennial favorite for its worldwide labor standards, which became the target of a hostile takeover in 2004. The key is that in a competitive marketplace, companies must pay attention to both SEERS and profitability or risk losing both.

In summary, from a finance perspective organizations must consider how SEERS creates value for both their customers and their shareholders. To do so they need to be aware of the competitive landscape and effectively communicate their social and environmental activities and anticipate customers' reactions to price increases or product functionality changes. Activities that reduce costs or directly increase revenues in a predictable way will yield the most immediate and tangible financial benefits. Furthermore the analyses of the cash flows should consider how these activities increase or decrease the risks.

Refer again to exhibit 7.3, our framework for reconciling SEERS and shareholder value. The figure establishes a context for making the connection between SEERS, financial performance, and shareholder value and also provides guidance on how SEERS might be incorporated into finance education.

Strategies for Integrating SEERS into Finance Education

Exhibit 7.3 provides a conceptual framework for incorporating CSR into finance pedagogy. The connection between SEERS and the prediction-based financial metric of shareholder value is through changes to cash flows and risk. By focusing on the clearest connections between these, we can incorporate social and environmental value creation into finance education without sacrificing analytical rigor. This means relying on examples and cases that emphasize SEERS impacts on the top half of exhibit 7.3. Today there are still very few cases or exercises that make this connection explicit. Until good teaching materials become more abundant, educators must be creative.

One way to do this is to focus on cost reduction. The easiest business case to make for SEERS is a direct reduction in costs. Our earlier discussion defined this as a cost savings that requires no additional investment or expense and also highlighted their infrequency. The more typical cost savings from social and environmental activity come when the firm makes an investment in new technology and incurs incremental costs or revenues elsewhere.

We use the *Acid Rain: The Southern Co. (A)* case (Reinhardt 1992) to illustrate this tradeoff. In the case, Southern Company, one of the largest power generators in the United States, is considering several options for complying with new pollution regulations at its largest coal-fired power plant. Although this is an older case, it provides an example of a cap-and-trade system for sulfur dioxide and analyzes new investment, input switching, and incremental costs and revenues. The case also enables students to engage predictive logic to quantitatively estimate the impact of various SEERS choices on profitability, cash flow, and value.

We use several cases on residential energy efficiency to connect financial analyses to SEERS. In one case students evaluate the costs and the benefits of adding insulation to an older home. In another case they compute the expected payback and current value of the investments in and savings from a residential solar photovoltaic installation. Although these activities are at the individual level, it is easy to scale up the exercises for a corporate scenario.

We also connect examples from the popular business news and corporate news releases of companies' SEERS initiatives that produce cost savings. Many companies issue annual sustainability reports that provide a wealth of ideas for the classroom.* Even though these reports are thin on financial metrics, they can be used to develop budding entrepreneurial leaders' understanding of the range of SEERS opportunities that companies are pursuing. This discussion can be used to press students about the impact that they think certain activities have on corporate financial performance and shareholder value (and how the connection might be measured).

After cost savings, direct revenue enhancement through SEERS activities has the strongest impact on corporate financial performance. Recall that direct revenue enhancement occurs when companies sell products with socially responsible attributes. These cash flows are more volatile and less certain because we must now incorporate the fickle nature of consumer behavior. To introduce students to these issues, we developed a case on bio-plastics to highlight the challenges of profitably developing and marketing a "green" product (Bliss 2007).

We are also in the process of developing an exercise to quantify the costs and the benefits of owning a Prius. This discussion raises the

---

*More than 1,300 companies from various industries around the world have reports that can be accessed at *http://www.globalreporting.org/GRIReports/GRIReportsList.*

important question of where boundaries can be drawn when evaluating SEERS initiatives. For example, from the driver's perspective owning a Prius may reduce fossil-fuel consumption and CO_2 emissions. When the entire environmental impact of producing the Prius and manufacturing and disposing of its batteries over the vehicle's life is included, however, the cost/benefit analysis becomes more muddled. By looking at the issue from multiple perspectives, students are forced to deal with the inherent ambiguity of analyzing SEERS using predictive logic.

As we proceed downward in exhibit 7.3, the connection between CSR and shareholder value creation gets weaker and there are fewer teaching materials that lend themselves to quantitative financial analysis. As such we have not yet focused our financial analyses with students on the link between CSR and indirect revenue enhancement, although we are trying to make these connections. For example, we are considering a case about an investment fund that purports to have CSR screening metrics that identify superior future stock returns. This case will make a contribution to the discussion regarding socially responsible investing and the ability to pick better-performing stocks using a combination of financial, social, and environmental measures.

Given the challenges of linking corporate social responsibility and shareholder value, we do not have a proven method based in predictive logic for quantifying the impacts of risk-reducing CSR activities. This is especially true when considering reputation risk. There are, however, many cases that highlight how a company's bad CSR practices negatively affect reputation. In the case of BP and the 2010 *Deepwater Horizon* oil rig explosion and spill, for example, there was a clear direct reduction in cash flow due to the cleanup and the legal expenses associated with the spill. The consumer boycotts and the damage to reputation also acted to indirectly reduce cash flow via lost revenues. In these instances the impact of poor corporate citizenship on shareholder value is both direct and indirect.

The final way that finance educators can help students develop their predictive logic assessment of SEERS activities is by including materials that may not emphasize the shareholder value connection quantitatively but that simply revolve around companies selling environmentally friendly products and services. For example, the topic of venture capital funding is popular with students, and using a green company for financial discussion can indirectly raise SEERS awareness with no loss of financial rigor.

Conclusion

The topic of SEERS should not generate anxiety or fear for finance educators. By using predictive logic and proven analytical tools with which we are already comfortable, SEERS and the existing tenets of finance can coexist with little conflict. The clearest connection between social and environmental initiatives and shareholder value are activities that directly increase cash flow.

There are numerous SEERS initiatives that reduce costs and increase revenues, and for these we can easily estimate their impact on corporate financial performance and shareholder value. By evaluating social and environmental investments in the same way we analyze other investments, we provide a rigorous financial assessment of the costs and the benefits of SEERS activities. Nonetheless we recognize that other aspects of SEERS are more difficult to connect to value creation. This is because their impact on a firm's cash flow—which ultimately is a key determinant of value—is less clear. For these SEERS activities, companies may need to postpone their adoption until there is more certainty around the financial implication and the impact on shareholder value.

When we discuss social and environmental issues and their economic impact in a free market, we believe that there will always be inherent tensions among these three dimensions. By subjecting the most extreme viewpoints—that is, that all SEERS activities are either universally good or bad—to a modicum of scrutiny and analysis, we can foster a fruitful and enlightening discussion and produce students who better understand how SEERS connects to shareholder value. These discussions, along with those suggested by our accounting colleagues, can raise awareness of a variety of SEERS issues and their financial implications and produce future entrepreneurial leaders who understand both the tensions and the potential synergies of social, environmental, and economic responsibility and sustainability.

References

Adkins, S. 2003. "Cause-Related Marketing: Who Cares Wins," in *The Marketing Book,* 5th edition, ed. M. J. Baker. Burlington, MA: Butterworth-Heinemann, 670.

Ailworth, E. 2010. "Wal-Mart Challenges Cape Wind's High Prices." *Boston Globe,* June 17. http://wap.boston.com/art/35/business/articles/2010/06/17/wal_mart_says_cape_winds_high_costs_will_hurt_retailer/?p=1.

American Beverage Association. n.d. "School Beverage Guidelines Ads." Accessed March 3, 2011, http://www.ameribev.org/nutrition--science/school-beverage-guidelines/ads--multimedia.

Bhanoo, S. N. 2010. "Products That Are Earth-and-Profit Friendly." *New York Times,* June 11. http://www.nytimes.com/2010/06/12/business/energy-environment/12sustain.html.

Bishop, S. 2008. "It's Green, But Will People Want It?" *Harvard Business Review,* September 10. http://blogs.hbr.org/leadinggreen/2008/09/its-green-but-will-people-want.html.

Bliss, R. 2007. *Socially Responsible Investing: Metabolix, Inc.* Babson Park, MA: Babson College.

Brammer, S., A. Millington, and B. Rayton. 2007. "The Contribution of Corporate Social Responsibility to Organizational Commitment." *International Journal of Human Resource Management 18* (10): 1701–19.

Cause Integration. 2010. "The Most 'Unethical Company' Is Also a 'Best Corporate Citizen.'" March 9. http://www.causeintegration.com/2010/the-most-unethical-company-is-a-best-corporate-citizen-what-gives.

Demetrakakes, P. 2007. "How to Sustain 'Green' Packaging: 'Sustainable Packaging' Is Getting a Lot of Attention. But What Does It Mean, and How Can It Appeal to Consumers?" *Food and Drug Packaging*, June. http://findarticles.com/p/articles/mi_m0UQX/is_5_71/ai_n19346051.

Eurosif. 2010. *European SRI Study.* http://www.eurosif.org/research/eurosif -sri-study/2010.

Herbert, B. 1996. "From Sweatshops to Aerobics" [op-ed]. *New York Times,* June 24, A.15.

Hill and Knowlton. 2008. "Reputation and the War for Talent: Corporate Reputation Watch 2008." http://www2.hillandknowlton.com/crw/charts.asp.

Kytle, B. and J. Ruggie. 2005. *Corporate Social Responsibility as Risk Management: A Model for Multinationals.* Corporate Social Responsibility Initiative working paper No. 10, John F. Kennedy School of Government, Harvard University, p. 15.

Luo, X., and C. B. Bhattacharya. 2009. "The Debate over Doing Good: Corporate Social Performance, Strategic Marketing Levers, and Firm-Idiosyncratic Risk." *Journal of Marketing* 73 (6), 198–213.

Margolis, J. D., and J. P. Walsh. 2003. "Misery Loves Companies: Rethinking Social Initiatives by Business." *Administrative Science Quarterly* 48 (2), 268–305.

Monster.com. MonsterTRAK Joins Forces with ecoAmerica to Launch Green Careers by MonsterTRAK [news release]. October 3, 2007. http://www .prweb.com/releases/monstertrak/green/prweb558374.htm.

Orlitzky, M., F. L. Schmidt, and S. L. Rynes. 2003. "Corporate Social and Financial Performance: A Meta-Analysis." *Organization Studies* 24: 403–41.

Pereira, J. 2003. "Doing Good and Doing Well at Timberland." *New York Times,* September 9.

Ravich, M. 2010. "CRO's New CSR Ranking." March 12. http://www.just means.com/CRO-s-New-CSR-Ranking/10707.html.

Reich, R. B. 2008. *The Case against Corporate Social Responsibility.* Goldman School of Public Policy working paper No. GSPP08-003, University of California, Berkeley. http://ssrn.com/abstract=1213129.

Reinhardt, F. 1992. *Acid Rain: The Southern Co. (A)*. Case 9-9722-060. Boston: Harvard Business School.

Renneboog, L., J. Ter Horst, and C. Zhang. 2008. "The Price of Ethics and Stakeholder Governance: The Performance of Socially Responsible Mutual Funds." *Journal of Corporate Finance* 14 (3), 302–22.

Social Investment Forum Foundation. 2010. *2010 Report on Socially Responsible Investing Trends in the United States: Executive Summary*. Accessed March 3, 2011, http://www.socialinvest.org/resources/pubs/trends/docu ments/2010TrendsES.pdf.

Towers Perrin Global Workforce Study. 2007–2008. "Closing the Engagement Gap: A Road Map for Driving Superior Business Performance." http://www.towersperrin.com/tp/getwebcachedoc?webc=HRS/ USA/2008/200803/GWS_Global_Report20072008_31208.pdf.

Wal-Mart Stores Inc. 2010. *Wal-Mart Global Sustainability Report: 2010 Progress Update*. Accessed March 3, 2011, http://cdn.walmartstores.com/sites/ sustainabilityreport/2010/WMT2010GlobalSustainabilityReport.pdf.

Weber, G. 2005. "Preserving the Starbucks Counter Culture." *Workforce Management,* February, 28–34. http://www.workforce.com/section/ recruiting-staffing/feature/preserving-starbucks-counter-culture.

Wikipedia. 2010. "Cause Marketing." Accessed March 25, 2011, http:// en.wikipedia.org/wiki/Cause_marketing.

Zmuda, N. 2010. "Beverage Giants Team Up to Remove Schools' Soda. *Crain's New York Business.com,* March 10. http://www.crainsnewyork.com/ article/20100310/FREE/100319988.

PART III

Self- and Social Awareness to Guide Action

CHAPTER **8**

Who Am I? Learning from and Leveraging Self-Awareness

James Hunt, Nan S. Langowitz, Keith Rollag, and Karen Hebert-Maccaro

AT THE CORE OF ENTREPRENEURIAL LEADERSHIP IS AN INDIVIDU-al's deep understanding of him- or herself, the context in which he or she is operating, and his or her network of relationships. Returning to the Clorox Green Works example discussed in the introduction, the success of the venture was dependent on a few entrepreneurial leaders' being deeply connected to their values regarding the environment and the safety of families. These leaders' passion to follow their values and put them into practice brought Green Works to market. Similarly, Robert Chatwani's passion for supporting artisans in developing countries was fundamental to the founding of WorldofGood .com (see chapter 4). Focusing on their own passions, these entrepreneurial leaders created teams who shared their vision for bringing a social and economic opportunity to fruition.

Beyond understanding themselves, these entrepreneurial leaders were also successful because they were aware of and responsive to the context in which they were operating. In the case of Green Works, the entrepreneurial leaders developed insight into why a certain population was interested in natural cleaning products. By connecting to the values and not the demographics of this group, they opened up a new market for Clorox and for the natural-products industry as a whole. Similarly, Chatwani's interactions with the local artisans in India helped him understand the needs of this community. His knowledge of eBay and its values also enabled him to garner internal support for WorldofGood.com by showing how the opportunity connected to eBay's culture.

Finally, these entrepreneurial leaders did not bring about these changes alone. They engaged others who co-created these opportunities. In the case of Clorox, the corporate marketing group, the new Clorox CEO, and the Sierra Club brought Green Works to market together. In Chatwani's case, he motivated co-creators inside eBay and connected with a critical outside partner, Priya Haji. For both sets of entrepreneurial leaders, these connections arose because they had passion for their ideas and they used experiments to build momentum for these initiatives. Network connections transformed how both of these innovative ideas developed.

In this chapter we explore how to teach entrepreneurial leaders to identify and engage their awareness of their passions, values, and skills. We focus on how budding entrepreneurial leaders can learn from and leverage personal and professional self-awareness.

Management Development and the Missing Focus on Self-Awareness

These examples indicate that the new entrepreneurial leaders need an extraordinarily strong and realistic understanding of who they are. They must understand their own identities in terms of their values, drives, and background and must be honest and open about their capabilities and limitations. This understanding provides the basis for their ability to build social and economic opportunity.

Consider, for example, John Chambers, CEO of Cisco, the largest networking communications firm in the world. Chambers has dyslexia, a condition characterized by difficulty reading written words and text-based communications. When he was growing up, the condition led him to appreciate the world of learning and human communication that existed outside of books. Chambers openly draws on this experience as he encourages employees to experiment and grow Cisco's video and web conferencing business, which aims to make virtual face-to-face meetings a more engaging alternative to sending long e-mails.

Similarly, Jeff Immelt, CEO of General Electric (GE), one of the most admired global corporations and known for its leadership, has newly refocused on what he describes as becoming "self-reflective on steroids." Immelt views his approach, and the one he hopes other leaders at GE will adopt, as a means to promote greater innovation to drive GE's performance (Brady 2010). While most entrepreneurial leaders do not have the high-profile roles of Chambers and Immelt, each has unique strengths and challenges as well as passions, values, and skills that he or she needs to understand and engage to drive opportunities.

Unfortunately, too many leaders have not done the work to know who they are and what they want. Worse yet, some even discount the inner voice that tries to inform them about their passions, strengths, and limitations. They have a poor understanding of their current strengths and weaknesses and have not given much thought to how to identify and improve on the critical competencies required to be successful in their current or desired careers. Even if they have done some self-reflection about their goals and abilities, few leaders understand how to engage their passion and goals to drive new social and economic opportunity. Thus to develop entrepreneurial leaders, management educators must help them assess their values, abilities, and interests. We need to educate these future leaders in how to improve their skills and competencies in ways that will enable them to create value for themselves and their organizations.

When individuals decide to enroll in business school or participate in a leadership development program, they are often looking to discover new ways of thinking, build new networks, and expand their horizons. Sadly, this is not the reality of what most individuals experience when they take a management development course and particularly when they enter an MBA program.

Both managers and academics have argued that MBA programs have become divorced from the realities of the workplace, disconnected from working students' day-to-day organizational experiences, and overly technical, teaching students concepts rather than introducing them to new ways of thinking and new insights to inform their leadership approach (Bennis and O'Toole 2005; Mintzberg 2004; Rubin and Dierdorff 2009). Organizations have complained that MBA graduates often emerge with unrealistic expectations of their self-worth and have not acquired the self-awareness and the social skills to quickly become effective leaders (Feldman 2005).

In essence most MBA students have not developed self-awareness of their goals and abilities in the context of their existing or future organizations. As such they are unprepared to help others build their self-awareness. What ultimately makes MBA graduates successful entrepreneurial leaders is their ability to not only proactively manage their own careers but also help develop the careers of others. Few MBA programs provide students with training and practice in talent development, particularly on how to prepare direct reports, identify personal career goals, assess and improve critical competencies, and provide coaching and support. This gap represents a largely untapped opportunity for management educators and leadership development professionals.

Linking Self-Awareness to Career and Talent Development

The context of talent and career management provides the perfect backdrop for introducing students to the importance of self-awareness and showing them the value that comes from a deep understanding of oneself. Against this backdrop we have developed an innovative course—Managerial Assessment and Development (MAD)*—which teaches future entrepreneurial leaders how to be more self-reflective and how to use that knowledge to guide their careers. The MAD course has the following objectives for students:

- Develop self-awareness by articulating their aspirations and gaining systematic insight into their strengths and weaknesses in relation to those aspirations

- Take ownership of their professional futures through a stepwise curriculum that leads to an individual development plan

- Take action to negotiate next steps with key stakeholders in their workplaces

- Learn to facilitate these activities with their direct reports

The learning experience in the MAD course deepens participants' ability to place themselves in context, whether for their own professional development or for working with and through others. This is particularly important in today's economic climate, where leaders are more likely to have protean careers that are self-determined and follow non-traditional paths (Hall 2002). This learning can be seen in the following quote:

> The MAD class taught me that I need to be challenging myself in a different way than I currently am in my role right now. . . .

---

*The course title draws on the work of Richard Boyatzis and his colleagues at Case Western.

Furthermore, by implementing my development plan, I had one of the best reviews I have had yet. My manager was totally amazed that I was able to implement her direct feedback so effectively from her last review. I knew that getting my MBA would help me grow my career in the long term but never in my wildest dreams would I have thought that coming to business school would help my career grow in the short term!

—Account executive, Internet portal company

As this feedback suggests, the MAD course helps leaders learn to explore talent management within their own careers and organizations. For organizations, sustainable competitive advantage frequently depends on the ability to innovatively select and deploy talent (Pfeffer 1998). Understanding how to attract, develop, and retain talented individuals is a strategic imperative for performance excellence, and understanding how to do this specifically with entrepreneurial leaders is all the more complicated. Furthermore, as demographic shifts continue in the United States and many other developed economies, the significance of talent management increases.

At the start of the twenty-first century, McKinsey and Co. reported on the "war for talent" and an updated report a decade later reiterated the importance of paying attention to the impacts that demographic changes have on human capital in organizations (Guthridge, Komm, and Lawson 2008; Michaels, Handfield-Jones, and Axelrod 2001). As populations age and become more diverse, shifting demographics also represent a new challenge for organizations (Guthridge, Komm, and Lawson 2008; Strack, Baier, and Fahlander 2008). These trends influence the selection, retention, and development processes in organizations and broaden the concept of fit. Entrepreneurial leaders will achieve great results only if they are able to carefully marshal and develop talent—both their own and that of their employees (Buckingham and Coffman 1999).

The basic concepts of talent management underlie the best practices of effective career management. For example, a fundamental concept underlying talent management is that of the fit between an individual's competencies and the role that he or she plays. Career development requires that one is aware of one's career and personal identity (Hall 2002), of the drivers that motivate the individual (Schein 1978, 2006), and of the relationship between oneself and one's context (Holland 1958). Developing self-awareness and the various aspects of emotional intelligence is a competency for professional success and leadership (Goleman 1995, 2000).

Developing talent also means that entrepreneurial leaders understand the issue of competency development and are capable of developing their own competencies and those of the individuals around them. Competency development, which helps the self adjust to a changing context, occurs largely through on-the-job learning and requires that employees have a chance to take on challenges, assess their progress in meeting those challenges, and have access to learning supports such as coaching, training, and continuing education (McCall, Lombardo, and Morrison 1988; Van Velsor and McCauley 2004).

By connecting competencies to the needs of the organization, entrepreneurial leaders are able to connect and build on employees' developmental interests, provide them with challenging work, and help them reflect on their efforts (Hunt and Weintraub [2002] 2010). All of this also requires self-awareness on the part of the employees, an awareness that can grow especially through dialogue with a manager who is self-aware. Talent management at its best is a negotiated outcome between two parties, both of whom understand what they want and need.

For future entrepreneurial leaders, career and talent management provide the ideal conditions to examine who they are in terms of their skills, values, and drives and how this connects to their careers and their life work. While entrepreneurial leaders are focused on developing their organizations and their teams, they are also driven by their desire to develop their own careers in a way that connects to their passions. Without this connection they are not likely to be successful. The MAD course facilitates the development of this critical connection.

Overview of the Managerial Assessment and Development Course

In our design of the MAD course, conceptual material regarding talent management is linked to a series of self-assessment and analysis exercises that lead to the creation of an individual development plan. In this process students focus on the following questions:

- Where and how should they invest their career energy?

- What do they have to invest (talent, values, competencies, and motivation)?

- What do they want in return for that investment (career and life aspirations)?

- How can they as managers maximize the effectiveness of the talent their organizations need to achieve business goals?

- What do they know about how their team members and colleagues would answer the first three questions, and how might that change the way they work with them or provide opportunities to them?

By focusing on these questions, participants learn to engage creation logic as they devise action experiments to assess and build their own personal talent, values, and drives and support others with the same approach.

The MAD course is taught in the context of our blended-learning MBA program designed for professionals with 15 years of experience.

As a blended-learning program, the course is delivered primarily online. Program participants meet in person only once, for a day-long session during the fifth week of the seven-week course. While many educators have questioned the use of distance learning to teach interpersonal concepts, we have found that this format provides new opportunities for students, as it enables them to wrestle with questions regarding their personal development in ways that better fit their individual learning styles and time frames.

Next we discuss in more detail the four central components of the course design: assessment, feedback and coaching, the development plan, and personal reflection. We conclude with a discussion of how these components work together to enhance participants' self-awareness and creation-oriented approach to career and talent management.

Assessment

The foundation of the MAD course is a diverse set of self-assessment activities. Students are required to complete three different assessments:

- The DISC Inventory, which provides insight regarding behavioral style tendencies (Target Training International, n.d.)

- The Career Anchors Self-Assessment, which provides insight into the motivations that drive career choices and satisfaction (Schein 2006)

- A Multi-Rater Survey (360-degree) that we have developed specifically for this program

Reading assignments and course discussion prompt students to assess their learning style (Kolb 1976), the structure of their social networks, and the strength of their networks and networking skills (Bolt 2005; Ibarra and Hunter 2007).

As the course progresses, we introduce new assessment data, and students make sense of its meaning for themselves through small- and large-group discussions and personal reflection. We remind students that no data or assessment tool is "the last word" on who they are. Rather students must interpret the array of data they receive to develop their self-awareness and establish their direction. Thus students are taught to engage a creation approach to building their careers.

One of the innovative instruments that students use in this self-assessment process is the Multi-Rater Survey. The strength of this instrument is that it provides feedback on five competencies that are central to entrepreneurial leadership:

- Creativity, innovation, and entrepreneurship

- Leadership, coaching, teamwork, and change management

- Decision-making and problem solving

- Business acumen

- Ethics, moral values, and law

These competencies connect to cognitive ambidexterity, SEERS, and self- and social awareness.

Course participants invite at least 10 individuals to participate in an anonymous online survey. We encourage students to seek feedback that can help them better understand their effectiveness in practice, not just in the classroom. We also encourage them to invite feedback from diverse work colleagues, who are likely to have different perspectives on their skills.

Even the process of inviting individuals to participate in the survey helps develop students' self- and social awareness because they are coached in how to invite their raters to participate, by explaining that the raters' feedback would be valuable to their learning. By understanding issues of reciprocity, the process of soliciting raters' feedback helps students develop their networking skills and encourages them to consider their raters as potential partners in their ongoing development. The effectiveness of this feedback is captured in one student's comment:

> The feedback was much more consistent and actionable than I had anticipated. This was my first time doing a 360, and the feedback was quite a bit more useful than manager assessments that I have received in the past. The 360 got into the details; there was a very consistent theme of my not expressing my opinions in meetings early on . . . Those stakeholders I will be keeping in mind are the same ones who filled out the 360, so they will certainly be a good sounding board for whether or not I am working toward improving this area of my work life.
>
> —*Vice president, investment management firm*

Feedback and Developmental Coaching

An important component of the MAD course is the notion that self-awareness and professional development do not just happen. Building this insight requires conscious effort and proactive negotiation with one's work context. Participants are taught to apply a creation approach to proactively drive their development. They also learn the importance of soliciting feedback through their network. This feedback enables them to evolve from not knowing what they don't know, to knowing they need to improve, to perhaps even becoming expert at a particular competency.

If talent is indeed a pattern of attitudes, behaviors, and skills performed at excellence (Buckingham and Coffman 1999), entrepreneurial leaders need to create a means for gaining feedback on how they are doing so that they can uncover and develop their talents.

In teaching participants to develop their self-awareness, the MAD course also shows them how to provide feedback to help others develop their self-awareness. Students learn the importance of separating observations from inference. This involves teaching them to suspend judgment and instead ask questions to gain clarification on how to interpret what has been observed. While this skill is particularly valuable in building social skills, it is also essential for entrepreneurial leaders to use when assessing and evaluating opportunities.

The final skill students learn in this phase is the concept of what it means to be a coaching manager and how this connects to entrepreneurial leadership. Through conceptual readings on the coaching manager (Hunt and Weintraub 2002, 2010), face-to-face faculty instruction, and a practice exercise aimed at reinforcing active listening and open-ended questioning, participants hone their coaching skills.

Later in the course when the 360-degree feedback reports are returned, students test their coaching skills by working in peer learning partnerships to help their counterparts interpret their assessment reports. The peer learning partnerships continue for the entire course, and participants say that this experience helps them make sense of the self-assessment process and prepares them for coaching others in the workplace.

Development Plan

The culmination of the course, and of developing participants' self-awareness and creation-based approach to career management, is the individual development plan. Creating the development plan requires students to reflect on the assessment results and feedback in the context of their professional aspirations. Given their aspirations, they are also asked to identify two to three competency-based development goals they need to make progress on their professional aspirations. This process of reflection and awareness of aspirations and competency-based development goals can be personally challenging to many participants. This exercise is often the first time that students have been forced to be intentional about understanding themselves and how this connects to their careers. As such they often need support from peer learning partners and faculty to do this self-exploration work honestly and thoughtfully.

In crafting their development plans, we encourage students to leverage the frame of challenge, assessment, and support—a concept they are introduced to early in the course (Van Velsor and McCauley 2004). While self-assessment in and of itself is valuable, entrepreneurial leaders gain true insight when self-assessment is connected with action. Thus as participants craft their development plans, we remind them that they will need to identify an opportunity that presents a challenge for their targeted developmental learning, specify how they will assess their learning along the way, and identify the resources or people available to provide support. Here again we remind students of the importance of connecting with other people when they apply this creation-oriented approach to their professional lives.

During the development plan creation phase, participants also learn to consider feasibility. They are asked to reflect on the political context of their proposed action so that they can create win-win opportunities, where moving toward their developmental goals and professional aspirations will benefit their organizations as well as themselves. If students can learn to frame their career aspirations in this way, they will have a better chance of gaining the opportunities, resources, and support they desire to enact their learning agendas and advance their career interests.

The final element of the development plan process involves engaging in a stakeholder conversation to "reality test" one's thinking. Participants identify a key stakeholder who has a vested interest in their development. In the final week of the course, students are required to discuss their development plan with this stakeholder. Reflecting on this conversation becomes the final input to their development plan as well as the topic of their final personal reflection blog entry. Participants learn that it is possible to have these conversations about self and career with key stakeholders. The following comment illustrates this point:

> I have to say that I was very pleasantly surprised with the meeting. She [the manager] really got into it and I ended up sharing a great deal more than I had planned. She also shared pretty openly about her own experiences. She was very supportive and committed to champion some of the opportunities I had outlined as well as suggested several which made their way into my final plan.
>
> Not only did we learn more about each other and our respective strengths and weaknesses but I think that seeing the strategic way I was approaching my career and tying it back to the organization's needs also increased her respect for me.
>
> *—Product marketing director, software firm*

Overall, for participants these conversations reinforce the need for self-awareness and to use this understanding to take ownership of their own career opportunities.

Personal Reflection

A key theme that runs through the MAD course is the importance of personal reflection to one's career and professional development as well as to one's development as an entrepreneurial leader. Participants learn that personal reflection is the foundational competency for developing deep self-awareness and for fueling a creation-oriented approach.

Personal self-reflection is developed in the course through the use of a blog. Every other week, students must respond to specific prompts that reference the week's work and ask for a reflection on its meaning to them. The faculty review these private blogs and provide students with feedback, questions, and insights. The personal self-reflection blog is instrumental in getting participants in the habit of making connections among different aspects of their professional lives as well as connecting their passions and interests to their careers. Faculty responses push students to reflect further or consider other possibilities.

The final reflection blog asks participants to reflect not only on the value of their stakeholder conversation for their own development but also on what they have taken away regarding how they will promote development for their direct reports. The dual focus of the course is brought full circle through the reflection blog. Students are reminded that as entrepreneurial leaders they must think about their responsibilities for development both as individuals and as talent managers.

Many participants incorporate the notion of perpetuating a weekly or biweekly reflection diary in their professional lives. Once they have gotten in the rhythm and have seen the power of personal refection, they don't want to lose the opportunities that personal reflection provides. This is a skill that entrepreneurial leaders can tap into throughout their lives as they consider how they take action and whether it is based on an open and inclusive view of the world.

Establishing Ownership for Self-Awareness

Since 2006 the Managerial Assessment and Development course has been taught more than 20 times to approximately 750 working professionals. The quotes in this chapter indicate how positively participants respond to the course. The personal self-reflections also indicate that participants use the learning experience to create new opportunities for themselves and to actively experiment with new approaches to talent management. Students' course assessments indicate that the MAD course gives participants a new way to understand themselves and others, and it teaches skills that are central to a creation approach to career development.

Beyond this immediate impact, evidence from follow-up research also suggests that MAD makes a difference in the long-term professional development of entrepreneurial leaders. In one study 90 course participants were asked to write an ungraded, confidential reflection on their development plan 18 months after taking the course. Specifically, students were asked to revisit their MAD development plan from the prior year and consider three points:

- The progress they had made

- The way their plans might have changed because of their experiences

- The challenges they were facing or expected to face

They were also asked to consider what had worked so far and what their next steps and commitments might be going forward. In recognition of their time, research participants received feedback from their professors on their self-reflections.

Our data analysis indicates that development planning is an invaluable action experiment that helps entrepreneurial leaders improve their understanding of their identities and their ability to use this understanding to achieve developmental learning outcomes and work toward their professional aspirations. Using content analysis, we examined students' post-facto reflections in comparison with the development plans written 18 months earlier. Adapting Hall's criteria for assessing career management activities and outcomes (2002), we coded the reflections with respect to career identity and work performance and then looked to understand how the development plans of those participants with strong identity and performance outcomes differed from those with weak identity and performance outcomes.

We found two distinct differences between the high-performance/high-identity and low-performance/low-identity groups. First, the high-performance/high-identity participants differed in the degree of *ownership* they displayed for their plans. These participants created development plans that exhibited strong evidence of insightful self-reflection, integrated use and personal interpretation of feedback and self-assessment data, and understood the connection between self-assessment and career goals. Second, high-performance/high-identity participants differed in the level of *proactivity and intentionality* demonstrated in their plans.

These results suggest that the MAD course has the potential to teach participants to develop the skills of ownership and intentionality—both of which are critical for entrepreneurial leadership. Ownership of one's development is not easy and requires personal investment. Students need to be passionate enough that they are willing to engage in self-reflection based on available assessment data and feedback. To develop skills around ownership, students need to connect their self-reflection to their career goals and take responsibility for closing competency gaps to achieve those goals.

Students learn the skill of intentionality by placing specific learning goals within the context of self-assessment and career aspirations and then identifying an action agenda to achieve those goals. They also develop intentionality in exhibiting creation-oriented behavior as they proactively seek input and feedback toward the implementation of their action agenda.

For the faculty who teach the MAD course, the follow-up research has provided an impetus for an even stronger emphasis on developing participants' competencies for self- and contextual awareness. It is important to reinforce to students that careers, like any other organizational endeavor, are often the result of a negotiated outcome, the implication being that entrepreneurial leaders must know what they desire and take action to further their interests.

The flip side of that message is that in their organizations these entrepreneurial leaders can drive social and economic opportunity by actively cultivating the talent of those they lead and manage. For both entrepreneurial leaders and the organizations in which they work, setting motivational goals, growing competencies through challenges, fitting individuals to roles, and providing both feedback and support along the way—all compose an essential recipe for strategic success. Engaging in and helping others with their self-awareness and development planning is an essential platform for entrepreneurial leadership in an increasingly ambiguous world in which careers are no longer linear but turbulent.

Conclusion

We began this chapter by discussing the apparent gap between the offerings of management education and the need to help students develop self-awareness of goals and abilities in the context of their existing or future organizations. Current criticisms of the relevance of management education, and of management development more generally, necessitate more than just the change of a single course.

Our experience suggests that the introduction of self-assessment and professional development work can be an important step for entrepreneurial leaders to take action to shape their careers and the talents of those they lead. Such opportunities, if they provide both the proper conceptual prompts and the mental and curricular space for reflection and planning, enable entrepreneurial leaders to develop the skills and the insight they need to shape social and economic opportunity that is connected to their personal passions and abilities.

References

Bennis, W., and J. O'Toole. 2005. "How Business Schools Lost Their Way." *Harvard Business Review* 83 (5): 96–124.

Bolt, J. 2005. "Networking Smarter: What's Your NQ?" *Fast Company,* October 10. http://www.fastcompany.com/resources/learning/bolt/101005 .html.

Brady, D. 2010. "Can GE Still Manage?" *Businessweek,* April 15. http://www .businessweek.com/print/magazine/content/10_17/b4175026765571 .htm.

Buckingham, M., and C. Coffman. 1999. *First, Break All the Rules: What the World's Greatest Managers Do Differently.* New York: Simon and Schuster.

Feldman, D. C. 2005. "The Food's No Good and They Don't Give Us Enough: Reflections on Mintzberg's Critique of MBA Education." *Academy of Management Learning and Education* 4 (2), 217–20.

Goleman, D. 1995. *Emotional Intelligence.* New York: Bantam Books.

Goleman, D. 2000. "Leadership That Gets Results." *Harvard Business Review* 78 (2): 78–90.

Guthridge, M., A. Komm, and E. Lawson. 2008. "Making Talent a Strategic Priority." *McKinsey Quarterly* 1: 49–59.

Hall, D. T. 2002. *Careers in and out of Organizations.* Thousand Oaks, CA: Sage.

Holland, J. L. 1958. "A Personality Inventory Employing Occupational Titles." *Journal of Applied Psychology* 42: 336–42.

Hunt, J., and J. Weintraub. (2002) 2010. *The Coaching Manager: Developing Top Talent in Business.* Thousand Oaks, CA: Sage.

Ibarra, H., and M. Hunter. 2007. "How Leaders Create and Use Networks." *Harvard Business Review* 85 (1): 40–47.

Kolb, D. A. 1976. "Management and the Learning Process." *California Management Review* 18 (3): 21–31.

McCall, M., M. Lombardo, and A. Morrison. 1988. *The Lessons of Experience: How Successful Executives Develop on the Job.* New York: Lexington Books.

Michaels, E., H. Handfield-Jones, and B. Axelrod. 2001. *The War for Talent.* Boston: Harvard Business School.

Mintzberg, H. 2004. *Managers Not MBAs: A Hard Look at the Soft Practice of Managing and Management Development.* San Francisco: Berrett-Koehler.

Pfeffer, J. 1998. *The Human Equation: Building Profits by Putting People First.* Boston: Harvard Business School.

Rubin, R. S., and E. C. Dierdorff. 2009. "How Relevant Is the MBA? Assessing the Alignment of Required Curricula and Required Managerial Competencies." *Academy of Management Learning and Education* 8 (2): 208–24.

Schein, E. H. 1978. *Career Dynamics: Matching Individual and Organizational Needs.* Reading, MA: Addison-Wesley.

Schein, E. H. 2006. *Careers Anchors: Self-Assessment,* 3rd ed. San Diego: Pfeiffer.

Strack, R., J. Baier, and A. Fahlander. 2008. "Managing Demographic Risk." *Harvard Business Review* 86 (2): 119–28.

Target Training International. n.d. Accessed March 3, 2011, http://www.tti disc.com.

Van Velsor, E., and C. McCauley. 2004. "Our View of Leadership Development," in *Handbook of Leadership Development,* ed C. McCauley and E. Van Velsor. San Francisco: Jossey-Bass.

CHAPTER 9

What Is the Context? Fostering Entrepreneurial Leaders' Social Awareness

Stephen Deets and Lisa DiCarlo

> We don't see things as they are, we see them as we are.
>
> —*Anaïs Nin*

B Y THE END OF CAITLYN'S FIRST EVENING IN THE COUNTRY, THE Ghanaian fishmongers had reduced her to tears. Caitlyn had traveled to Ghana excited about the opportunity to advise Ghanaians on how to improve their businesses. During her first evening of consultations, however, the women in her small group openly mocked her. Whenever she offered a new idea, the women laughed, "What do you think this is— America?"

The next day Caitlyn took a different approach. She asked questions and listened intently. The women slowly opened up and explained the entire process—from how fish are caught to how they are sold at the market. More importantly, they helped Caitlyn understand how the community operates and the social relations and practices that surround the fishing industry. Although Caitlyn did not solve these business owners' problems, by listening and learning about the Ghanaian context she was able to advise the group in a way that was consistent with the social processes that make the Ghanaian fishing industry work.

It is not radical to argue that understanding self- and social context is a prerequisite to addressing social problems, embarking on new expansion opportunities, and making global business initiatives work at the local level. This principle forms the basis of many organizational strategies. For example, HSBC, which brands itself as "the world's local bank," built this idea into its ubiquitous "Different Points of Value" 2009 ad campaign (Financial Brand 2009). Building on its belief that "differences create value," HSBC developed a highly successful ad campaign that challenged the viewer to consider personal points of view on a number of topics and to recognize the many contradictory points of view that exist around the world.

For example, one print advertisement features three identical photographs, arranged side by side, of a finely detailed Persian carpet. The word *décor* is superimposed over the first, *souvenir* over the second, and *place of prayer* over the third. In another print ad, *freedom* is superimposed over the photo of a classic American sports car zooming down a tree-lined road, *status symbol* is over the second photo, and *polluter* is over the third. HSBC has stated that this ad campaign echoes the same dilemmas the organization faces as it tries to be aware of and responsive to the viewpoints and the practices of local communities (Green 2008).

As these examples illustrate, it is not enough for entrepreneurial leaders to simply recognize different viewpoints and the contextual differences of the local environment; they must also know how to engage this understanding to guide their actions. To develop this understanding, we work with students to reflect on their own identities, biases, and assumptions of the way the world works and to consider how this worldview compares with that of the context in which they are operating. When entrepreneurial leaders consider the unique perspectives and practices that embody a local context, they are able to successfully and responsibly discover avenues for change.

In chapter 8 we outlined the innovative approach we take to nurture entrepreneurial leaders' self-awareness. In this chapter we expand beyond the individual focus to explore the importance of cultivating social awareness.

The Need to Consider Social Context

Over the past 20 years, we have moved from a single view of the "objective" reality of business and management practices to an increased emphasis on how individual perspective and culture shape our "objective" realities. Behavioral economics, for example, arose out of the recognition that individual desires, emotions, and psychological traits have an impact on economic decision-making (Kahneman and Tversky 1979; Simon 1996). This has expanded into broader recognition of the roles that culture and social norms play in determining what individuals consider valuable during economic interactions.

The work of the French sociologist, anthropologist, and philosopher Pierre Bourdieu has been particularly influential in enhancing our understanding of the relationship between individual action and the construction of society. Seeking to bridge arguments about the relationship between individual action and social structure, Bourdieu and Wacquant (1992) begin with the idea that most of what we do every day is governed by informal rules and unconscious decision-making. Our individual actions reflect our socialization into the diverse "fields" in which we act; a "field" can be anything from a community to an academic discipline to a corporate department to a country.

Students, for example, easily recognize that their goals and behaviors in a nightclub on Saturday differ from those with their families on Sunday, which differs from those in the classroom on Monday. They also realize that they generally do not consciously think about how they act in each setting. Thus for entrepreneurial leaders to understand how individuals conceive of their interests, it is critical that they learn about the beliefs, norms, and perspectives that shape perceptions of behavior.

Bourdieu's views on the relationship between the individual and the social structure are already embedded in many important management principles. For example, when academics and managers discuss organizational culture, they are referencing the relationship between the individual and the social structure. In connecting culture to strategy, we are educating students on how cultural values and norms guide individual behavior toward collective action. In discussing socialization, we teach managers how to proactively introduce individuals to the organizational context and help them quickly and easily adapt their actions to fit that context (Rollag, Parise, and Cross 2005).

These discussions are useful for introducing management students to the concept of context, but they often don't go deep enough. Entrepreneurial leaders need to develop the skills and the knowledge to fully understand how social identity is created, how identities are important to the construction of social networks, how rules and institutions shape behavior, and how context affects decision-making. By understanding the ways in which social identities—both our own and those of others—are constructed, entrepreneurial leaders explore the normative assumptions and behaviors that affect their ability to move new ideas forward.

Better Place CEO Shai Agassi, for example, has railed against groupthink in the auto industry. He believes that major car companies assume that the way people use cars will remain the same. As a result, companies are overly focused on increasing fuel efficiency and maintaining financial models based on selling cars. Agassi argues that electrification of vehicles could cause a paradigm shift in the way people use and fundamentally think about cars. We use the term *cognitive locks* to describe situations in which decision-making fails because individuals, individually or collectively, fail to examine an issue in an innovative way. When cognitive lock sets in, an individual will simply try harder rather than recognize that the causal effects of our actions may be historically or culturally contingent and our actions may need to change in light of changing contexts (see, for example, Blyth 2001).

Moreover, socially constructed identities create advantages and disadvantages when entrepreneurial leaders try to move an opportunity forward. Understanding the privilege granted to some perspectives means becoming aware that certain kinds of knowledge, insights, and ways of acting have been undervalued or even silenced. This is also true when thinking specifically about social positioning, which has significant implications for individuals' ability to access various social networks, for how social networks can be used as a resource, and for how resources can be mobilized through social networks. For example, organizational initiatives around diversity and inclusiveness are about recognizing the value of those who historically have been marginalized, and they provide insight on what we are losing by not having networks that include diverse perspectives.

Developing a deep understanding of identity and context is therefore important to releasing creativity in problem solving. In this respect it is important to note that Bourdieu speaks not just of how our actions reflect and reinforce social norms but also how we can act in ways that modify and challenge such norms. Entrepreneurial leaders need to view culture and social practice as both a constraint and a resource. Thus when embarking on new endeavors, entrepreneurial leaders can decide whether to accept culture as a constraint or to act in ways that can modify existing social practices and beliefs.

Teaching Entrepreneurial Leaders Social Awareness

While it is clear that entrepreneurial leaders need to understand their identities and develop their social awareness, the challenge is that these ideas are rarely taught in business schools or management development programs. The lack of deep understanding of social context and perspective is at the heart of recent criticisms of management education that focus predominately on maximizing economic profit.

One reason for the dearth of contextual learning opportunities in business curricula is the suspicion with which the related research in the realms of management context, organizational culture, and employee perspectives is regarded. For researchers to capture, study, and translate the gray area of context, they usually have to do so through qualitative, ethnographic research methods. As quantitative research remains the dominant paradigm in most management disciplines, this qualitative research is often dismissed as anecdotal. Until management disciplines learn to embrace and value qualitative social science methods, we do not expect that management students will find many learning opportunities that will enable them to investigate a corporate or industrial context through a contextual lens (Van Maanen 2011). Of course, another possibility is to open up management education to other disciplinary perspectives such as the social sciences, design research, or courses like the ones described later in this chapter.

We recognize the complexity of teaching any individual, particularly management students, how to consider identity, context, and perspective in their decision-making. As students learn about perspective, they must acknowledge their own biases and assumptions and be willing to challenge them in light of new data. As such, learning opportunities regarding perspective and context must be well crafted to achieve these goals. This chapter focuses on learning opportunities that are designed to build social awareness through encounters with "exotic" cultures, yet we want to acknowledge that it is also possible to create these same experiences close to home.

For example, in our course The Enlightened Entrepreneur, we have found that local cultural studies provide a powerful learning opportunity. In one exercise students choose a person to investigate and inquire about the frequency of a particular behavior, such as study or eating habits. After a week of observing that specific behavior, students discover the discrepancy between statements about behavior and the actual behavior. As a class we discuss what motivates people to consciously or unconsciously misreport and how those tendencies are socially constructed and embedded in notions of what is acceptable or desirable in a given culture.

This exercise conveys the essence of storytelling truth—that a narrative can be as much about *what we want* as it is about *what is*. The exercise prepares students to then approach, infiltrate, and shadow the daily activities of a local social venture to capture the essence of the lived world of social entrepreneurs. In this "familiar" context, students anticipated that they would not discover anything new because they had read about social entrepreneurship and believed they knew the terrain. This exercise proves to be a valuable lesson in accepting text as only one of the many crucial sources in their search for understanding the world around them.

In the next section, we highlight two other learning programs we created to teach future entrepreneurial leaders how to be aware of and responsive to social context. One course engages a liberal arts orientation and the other a business orientation. As such they are designed differently and follow different conceptual structures. Despite these differences, you will notice many parallels between the programs. Both start with on-campus meetings to provide an overview of context and then follow with a short trip to explore another country and context. While in-country, students are encouraged to observe, listen, and engage. In this way the programs encourage epiphanies and reflection. The natural toggling between being an observer and being a participant helps students identify the exotic in the local and the everyday in the global and to fully examine the social construction of local norms and values. By developing an understanding of the origin and the nature of identity and behavior, it became possible for these

future entrepreneurial leaders to imagine creating new ways of interacting within both their own and very different contexts.

Supporting Local Development Opportunities in Ghana

For five years we have run a short course in which our students teach
entrepreneurship and basic business planning in Sekondi-Takoradi,
Ghana. Most course participants encounter a social context in Ghana
that is radically different from their own, forcing them to question
and reconstruct some of their basic beliefs about business and entrepreneurship. They learn that their knowledge about what constitutes
economic rationality, marketing success, and financial management is
culturally contingent. In other words, what are assumed to be univer-
sal laws in the United States, or even in developed countries, simply do
not work in a Ghanaian town.

This overseas course is structured around a one-week experience
in Ghana during which participants work in high schools, teaching
students how to write a business plan and preparing them to participate in a business plan competition created for the program. Course
participants also provide business consulting to adults. Outside of the
program requirements, participants have also established a microfund
and expanded an existing program for local high school students to
teach elementary school students the importance of saving and other
basic economic lessons.

Prior to traveling to Ghana, participants attend three weekend
preparation classes in which they are introduced to the historical,
political, and cultural context that surrounds Ghana and Africa more
broadly. Discussions focus on the broader theoretical perspectives
on state capacity, contentions between identity groups, and evolving
debates on development. Finally, we discuss the business climate and
the educational system in Ghana, as these are the aspects of the social

context with which participants will interact most. While these discussions provide background, we know it is difficult to fully appreciate differences in context and perspective until one confronts those differences in person. As such, when one is focused on helping entrepreneurial leaders understand perspective and context, it is essential to provide them with opportunities to experience different social contexts firsthand.

There are a number of unique ways in which we structure the program in Ghana to help participants develop skills to recognize and respond to differences in context and perspective. Participants confront myriad situations that do not conform to their own mental maps of how the world operates. The entire experience provides these provocative challenges to students' entrenched ideas. Reflecting on his experience teaching high school students, one participant said:

> Before leaving, I mapped out how to teach our Ghanaian students entrepreneurship. However, as with any journey of discovery, at some point you must leave the map behind. It was not enough to simply understand entrepreneurship or to know there would be differences in culture and values. We had to understand our Ghanaian students. What motivates them to learn? What do they value? How do they view the world in which they live? What events have shaped their lives? Only after asking ourselves questions like these could we truly stand before our students and engage them.

Working with the adults also fosters intense learning opportunities. During these sessions course participants are on their own with individuals who have businesses that they and their families depend on for survival. Below we share two such learning moments to illustrate how these situations enabled participants to break out of their cognitive locks and understand the importance of social awareness to engaging in entrepreneurial leadership.

In the first situation, course participants consulted with a woman who sold chips made of flour and butter. The woman put the chips into small bags, placed the bags into a giant bowl that she carried on her head, and, like many women in town, wandered around selling them. She asked the consultants to help her explore how to better promote her business without spending any money.

In considering this issue, the students initially focused on the fact that there was no company name, no location, and no way to differentiate the product. The business was so unlike any that the students studied that branding and marketing lessons were irrelevant. The woman's complete lack of financial resources only compounded the problem. She was selling just like everyone else in town and had a difficult time imagining another approach. As the students focused on the woman's identity and context, they moved away from a predictive orientation to a creation orientation to consider the resources that she could garner. Because the woman had a beautiful voice, the students encouraged her to use this resource and sing during her route so that she might be easier to find and could become known as the "gospel-singing chip lady."

In another situation, course participants worked with a woman who bought shoes in town for 5 Ghana cedis (GhC) and sold them in rural areas for 5.50 GhC. All of her customers wanted to purchase shoes on credit, however, and promised to pay her in two weeks. Two weeks later her customers would tell her they could not pay the full amount but would pay in another two weeks. Everyone paid eventually. In the meantime the woman had no cash to buy more shoes or to buy food for her children. If she didn't sell on credit, she believed that her customers would buy from another vendor who would sell on credit. While this was difficult for course participants to understand, as they asked more-insightful questions they identified a deeper issue: the woman was fundamentally afraid that people would call her a bad Christian and ostracize her if she didn't sell on credit. Because the norms of selling were a constraint that could not be changed, participants explored with her ways she could better save money to create a cushion.

Through a process of questioning and reflective listening, participants came to understand the different role that religion plays in Ghanaian culture. Ghana has few active civil society organizations outside the church or mosque, particularly in the region where the course operates. Low crime rates and enforcement of contracts, as this example illustrates, seem to reflect religious values and the ability of churches and mosques, instead of civic culture, to enforce norms on members. Religion is also central to Ghanaian social networks. Over the years multiple Ghanaians have told the students that while they do not really trust anyone in their own church, they would never even consider going into business with someone of another faith. For North American students who rarely consider how religion and religious context factor into a business decision, understanding the importance of religion enables them to explore fundamentally different solutions to the problems facing many Ghanaian entrepreneurs.

Through these experiences students also learn why contextual differences exist. While some reflect primarily differences in the role of religion or the fact that most people are perpetually short of cash, others arise due to differences in government policy. For example, very few people in Ghana maintain business records. Because sole-proprietor businesses in Ghana do not have to pay taxes or comply with other regulations that would necessitate bookkeeping, it does not occur. Consequently, businesses are often extensions of the household.

For example, if one has a "provisions store" (often a tiny kiosk in front of the house that sells such things as beverages and soap) and the children are thirsty, they take a soda from the store. As there is no accounting for what the household consumes, it is difficult to determine the profitability of this business. Our students learn that how they respond to these local differences will vary depending on whether the actions are connected to social behavior, government policy, cultural history, or some other contextual factor. This learning is essential, as it helps students establish strategies for how to respond to differences in identity and context.

The final component of the program design occurs when participants return home. After the overseas experience, they are required to write a paper that explores themes from the previsit work in conjunction with their observations, interviews, and experiences in Ghana. As most of the student-selected topics are related to issues of social practice, it gives students a focus for their observations and provides a route to engage Ghanaians in conversation about their lives. This paper cements students' learning, as it forces them to critically reflect on their experience and really explore the deep and diverse perspectives that exist in Ghana. As one student noted, "Only after reflecting on our experiences could the lessons we learned be truly appreciated." With a little distance from the experience, participants can reflect on their own assumptions about Ghana and explore how they will approach context and perspective differently in the future.

Encountering Social Entrepreneurship in Turkey

In another short-term offshore elective, we have used a different learning experience to teach students the importance of social and contextual awareness. In this elective, which is centered in cultural anthropology, participants spend three weeks in Turkey doing research with a for-profit social venture, *çöp (m)adam*. At *çöp (m)adam* women who have never worked for pay learn to make marketable goods out of garbage. While the explicit program objectives are to learn about social venture and Turkish culture, the implicit focus is to teach participants to recognize the complexities in unfamiliar contexts, to suspend judgment, and to take action. As such there are a number of social experiments designed into the course to facilitate this learning.

Before leaving for Turkey, course participants attend a number of workshops designed to illustrate some of the implicit assumptions students are making about the program and their own value and impact on the women who work at *çöp (m)adam*.

For example, in one session we discussed the concept of reciprocity and how we could contribute to these women who are opening up their lives for three weeks. As this course is explicitly about social entrepreneurship, some students suggested that they could provide the most value to these women by teaching them about entrepreneurship. This response yielded a lively discussion about some of the implicit assumptions we make about the needs of others to be entrepreneurs and the importance of recognizing that these assumptions are not universally held. The students eventually realized that they needed to ask questions to understand how best to help someone else. As a result, they considered identity and social awareness through discussions that engaged others' perspectives and reality.

In a later session, when students posed their questions to one of the founders of *çöp (m)adam*, Tara Hopkins, she responded to their offers of assistance by suggesting that they could help the most by collecting corks. There was a palpable drop in energy level when students heard that their biggest contribution would be serving as cork mules. These budding entrepreneurial leaders wanted to go to Turkey to change lives, to make a difference. They were not ready to ponder the possibility that the country would change them, that the experience would change their perspectives and their lives.

Upon arriving in Turkey, students participate in another ethnographic experiment designed to further complicate their understanding of social context. The students participate in a citywide scavenger hunt in which a small group is paired with a local Turkish-speaking university student. When the group reconvenes, participants share adjectives that they believe describe Istanbul. With one student group, the list that was generated included:

- Crowded
- Clean
- Old
- Lots of soccer
- Lots of miniskirts
- Beggars

- Rich
- Ghetto
- Huge
- Lots of headscarves
- Dirty
- Lots of poverty

As we reviewed our joint description of the social context, we asked participants if they agreed that these adjectives described Istanbul. Not surprisingly, they were quick to point out their disagreements with the list. The participant from Pakistan thought Istanbul was clean, while the participant from New Hampshire thought it was filthy. The participant from North Dakota saw a great deal of wealth, while the participant from New York City saw poverty. Through this discussion participants understood how their own individual identity affects their interpretation of the social context. This reiterates the importance of understanding one's own identity before one can understand others'.

Course participants also come to understand the variance of experience that underlies a social context. Those who visited more-conservative neighborhoods were thrilled to hear about pierced navels, hot pants, and rock music on the other side of town. Those who traveled to the wealthier districts were surprised to learn that their nascent understanding of Istanbul as a beautiful city of yachts and luxury shopping malls did not reconcile with those who reported seeing begging women with undernourished children.

While participants may have been initially applauding themselves for paying attention to the social context, they soon recognized the diversity of experience that underlies any situation; they also realized that they made uninformed assumptions about the context and that if they wanted to understand a local context, they needed to engage those who went beyond their own experiences. Participants learn that there is no one truth to the context and that it is possible to look at something without really seeing it. Through these experiments students develop the skills to ask questions and engage others to understand the variance of the social context before they begin a course of action.

Once students understand the concept of differing perspectives, they must develop the skills for suspending judgment as they explore those perspectives. For example, one course participant was interested in learning how one woman's life had changed as a result of new employment and income. When she asked an interpreter for help asking this question, the interpreter checked to make sure that the student meant to convey her unquestioned assumption that change had indeed occurred. A response to this question would require the interviewee to report change. What if she had not experienced change? The student learned to rephrase the question without bias by asking, "Has your life changed since you started working for pay?" Through this experience the student not only learned about how to pay attention to context but also how to develop the skills for learning about contextual differences in a way that is not laden with value.

Often contextual learning cannot be predesigned by the professor; rather it emerges from the situations in which participants find themselves. In one conversation a student mentioned her anger and deep frustration that these women live in a "state of oppression" as indicated by their clothing and headscarves. After discussing the multiple ways in which female dress in Turkey is a type of cultural text that can convey political beliefs, regional identity, family position, religious beliefs, or just aesthetic preferences, we encouraged this student to explore this issue with the women who came to work at *çöp (m)adam*. In discussions these women stated that they preferred being covered up. The student, however, still did not fully believe they were basing their responses on a conscious personal choice.

Later, during a visit to Bergama, a shopkeeper invited the student to sit in his tent and have a glass of tea. As he spoke to her in broken English, he approached her and stood over her left shoulder. When she turned to look at him in conversation, she realized that he was staring straight down her tank top. Disgusted, she got up and left, returning to the group and reporting in a derogatory manner, "That perv was staring straight down my tank top!" In a small town in Turkey, where genders seldom mingle between puberty and marriage, the choice for a female tourist is between dressing modestly or being ogled in a most obvious way. This young American in shorts and a tank top, traveling through small-town Turkey, was now in a position to understand how women in different societies have, and must negotiate, very different choices.

Conclusion

Entrepreneurial leaders consider their impact on their community, understand the potential of their talents, and are mindful of their potential impact as members of society. The examples in this chapter highlight the creative approaches that educators can take to develop entrepreneurial leaders who consider context and perspective and understand how that knowledge is central to their actions. These examples rely on similar pedagogical tools to encourage students to appreciate the context under examination and to explore how their own identities and context affect how they view the problems and the feasible solutions.

Entrepreneurial leaders must be conscious of the roles of different types of learning, including participant observation. They must be prepared to observe, listen to, and engage individuals in conversations on perspective and practice. In both learning experiences discussed here, the initial response of many course participants to epiphanies about context was anger: "Why aren't they more rational?" "Why aren't they like us?" Only through further reflection do they realize how they have privileged their own perspective—that their beliefs and behaviors may not be "right" but simply one set among many. It is then that the students are on their way to becoming "enlightened" entrepreneurial leaders.

Through these experiences entrepreneurial leaders come to understand that their focus on enthusiasm and passion, while important, is not the entire story for imagining an entrepreneurial solution to a problem. Even when considering SEERS, entrepreneurial leaders cannot just assume what other people want and value. Context and perspective are fundamental to a solution, and the wrong kind of solution can be offered too easily for the right reasons. Entrepreneurial leaders must develop the skills to explore perspective and context, to understand deeply entrenched but unexamined behavioral patterns, and to consider how to deconstruct and reconstruct behaviors and attitudes in useful ways. The experiences described in this chapter enable entrepreneurial leaders to develop such skills.

References

Blyth, M. 2001. "The Transformation of the Swedish Model: Economic Ideas, Distributional Conflict, and Institutional Change." *World Politics* 54 (1): 1–26.

Bourdieu, P., and L. Wacquant. 1992. *An Invitation to Reflexive Sociology.* Chicago: University of Chicago.

Financial Brand. 2009. "HSBC 'Different Points of Value.'" *FinancialBrand.com*, July 6. http://thefinancialbrand.com/6361/hsbc-brand.

Green, S. 2008. "A Conflict of Interests? Reconciling the Interests of Shareholders and Stakeholders." Speech given to RiskMetrics Conference, Lausanne, Switzerland.

Kahneman, D., and A. Tversky. 1979. "Prospect Theory: An Analysis of Decision under Risk." *Econometrica* 47 (2): 263–91. http://www.princeton.edu/~kahneman/docs/Publications/prospect_theory.pdf.

Rollag, K., S. Parise, and R. Cross. 2005. "Getting New Hires Up to Speed Quickly." *MIT/Sloan Management Review* 46 (2): 35–44.

Simon, H. A. 1996. *The Sciences of the Artificial,* 3rd edition. Cambridge, MA: MIT Press.

Van Maanen, J. 2011. "Ethnography as Work: Some Rules of Engagement." *Journal of Management Studies* 48 (1): 202–18.

CHAPTER **10**

Whom Do I Know? Building and Engaging Social Networks Using Social Media Technology

Salvatore Parise and PJ Guinan

I N THE PREVIOUS TWO CHAPTERS, WE CLARIFIED THE IMPORTANCE of knowing oneself and one's context as cornerstones of being an entrepreneurial leader. Beyond the ways that have already been discussed, this awareness is essential, as it supports one's ability to build relationships and enlist social networks to garner support for new ideas and organizational initiatives. Entrepreneurial leaders—with a deep understanding of their capabilities, weaknesses, values, and drives— use this understanding to connect with others who complement and supplement their own skills and share their own passions. Even within traditional bureaucratic decision-making contexts, entrepreneurial leaders can learn to develop and tap social networks to build momentum for ideas and strategic initiatives that they are passionate about. Finally, understanding their own position within networks enables entrepreneurial leaders to discern and build connections in a way that is sensitive to the interests and the perspectives of those who are situated in the particular cultural context.

Building networks and engaging relationships is foundational to cognitive ambidexterity. By engaging others in co-creation, entrepreneurial leaders identify and follow new directions in the pursuit of economic and social opportunity. Engaging social networks was critical to Robert Chatwani's work in building WorldofGood.com. His passion and communication of the idea to both friends and colleagues is what led him to Priya Haji, who helped him refine the idea; and together they created WorldofGood.com.

Engaging social networks has also been essential to the work Alan Mulally has accomplished in revitalizing and increasing profitability as CEO of Ford Motor Corporation. Mulally has used social networks to improve communication with employees, personalize the brand, and build more-engaging relationships with new customers. One such customer effort, the Fiesta Movement, focused on using social networks to market the US launch of the compact Ford Fiesta. During the six months that Mulally championed the Fiesta Movement campaign, Ford was able to expand its network of customers and brand advocates. The company reports a number of measurable marketing results, including 37 percent prelaunch brand awareness among millennials. Moreover, the social networking campaign resulted in 50,000 sales leads to first-time Ford customers and 35,000 test drives.

In today's world, technology is a central tool for entrepreneurial leaders in building and engaging social connections. Social networking technology—comprising social media, Web 2.0, and Enterprise 2.0—has fundamentally shifted whom we can connect to, how we maintain our connections, and how we envision connections between our organizations and stakeholders. Internet tools such as blogs, wikis, rating systems, tagging and bookmarking systems, and social networking platforms allow entrepreneurial leaders to build connections with others who share a common interest. Through the richness of social media, entrepreneurial leaders can easily share their passion for an idea and build others' passion for the idea as well.

Because users can easily and rapidly produce and consume content through social media technologies (such as YouTube videos, web

links from Twitter followers, and the like), there has been an expo-
nential increase in the use of social media. With Facebook alone,
it is expected that by 2012 one out of every six people on the planet
will be a member. These technologies create unparalleled access to
social networks.

One of the challenges for the entrepreneurial leader is to determine how to engage social media in a way that provides access to
individuals and innovation but doesn't excessively waste energy and
resources. Individuals and organizations need to develop a social technology strategy that includes a suite of technologies, processes, and
ultimately management practices that enable them to greatly expand
the potential size and reach of their personal networks and dramatically reduce the "costs" of collaboration (Dutta 2010; Li and Bernoff
2008; McAfee 2006; O'Reilly 2005).

In this chapter we explore how entrepreneurial leaders can use a
social media strategy to build and leverage relationships to move new
ideas forward.

Social Media and Cognitive Ambidexterity

Organizational use of social media is not a new phenomenon. Approximately 65 percent of today's organizations have adopted at least one
social technology, with blogs, wikis, and discussion forums leading the
way. Organizations are using these technologies to capture and share
knowledge inside their organizations, to foster collaboration within a
division or group, and to improve external corporate communications
(Keitt 2010). Wiki software has proven to be a particularly valuable
tool, as it enables a large community of knowledge workers to generate, share, and maintain content and to coordinate activities. By 2010
nearly 50 percent of organizations were using wikis (Koplowitz 2010).

Organizations are increasingly finding ways to incorporate social
technologies into their business functions, often employing both

prediction and creation logics. On the prediction logic side, employees use these tools to systematically analyze and locate subject-matter experts or workers with similar interests, helping themselves overcome physical or organizational boundaries. As a result, these technologies are integrated into structured talent and knowledge management practices and processes. For example, when these technologies are incorporated into the on-boarding process, new employees are able to build relationships and integrate into the organization more quickly.

At the same time, additional benefits stem from the link between social networks and creation logic. When entrepreneurial leaders need to engage a creation approach to decision-making in which they are acting their way into new situations, social networks and specifically social media become fundamental to these actions. Numerous marketing campaigns we have studied use social media platforms such as Twitter and Facebook to experiment with new ideas and test potential solutions to customers' needs wherever they live. Returning to the Clorox example, YouTube and Facebook were used extensively to determine potential interest and to identify the market for Green Works. Below we highlight three unique ways in which social media is particularly advantageous to a creation approach to decision-making.

One of the first beneficial uses of social media is as a means to help entrepreneurial leaders work through both uncertain and unknowable situations. Researchers have found that those who adopt social media are more effective at dealing with high environmental uncertainty and in adapting to customers' changing demands (Wilson and Eisenman 2010). In unknowable situations, social media enables entrepreneurial leaders to act first and experiment to move toward a solution. For instance, social media enabled EMC, a global technology firm, to identify pockets of "free work"—self-forming groups of employees working on emergent opportunities not forecasted during planning or strategy sessions. According to an EMC manager we interviewed, unpredicted issues that these groups were working on included "global cultural awareness, green and sustainability, markets around data warehousing, and virtualization."

Second, entrepreneurial leaders can draw upon social media to enlist others in co-creation. This model is different from shared decision-making because with co-creation others are fully involved in shaping and directing the outcome. In this process of co-creation, the outcome is likely to be very different from the entrepreneurial leader's original ideas. The challenge for an entrepreneurial leader is how to activate co-creation. Social media can be a useful tool for leaders to connect with their networks and engage others in co-creation. For example, in the marketing area, entrepreneurial leaders are using web-based customer communities to gain real-time feedback on potential product ideas. By launching contests and promotions on social networking sites such as Facebook and Twitter, entrepreneurial leaders are enabling customers to help them co-create new opportunities to meet customer needs that the organization might not have known existed.

Third, entrepreneurial leaders can use social media to enlist stakeholders to help them achieve business goals with minimal investment. For example, in 2007 as Facebook was expanding the number of languages it supported, it could have paid a dozen professionals hefty fees to translate the site. Instead Facebook used social media and, specifically, crowdsourcing as a less expensive alternative with more value-creation opportunity. Crowdsourcing is the process of taking work that would traditionally be given to a designated agent and instead outsourcing it to a large, unidentified group. Facebook users could join the "community of translators" and begin translating Facebook into new languages.

The power of this approach can be seen in the site translation into French, which occurred over a 24-hour period and was supported by 4,000 users (Sawers 2009). Through its Facebook Translations application, Facebook has used crowdsourcing to have its members translate the site into 100 different languages. Beyond saving money, this approach has enabled entrepreneurial leaders at Facebook to move the organization into diverse markets and to do so in a way that is customized to the needs of the local context, as it is created by local agents (Holahan 2008). Most importantly, by developing translations through the use of social media, Facebook has been able to tap into the enthusiasm and the passion of its social network so that these users attract new users to the site.

Educating Entrepreneurial Leaders about Social Media

When we introduce entrepreneurial leaders to social media and engaging social networks to support prediction and creation logics, we focus both on modeling how to use these technologies to connect with others and how to build passion through networks. As in organizations, social media applications in a management course can foster dynamic collaboration among learners, and this experience can be used to connect back to the real world (Wankel 2009).

In this section we describe two learning projects we have developed that enable participants to work with social media, such as user-generated video, wikis, tagging and bookmarking systems, and social networking sites, to create new opportunities. As we present these learning projects, we also provide research data to show the effect these experiences have had on students' understanding and use of social media.

Reinventing Case Discussions through Wikis

Case-based discussion is fundamental to every MBA program and to every management development program. The notion of bringing together leaders to collectively make sense of a real-world experience is a hallmark of management education. Beyond introducing managers to new models of decision-making, case-based teaching also enables managers to build connections and to see alternative points of view of the same material.

One of the easiest ways to introduce entrepreneurial leaders to the power of social media is through the use of wikis to deliver case-based materials. We have adapted a traditional case involving the diffusion of tagging and bookmarking technology in the MITRE Corporation (Parise et al. 2009) to deliver it using a wiki-based platform. With a standard teaching case, the case authors would have simply interviewed stakeholders in the MITRE Corporation and written a paper-based case. Students would read the case and then participate in a face-to-face discussion to explore solutions to the problems presented. Using the wiki software, we have fundamentally shifted how we teach this case.

First, the wiki platform enables us to provide supplemental information from MITRE employees and from IT industry experts. For example, an expert in the knowledge management field created content that describes the knowledge management software, infrastructure, and marketplace. This content is placed in a supplements menu option on the home page of the case. The two main protagonists of the case created a Class Prep section, which includes discussion questions and action items from their perspective. Beyond this additional case content, the faculty used the wiki technology to create hyperlinks between the case and related digital materials. We can update these links every year as relevant new articles appear.

As course participants use the wiki technology to engage in case preparation and discussion, they also learn how to successfully leverage social media to make decisions. For example, as a part of the case discussion, each participant bookmarks, tags, and comments on an article (or a video or audio clip) related to the case. Participants then comment on their own and others' bookmarks based on what they found interesting in the case. A tag cloud appears to the right of the case and is updated in real time so that participants can see popular themes emerging. Participants learn to use social media tools to more effectively communicate and generate enthusiasm for their ideas.

In the action-planning section of the case, participants learn how to engage others in a co-creation process through the use of social media. As in traditional case discussion, students are assigned to small groups to generate action plans. Instead of working face to face, these groups use a wiki to generate an action plan electronically. When the final action plans are posted to the class wiki, two MITRE decision-makers read each plan and respond to the group. These comments can include strengths and critiques of each plan as well as follow-on questions. Course participants can respond to the decision-makers' inquiries and ask additional questions regarding the case or the company. At this point the course instructors become part of the discussion thread.

In teaching this case recently, the instructors modified the teaching model to enable course participants to present their action plans to the two case decision-makers in a live setting using Elluminate Live!, a web conferencing program used in higher education. From disparate locations, course participants, instructors, and case decision-makers were able to give PowerPoint presentations and receive feedback and questions from the decision-makers in real time. The MITRE decision-makers followed with a description of current social media and knowledge management practices at MITRE, and instructors ended the session with a debriefing of lessons learned.

From the post-course survey data we gathered, it was clear that students learned more than just action planning regarding MITRE's use of social media. Through the wiki technology, they learned how to more effectively use social media to initiate a co-creation process. First, students learned how to use technology and social media to effectively gather information as they began to formulate an idea. By having to use the Internet, articles, videos, and blogs to prepare for the case, participants developed strategies for how best to leverage the vast resources and information that can be used to inform their ideas. Rather than become hamstrung by the high levels of uncertainty resulting from all these data, however, students learned to reduce uncertainty by testing and learning from specific media formats to gather information. For example, they discussed the value of hyperlinks and multimedia content as essential to helping them make sense of and internalize the material available.

Through the use of the wiki platform, students also learned how to connect with and involve others in a creation approach. They learned how to effectively communicate their ideas, respond to others, and generate momentum for new ideas. They also learned how to use social media to find out what other course participants knew and were interested in and how to tap in to their colleagues' knowledge to move an idea forward. For example, one course participant commented,

> I always had an interest in cloud computing, but everything I read on the topic seemed foreign or overly complex. There was a cloud computing tag on the wiki. From that I watched a video posted by Bill, who was in another section. The video was great, as it explained what a cloud was in terms I could understand. I barely knew who Bill was, and I didn't realize he had done an independent study project on cloud computing. Since the case, we've met several times, and he was more than happy to share his project report with me.

As this quote illustrates, many times entrepreneurial leaders don't know who knows what in their network. This student learned how to use social media to supplement his knowledge and engage the knowledge of others to move forward with a new idea.

The other key learning about networks and social media came from watching the faculty use the social media. Faculty modeled for students the opportunities that a blended learning format (including online and in-class formats) provides for diverse types of learning and knowledge sharing. While there is a tendency to believe that asynchronous technology is most useful for conveying technical content such as financial and accounting metrics, the experience with this case shows how beneficial social media can be for knowledge sharing that relies on engaging others in a social constructionist approach.

With a social constructionist approach, social media can be used to have participants learn from each other and to challenge and expand each other's ideas. The asynchronous format supported rich, diverse conversations in which participants could more easily access and share other related knowledge. For example, in a traditional face-to-face case discussion (or even a meeting), the program leader is often constrained in terms of how many ideas can be discussed and how many others can participate. With the wiki case discussion, participants felt they had more opportunity to offer their perspectives and, more importantly, to learn from their classmates.

Many students indicated that in a face-to-face classroom they were sometimes intimidated by the more vocal students, but in an online discussion they felt more comfortable replying to and engaging all of their classmates. As one participant commented, "There were so many interesting threads to participate in, and more participants were engaged." Both the faculty and the students learned to use the technology to co-create an experience that parallels future situations that students will face as entrepreneurial leaders.

The one challenge to the use of a wiki-based case discussion is that there is a learning curve for most students before they can use the technology to its full capabilities. When using a wiki platform, professors need to build time into the course to teach participants how to use the technology. Yet here too there were hidden advantages of this learning-by-doing experience. Some students talked about the benefits of learning firsthand how to use the wiki platform for joint content creation and online discussions. By learning how to create content in the context of this program, participants were more confident with engaging social media in the real world to explore and build support for their ideas.

Social Media Simulations

With all the popular press on the good, the bad, and the ugly of social media, we have found that some entrepreneurial leaders are reluctant to use these technologies. Entrepreneurial leaders who are not a part of the millennial generation often have well-established ways of networking and leveraging social connections and well-practiced scripts that often ignore the power of social media. These leaders don't fully understand the diverse and complex ways that social media can be used to gain access to new ideas, to engage others who share their passion for an idea, and for complementing their knowledge and skills with those of others. For example, one entrepreneurial leader we worked with stated: "I thought that social media was a 'checkmark' with very little relevance to the overall organization's existence. The course opened my eyes to how my organization could leverage social media platforms for functions such as marketing, branding, and customer service and engagement."

To develop entrepreneurial leaders who can leverage social media, we had to find a novel way to teach new scripts for working with and through social media. We created the Boston Advertising Simulation, an experiential exercise that teaches budding entrepreneurial leaders to use social media to generate new ideas and work toward innovations with their established and new social connections.

In this simulation course participants work for a fictional advertising agency in which they must create an external social media campaign for one of Boston Advertising's clients. To introduce students to the power of video in social media, we use video as the primary means of communicating with students around the simulation. Each week the students are given a new video from Miranda Priestly, the

CEO of Boston Advertising, with a new assignment for the campaign. Through these videos, course participants are introduced to the value of video to engage colleagues who are geographically dispersed.

As this is a real challenge for many entrepreneurial leaders, students immediately get to wrestle with how to best activate others' passions in a disparate work environment. Furthermore, because each video introduces new demands, new situations, and new requests, students also learn the challenge of working in unknowable and fast-changing environmental conditions. All of these unknowable environmental components are critical to building entrepreneurial leaders' understanding of how best to utilize social media.

In the simulation, participants must work with a number of social applications, including Twitter, LinkedIn, YouTube, and Facebook, as they conduct research and build their advertising campaigns. Through this activity, students learn how social media can be used to reinvent traditional analytical approaches to market research. They also learn to engage a creation approach as they interact with customers and encourage them to share data and ideas that they might not have otherwise known. As such, participants learn to engage social media to develop a cognitively ambidextrous approach to action.

Students also learn that social media can be a unique tool for generating fun, passion, and excitement about an idea. Because social media is technology-based, many course participants initially assume that it is a weak form of communication that doesn't build bonds or convey passion. They quickly discover that the fun and the excitement of social media can be easily harnessed to create emotional connections among people and build momentum for a new idea, sometimes in more powerful ways than with face-to-face communication. Students develop strategies to share their passion and enthusiasm through the use of Twitter and other social media tools. In so doing they develop new scripts for engaging social media in a co-creation process.

Twitter is a unique tool that course participants can use to stay connected and to share content. As one executive stated:

> Each section had its own [Twitter] hashtag.* I know our section had the highest adoption rate of the three sections and someone posed a challenge to the other two sections to catch up to us! It was fun to stay engaged with classmates, and I found some very useful links from others that I used for my project.

Through this simulation participants realize the ease with which they can tap into a network and generate new levels of engagement within it.

With the simulation entrepreneurial leaders also learn that social media is particularly powerful for receiving quick, immediate, and often brutally honest feedback that they can use to move forward on a new idea faster and with greater success. We introduce students to this component of social media by inviting social media experts to comment on the participants' social media campaigns, which they deliver using multimedia (voice, video, and presentations with notes) via Adobe Connect. Using video, these experts provide feedback on the presentations, and students are invited to use web rating systems to vote and comment on their favorite social media campaign. Beyond simply providing data on which campaign has the most votes, course participants often receive new insights from the data in the web rating systems that enable them to examine their campaigns in new ways. As such they become skilled in using social media to examine an idea from different perspectives and to use others' insights to modify their own thinking.

One of the challenges of launching entrepreneurial leaders' use of social media is to help them recognize the biases that others, particularly those of different generations, have for and against social

----

*A *hashtag* is a keyword that describes a tweet message and helps people search for tweets that have a common topic.

media. If entrepreneurial leaders are to use this technology, they must know how to respond to these differing perspectives. When students from different generations and backgrounds work together on a social media project, they are able to gain insights into others' perspectives. As one younger course participant explained,

> In my job I have to convince decision-makers and dollar owners that they need a social software framework. Discussing and implementing change management, leadership, and cultural ideas with respect to social technologies really helped me think about how I could be successful in getting others to adopt social media in my job.

Some educators are often concerned about the potential problems with online teaching, but we believe that these examples illustrate that online cases and simulations can effectively engage students in learning experiences that mimic the co-creation method they will need to generate social and economic opportunity.

Conclusion

Entrepreneurial leaders who engage cognitive ambidexterity must know how to connect and use their social networks. These networks give leaders access to knowledge and resources that both supplement and complement their skills and are instrumental to creating a new opportunity. These networks can also foster productive relationships with others who hold similar passions and share a new world perspective. In today's technology-enabled environment, social media is the fundamental means by which entrepreneurial leaders can connect and activate their networks. It is therefore vital that we teach future entrepreneurial leaders the skills to leverage networks in co-creation and to use social media to do this. When entrepreneurial leaders tap the power of social media, they expand their ability to co-create social and economic opportunity.

References

Dutta, S. 2010. "Managing Yourself: What's Your Personal Social Media Strategy?" *Harvard Business Review,* November.

Holahan, C. 2008. "Facebook's New Friends Abroad." *Bloomberg Businessweek,* May 14. http://www.businessweek.com/technology/content/may 2008/tc20080513_217183.htm.

Keitt, T. J. 2010. *Business Web 2.0 Buyer Profile: 2010* [Forrester Research report], April 28.

Koplowitz, R. 2010. *Enterprise Social Networking 2010 Market Overview* [Forrester Research report], April 22.

Li, C., and J. Bernoff. 2008. *Groundswell: Winning in a World Transformed by Social Technologies.* Cambridge, MA: Harvard Business School.

McAfee, A. P. 2006. "Enterprise 2.0: The Dawn of Emergent Collaboration." *MIT Sloan Management Review* 47 (3): 21–28.

O'Reilly, T. 2005. "What Is Web 2.0: Design Patterns and Business Models for the Next Generation of Software." *O'Reilly,* September 30. http://oreilly .com/web2/archive/what-is-web-20.html.

Parise, S., P. J. Guinan, B. Iyer, D. Cuomo, and B. Donaldson. 2009. "Harnessing Unstructured Knowledge: The Business Value of Social Bookmarking at MITRE." *Journal of Information Technology Case and Application Research* 11 (2): 51–76.

Sawers, P. 2009. "Facebook's Un-Rebellion." *Multilingual,* April/May. http:// multilingual.texterity.com/multilingual/200904/?folio=62#pg62.

Wankel, C. 2009. "Management Education Using Social Media." *Organization Management Journal* 6 (4): 251–62.

Wilson, H. J., and E. J. Eisenman. 2010. *Business Uncertainty: 2010 Global Survey Results.* Babson Executive Education report. Accessed March 3, 2011, http://www3.babson.edu/bee/uncertainty.

PART IV

Management Educators as Entrepreneurial Leaders

CHAPTER 11

A New Pedagogy for Teaching "Doing": Preparing Entrepreneurial Leaders for Values-Driven Action

THUS FAR WE HAVE PRESENTED THE THREE PRINCIPLES OF ENTRE-preneurial leadership—cognitive ambidexterity, SEERS, and self- and social awareness—and have provided examples of how these principles can be taught through various exercises, cases, and courses. For most readers, however, one nagging question remains: *How can I get started?*

Can it be done only through a radical change to management education that is driven from academic leadership, or can it begin with individual faculty members who act as entrepreneurial leaders? We believe that faculty must walk the talk. If we believe that our students need to learn entrepreneurial leadership, we should model that behavior as we develop our courses and engage students outside of the

We would like to thank Mary C. Gentile for her assistance in developing this chapter. Mary is the creator and director of Giving Voice to Values (*http://www3 .babson.edu/babson2ndgen/GVV/default.cfm*) and a senior research scholar at Babson College. She has authored many books, including *Giving Voice to Values: How to Speak Your Mind When You Know What's Right* (New Haven, CT: Yale University Press, 2010).

classroom. We can take action and modify individual class sessions or develop our own courses, as we have illustrated throughout this book.

In this chapter we present another pedagogical approach—a new case method—for teaching management students the principles that underlie entrepreneurial leadership. This pedagogical approach is an alternate case method that we believe is particularly valuable for teaching students the principles that are outlined in this book. What is unique about this approach is its flexibility and adaptability—an educator can adopt it as an alternative way to teach existing cases or topics. By modifying a case discussion using this approach, an educator is able to reorient students' thinking toward engaging action and analysis; toward engaging values that consider social, environmental, and economic impact; and toward aligning who they are with what they say and do.

A New Case Approach for Developing Entrepreneurial Leaders

For years management educators have relied on the case-based method of teaching. The case method was designed to simulate action in the classroom so that business students would learn to *apply* theory and analytics rather than simply read and talk about them. A favorite metaphor, attributed to Benson Shapiro, is that case-based learning is akin to jumping—or being thrown—into the pool rather than standing poolside, talking about the breaststroke. This all made sense, and many management educators committed to this approach.

Today new cases are being developed that include a wide variety of organizations (nonprofits, for-profits, and government and non-government organizations); discuss scenarios with various social, environmental, and economic implications; and examine global issues. These cases develop an awareness of the challenges faced by all organizations, the rights and interests of a variety of stakeholders, and the possibilities of simultaneously creating social and economic value. Many of these cases present students with a decision that needs to be made and require detailed analysis of the situation to arrive at the decision. By introducing these cases, we expose students to new business models, new corporate responsibilities, and examples of various leadership approaches. This pedagogical approach can be used to expose students to some of the principles of entrepreneurial leadership and is an easy first step for educators.

When trying to teach a creation logic that should be embedded in an action-based pedagogy, however, the traditional case method can be limiting. Rather than true *action* learning, the focus of the case methodology is on *awareness* and *analysis;* that is, it familiarizes students with the types of challenges they are likely to encounter and it provides opportunities for them to analyze—applying quantitative methods or frameworks in a prediction approach—and discuss different arguments for and against various choices.

In some instances—particularly for the cases that pose ethical decisions or discuss the tradeoffs among social, environmental, and economic value creation—this traditional case method approach feels as if it were focused on teaching students the "professional rationalizations" (as one professor named them) that would enable them to defend their focus on short-term shareholder wealth creation in spite of negative social and environmental effects or their decision to take questionable actions.

The question then becomes: How can we build on the traditional case methodology that focuses on *awareness* and *analysis* to focus on *action* and *implementation?* The solution to this teaching dilemma seems quite clear: instead of focus on the decision-making, we need to focus on post-decision-making. Rather than decide the right thing to do, we need to develop cases in which the protagonist has already decided what to do and needs to follow through on the decision. In the place of cases that help students arrive at decisions that maximize only economic value, we need to offer cases that consider social and environmental value as well. Finally, instead of considering one way to implement a decision, we need students to develop implementation-scripts based on their own skills, relationships, and style as well as on the situation or context of the protagonist.

Implementation-scripting cases, a new case pedagogy developed by Mary Gentile, can be used to teach these missing elements. This curriculum is called Giving Voice to Values (GVV, GivingVoice ToValues.org). The GVV approach was initially developed to teach business ethics and value-based leadership. Rather than ask students *whether* to do what they think is right, GVV cases ask them *how* to do it. Employing a creation approach, students act themselves into new ways of thinking by actually saying and doing what we want them to learn to do—rather than talk about it or, worse, talk themselves out of it. Instead of using the language and the tools of philosophy and ethics to address business issues, they develop scripts that use the language and the tools of the discipline wherein the problem lies. For example, if they are being pressured to "cook the books," arguments that use the language of the Financial Accounting Standards Board—or even more persuasively, ROI—will be more effective than allusions to philosophers Singer or Aristotle.

As we prepare leaders to make decisions based on a fundamentally different worldview, we need to enable them to practice and develop their skills for acting on and implementing their decisions. We believe that the GVV implementation-scripting case approach can be an effective tool for engaging students in action-based learning across disciplines and programs.

GVV Implementation-Scripting Cases

Like traditional decision-making cases, an implementation-scripting case focuses on a particular business challenge, set within an entre-preneurial venture or existing organization, and presents the situation from the perspective of an individual case protagonist or actor. Unlike traditional cases, where a decision is required and a thorough analysis would lead to a solution, the implementation-scripting case study ends at the point where the protagonist has already decided what to do and needs to build an action plan and a script to get it done. The implementation-scripting cases present students with a series of scenarios in which the protagonist already knows what he or she believes is the ethical or right decision, but it is unclear how this decision will be accepted by the various stakeholders and what the first steps should be. The GVV cases are about how a manager raises these issues effectively; what he or she needs to do and say to be heard; and how to correct an existing course of action when necessary.

A GVV Case Example

"This Whole System Seems Wrong": Felipe Montez and Concerns about the Global Supply Chain is a wonderful GVV case for a core operations management or supply-chain management class. It helps students consider issues of social responsibility and supplier management as well as the challenges of managing a global supply chain. Most importantly, it asks students to develop a script and experiment with taking action.

The case presents a situation in which Felipe Montez was hired to be a purchasing director and product designer for a Spanish electronics company. The company has a 27-year history of working with a Hong Kong distributor. On Felipe's first trip to China, he visited several factories and found a wide range of conditions. He was most concerned about the conditions (which included child workers and unsafe working conditions) in the factory that produced the majority of his company's goods. When he returns from China, he speaks with his manager, who largely dismisses his concerns. After reviewing other industry practices, Felipe decides that he would like the company to develop more-stringent requirements for its factories.

The focal questions for this GVV class discussion become: How can Felipe get this done? What information will be needed? What arguments will be effective? What allies are needed? What steps should be taken—and in what sequence?

Source: *Gentile and Klepper 2010.*

The implementation-scripting case study is typically much shorter than traditional decision-making cases. It may be as brief as a paragraph or as long as three or four pages. Because the cases are shorter, they are more suggestive, relying on students' own experience and knowledge as well as outside research (such as reading and practitioner interviews). For this reason students often benefit from team preparation of their action plans so that they can share data-gathering and interviewing tasks. They can also use peer coaching and brainstorming to generate effective and persuasive scripts for building support for the protagonist's decision.

With this team-based approach, the class discussion begins with structured questioning wherein students anticipate the arguments they are likely to face when they propose their values-based positions. Here students can apply their prediction logic, assess the social contexts, and consider arguments from many perspectives. They then work together to craft the most effective scripts for how to respond to those arguments, and they practice voicing the scripts out loud in front of their peers, who stand in for the audiences they will need to persuade in the workplace. Finally, rather than critique classmates' scripts, as would be the process in traditional adversarial role-playing, students use peer coaching to refine and enhance each other's arguments. By the end of the class, all students have created a credible and workable set of arguments and implementation plans for values-based action.

Here are just some of the benefits of the GVV case approach:

■ It focuses on *positive examples* of times when folks have found ways to voice, and thereby implement, their values (or worldview) in the workplace.

■ It emphases the importance of finding an *alignment* between one's individual sense of purpose and that of the organization (an alignment that involves self-assessment and a focus on one's individual strengths).

■ It provides the opportunity to *construct and practice responses* to the most frequently heard reasons and rationalizations for *not* acting on one's values.

■ It challenges leaders to *build commitment* by providing repeated opportunities for them to practice delivering their responses and to learn to provide peer feedback and coaching to enhance effectiveness.

With its focus on action, the GVV methodology allows students to practice responding to the question *What do I do next?* (as opposed to *What do I do . . . permanently?*), which is at the heart of cognitive ambidexterity.

Conclusion

In teaching future entrepreneurial leaders to engage a cognitively ambidextrous mindset and to articulate a SEERS worldview, the Giving Voice to Values curriculum can be a central component of the "pedagogical portfolio" discussed in chapter 1. GVV is a thought experiment, an iterative process, and a method for both developing and practicing values-driven leadership—all elements that are important in a pedagogy for teaching entrepreneurial leadership. GVV cases help students apply prediction logic to anticipate arguments from stakeholders and pose counterarguments. They also help students use creation logic to develop new and innovative approaches to practice problem solving by taking action.

While education for action is essential, that action must be guided by the principles, objectives, and means of our individual identities, our organizations, and our entrepreneurial ventures. And these principles, objectives, and means—this *purpose*—brings us to SEERS. The raison d'être for GVV is the development of a pedagogy that engages students in the response of creative thinking and practice around the pursuit of social, environmental, and economic responsibility and sustainability. GVV asks students to develop practical scripts and action plans for values-driven entrepreneurial leadership. Furthermore, it asks students to consider how to respond to the various demands and perspectives of the stakeholders in the case. This shift from asking *whether* SEERS can be addressed to asking and answering *how* it can be done is a fundamental premise of the GVV pedagogy.

Finally, as we turn to the third principle behind entrepreneurial leadership—self- and social awareness—we see how it too is aligned with the GVV approach. Entrepreneurial leaders are more likely to be able to voice and act on their values if they frame their choices in ways that play to their strengths: *If I see myself as a pragmatist, I will work best if I find ways to frame my actions on my values as pragmatic. If I see myself as a risk-taker, I will frame the values-based choice as the bold move. If I see myself as cautious, I will frame my values-driven decision as the conservative choice.* Through implementation and scripting, GVV helps entrepreneurial leaders find alignment between who they are and what they say and do.

Thus, when the only way to lead in an unknowable world is through action, GVV is all about action—but it's action that is informed by analysis and planning and the lessons of research about decision-making biases and heuristics and that is enabled by prescripting and literal practice. If global business leaders are "redefining the context" for their decision-making, as Wilson and Eisenman (2010) point out, the GVV approach is entirely suited to this endeavor. GVV enables students to learn the "new narrative" about the choices entrepreneurial leaders face and to be empowered and enabled to shape social and economic opportunity in creative and responsible ways.

While the GVV curriculum is but one approach, it is one that we can easily use in our classrooms. In fact, all cases are free and available to all. We hope that this discussion will encourage you to act as entrepreneurial leaders who create new GVV cases, traditional cases, and other teaching materials for educating our students and future leaders.

Whether they center around the principles of cognitive ambidexterity, SEERS, or self- and social awareness, if materials are developed, tested, and shared across the academic community, we can change the course of management education.

References

Gentile, M. C., and W. Klepper. 2010. *"This Whole System Seems Wrong"*: *Felipe Montez and Concerns about the Global Supply Chain,* Columbia CaseWorks Collection (#081803) and Giving Voice to Values program, available at *http://www.babson.edu/GVV/Student/4_Individual-Cases -and-Modules/Felipe-Montez_S.pdf.*

Wilson, H. J., and E. J. Eisenman. 2010. *Business Uncertainty: 2010 Global Survey Results.* Babson Executive Education report. Accessed March 3, 2011, http://www3.babson.edu/bee/uncertainty.

CHAPTER **12**

Curriculum-Wide Change: Leading Initiatives to Develop Entrepreneurial Leaders

THROUGHOUT THIS BOOK WE HAVE PROVIDED PEDAGOGICAL examples to illustrate how individual faculty from diverse disciplines and programs can teach students to make decisions guided by cognitive ambidexterity, a SEERS worldview, and self- and social awareness. Yet the largest opportunity for shaping entrepreneurial leaders comes when we consider how to reorient our entire curriculum. We have the most power to change management education when faculty from diverse disciplines work together to develop entrepreneurial leaders who possess both core disciplinary knowledge *and* a new way of thinking based on a new worldview. By working together management educators have the opportunity to develop the next generation of entrepreneurial leaders who will shape social and economic opportunity across diverse contexts.

Thus the challenge becomes: How can management educators introduce systemwide changes to reorient student learning toward educating entrepreneurial leaders? We recognize that the answer is both simple and quite complex: we advocate that management educators need to become entrepreneurial leaders. Just as we are teaching students to engage a different way of thinking and a different worldview, management educators need to do the same as we test and build new models of management education in our own universities.

In this chapter we provide examples of curricular and co-curricular changes that are enabling us to move our curriculum toward this new model of educating entrepreneurial leaders. It is important to note that ours is a work in progress. Here we share some of the changes that we have made as well as some proposed changes we are designing into our curriculum that we believe will be most useful to reorienting management education toward entrepreneurial leadership.

Curriculum-Wide Opportunities to Develop Entrepreneurial Leaders

Just like any college or university, we struggle at times to bring desired changes to fruition. The challenges of engaging all faculty and staff and squeezing more content into fewer classroom hours plagues us just as it does other management education institutions. Yet we press on, as we believe in the power of teaching entrepreneurial leadership. In this section we highlight curriculum-wide opportunities that we have thus far had the most success with implementing: redesigning the core curriculum, introducing signature learning experiences, integrating co-curricular learning opportunities, and leveraging entrepreneurial leadership in how university operations are managed.

Core Curriculum Redesign

The boldest and most dramatic way to reorient a management curriculum toward developing entrepreneurial leaders is to closely evaluate one's core curriculum to identify areas that integrate the three principles of entrepreneurial leadership. While this approach is similar to any major curriculum redesign, it differs in a fundamental way: Rather than attach the three principles of entrepreneurial leadership to the core by introducing additional core courses, we consider how to integrate the principles into existing discipline-based courses.

If entrepreneurial leadership is to become an objective that unites management pedagogy, faculty must collaborate to develop students' understanding of and skills with its fundamental principles.

We recently embarked on such a redesign in our graduate program, and there are a few key actions we have taken to facilitate this process. We began by assembling a committee of faculty members who had different levels of experience with the graduate program. In this way we ensured that we could learn from the past but also be open to new ideas. The group was asked to redesign the MBA curriculum to develop "entrepreneurial leaders who create great economic and social value." In so doing they focused on how best to integrate the principles of entrepreneurial leadership into the new discipline-based course structure.

To reorient our curriculum toward developing entrepreneurial leadership, the redesign committee surveyed the curriculum design and found that many courses focused on prediction logic. At the same time, there were no clear touch points where students would learn cognitive ambidexterity and how to cycle between creation logic and prediction logic. So, early in the first year of our MBA program, we are introducing an entrepreneurship course, a portion of which focuses on developing students' cognitive ambidexterity. Also, at the end of the first year, our information course now engages students in using information technology to support both prediction and creation logics.

To teach the SEERS worldview, we have integrated this principle into many core courses. We are carefully reviewing cases and teaching examples to ensure that students are exposed to a diverse set of contexts that consider social, environmental, and economic value creation simultaneously. Discipline faculty are also considering how to engage SEERS into discussions of other discipline concepts. For example, the technology and operations management course is likely to include a module on sustainable operations, the marketing course may consider marketing "green" products, and the accounting course may incorporate the sustainability metrics discussed in chapter 6.

To develop students' self- and contextual awareness, we have modified our core organizational behavior course to align with the Managerial Assessment and Development course discussed in chapter 8. In other courses that consider global issues explicitly, such as economics and strategy, we are using conceptual materials to develop students' contextual awareness to successfully navigate changes in industries, nations, and the global environment. In our IT course, we are introducing the social media ideas discussed in chapter 10 to highlight the importance of networks and co-creation to entrepreneurial leadership and to show how students can leverage technology. The three principles behind entrepreneurial leadership are then tied together into signature learning experiences.

Signature Learning Experiences

Signature learning experiences (SLEs) represent a distinct curricular design to inculcate the principles of entrepreneurial leadership. Although the MBA Oath (Khurana 2007) is an innovative way to encourage newly minted MBA graduates to feel committed to a professional identity and to the established norms of that identity, we are not confident that signing an oath is enough to assist students in developing a new worldview of business. We believe that action and discussion must be embedded in learning for students to adopt a new worldview and to engage a new level of self- and social awareness.

Based in the theory of organizational socialization, SLEs are designed to socialize students into the principles of entrepreneurial leadership and to teach them to use cognitive ambidexterity and to make decisions by considering self, context, and a SEERS mindset. SLEs can come in a variety of forms; the Foundations of Management and Entrepreneurship course discussed in chapter 1 is one example. This yearlong first-year course is designed to teach integrated management concepts, and one of its primary objectives is to teach students what it means to be an entrepreneurial leader. Through the experience of building their own businesses, students learn to engage cognitive ambidexterity and a SEERS mindset.

While introducing students to the principles of entrepreneurial leadership is important, it is equally important to reinforce those principles throughout the curriculum. Just as a class is designed by telling students what you are going to teach them, teaching them, and then telling them what you have just taught them, a strong curriculum follows the same model. We believe that there needs to be a learning opportunity later in the curriculum that again emphasizes entrepreneurial leadership. The most straightforward way to do this is to take an existing discipline capstone course and reorient it toward teaching the entrepreneurial leadership principles.

A capstone course can often signal to students that their learning is complete, however, so with entrepreneurial leadership we want to reinforce the underlying principles but also remind students that their learning will never be "complete." In both our graduate and undergraduate curricula, we are proposing new upper-level signature learning experiences that are focused on reinforcing the principles of entrepreneurial leadership.

One proposal in the undergraduate program is to have faculty teach different disciplinary-based courses on a "big idea"—a challenging social or environmental issue. For example, a big idea might be education, hunger, or climate change. Instructors would explore the big idea from their disciplinary perspective, but they would also focus on teaching students to engage the principles of entrepreneurial leadership as they reflect on and consider how to respond to the challenge. Students learn to employ cognitive ambidexterity, a SEERS mindset, and their understanding of self and context in their decision-making.

For some management education curricula, it may be very complex to introduce an SLE as a new course. The battle for disciplinary credit and the constant demand to add more to a curriculum may reduce buy-in from faculty. In such cases, faculty champions may have to consider other creative ways to build SLEs into their curricula.

In our graduate program, SLEs are being designed as shorter experiential exercises within a course, as co-curricular experiences, as daylong events, and even as components of orientation. For example, one might consider replacing the ubiquitous casino night during graduate school orientation with a presentation by an entrepreneurial leader in a nonprofit or an NGO. An afternoon or evening of community service activities could follow. One can only imagine the different imprinting that comes from a day of community service compared with an evening of gambling.

Co-Curricular Learning Opportunities

Another method for embedding the concept of entrepreneurial leadership across a curriculum is by engaging co-curricular experiences—any activities outside of the classroom that complement the general curriculum. Examples include student organizations, honor societies, and athletic and social clubs such as fraternities.

Moffatt (1988) states that 40 percent of college students report that activities outside of class constitute the most significant part of their educational experience. Higher education is placing more emphasis on providing students with both curricular and co-curricular experiences to support their learning (Ahren 2009). Following this perspective, we see co-curricular learning as an opportunity for students to practice being entrepreneurial leaders. Through co-curricular experiences, students are able to test out prediction- and creation-oriented decision-making and further develop their understanding of SEERS and self- and contextual awareness as the basis for action.

One co-curricular learning experience we launched recently is the Venture Accelerator. Designed by Professor Candida Brush and other Babson entrepreneurship faculty, the Venture Accelerator is for

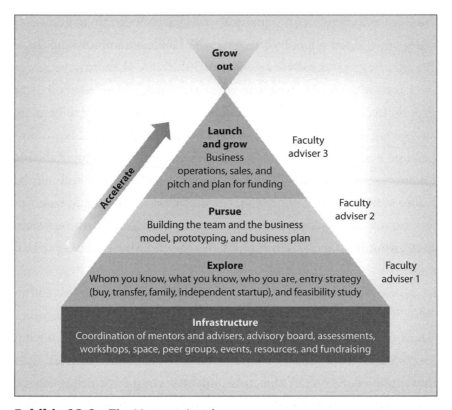

Exhibit 12.1 The Venture Accelerator

students interested in starting or running a new venture. The experience is divided into three phases: explore, pursue, and launch and grow (see exhibit 12.1).

Using self- and social awareness, students "explore" what they might like to do, what the opportunities are, and what the appropriate mode of action might be. They also consider how to engage SEERS as they pursue social and economic opportunity simultaneously. In the "pursue" phase, students combine creation and prediction approaches by taking action to test the market, develop prototypes, shape opportunities, and write business plans. They also consider their social networks as they assemble a leadership team. Finally, in the "launch and grow" phase, the students launch their ventures and "live" the experience as they create a revenue stream, find investors, and market their products and services. As students "accelerate" through these three phases, they have the opportunity to "earn" additional resources such as office space and mentoring by pitching ideas to faculty.

Although this is a co-curricular experience, it does involve some structuring and oversight from faculty outside of the classroom. There are specific deliverables for each stage. In the "explore" phase, we offer free workshops on establishing a legal form of business, technology commercialization, searching for business opportunities, and research techniques to determine market and industry feasibility. These workshops are led by faculty and external business leaders. For the "pursue" phase, we assign mentors to oversee a cluster of students. We also tailor panels and workshops around relevant issues, such as investigating feasibility, determining customer demand, building a team, crafting a business plan, and protecting intellectual property. Finally, for the "launch and grow" phase, we assign dedicated mentors to work with students to execute their plan, meet milestones, and acquire resources (space and equipment) and funding. We are also working to develop relationships with local incubators that might fast-track these student businesses upon graduation.

Living-learning communities   A very different model of co-curricular learning comes from living-learning communities, where students can apply their values and passions by living in a designated area with others who share that focus. Even the process they go through to create these communities involves practicing entrepreneurial leadership. Students create new living-learning communities by co-creating and building interest among their classmates for a particular idea. In so doing they learn about the importance of passion to engage others' interests in a particular community and how the idea of a community may shift as others become involved. Self- and social awareness and creation and prediction logic are fundamental to the creation of new living-learning communities.

As members of these communities, students are expected to engage in action both on and off campus. The Green Tower, which was mentioned in chapter 5, has undertaken action that has created systemic change on our campus. Green Tower members are required to sign and uphold a Sustainable Living Pledge and a vow to minimize their personal carbon footprint. Residents are also required to participate in at least one of the Green Tower's two working groups: green living and green business. The green living group focuses on campus initiatives around recycling and conservation. The green business group develops research and education projects on green industries and careers; this group has founded a Sustainable Idea Lab on campus to incubate scalable green businesses.

Green Tower residents understand that environmental initiatives and discussions shouldn't be located in just one dorm. "There was a lack of consciousness among the students," a Green Tower student leader explained. In response, Green Tower inhabitants have designed various events to democratize campuswide dialogue around environmental themes. These events include movie nights featuring films with environmental topics as well as Zero Waste fashion shows spotlighting attire made from recycled or sustainable materials.

In starting these initiatives, Green Tower members learned how to connect others to their SEERS worldview and to use a creation and prediction orientation to bring these changes about.

Modeling Entrepreneurial Leadership through University Management

Similar to the concept of "walk the talk," student learning also arises from observing how we as educators lead our own colleges and universities. By reflecting on the three themes, administrators will find opportunities to model entrepreneurial leadership in key institutional decisions and operational practices.

For example, we have worked hard to make SEERS evident in all aspects of the university, particularly those that are most visible to our students. We are partnering with facilities managers and outside service providers to design offerings that resonate and communicate SEERS values. In collaboration with our food services company, Sodexo, we have implemented a tray-free policy in our dining halls, which has reduced water usage as well as food waste. We are trying to source food locally, we are conducting food waste audits of all campus dining facilities, and we are testing approaches to reduce food waste and produce compost on campus grounds. This partnership has also yielded a number of other results that students see or that we report to them:

■ An 11 percent reduction in energy consumption versus the baseline year

■ A reduction in CO_2 emissions of more than 5,700 tons during the same period, equivalent to removing 961 cars from the road for one year

■ A 51 percent recycling rate for the campus

■ Reduction of trash tonnage by more than 200 tons annually

Part of our success with these programs is because these campus initiatives fit with our school, our community, and the overall Babson culture. As management educators take action to bring about campuswide reform, it is critical that they consider their school's strengths, partnerships, financial and human resources, and culture and customize the type and the scale of initiatives to best fit with the school's context.

Engaging Cognitive Ambidexterity to Lead Management Education Reform

Beyond thinking about *what* to reorient in management curriculum and co-curricular initiatives, we need to consider *how* to do it. As entrepreneurial leaders, management educators will need to employ both creation and prediction approaches and become adept at cycling between the two as they introduce new initiatives and update and reform curricula. Through a continuous process of engaging creation and prediction approaches to thought and action, management educators can innovate and manage change effectively.

A Prediction Approach to Management Education Reform

The more common approach for academics is prediction logic. In fact, the Association to Advance Collegiate Schools of Business requires this type of approach when preparing for accreditation. The alignment between the college mission, the resources (or inputs), and the outcomes (student assessment) is closely reviewed. It is also expected that clear processes are used to strengthen curricula, develop faculty, and improve instruction. For any management program, the goals must be established, the resources must be available and of high quality, outcomes need to be assessed, and improvement plans must be established and implemented. These checks and balances help ensure the quality of the program.

When schools' goals are certain, the business and management education environments are stable, and data are available, prediction approaches to management education reform can be very effective. A few prediction tools—goal establishment, resource identification, and data collection and analysis—informed our curriculum revision efforts.

Goal establishment   When we considered how to develop entrepreneurial leaders, the school established a task force of faculty and staff members to identify the key concepts or principles that needed to be included in our curriculum: cognitive ambidexterity, a SEERS worldview, and self- and social awareness. Once these principles were developed and approved by our faculty senate, curriculum redesign task forces were established for both the undergraduate and graduate programs. Each task force was given the goal of integrating the three principles into a newly designed curriculum.

Resource identification   In good economic times, there had been relatively unrestricted resources to design and implement new curricula at our school. Today's economic environment, however, requires us to be fiscally conservative in our revisions. Our curriculum redesign task forces were asked to maintain, and in some cases reduce, the current cost of delivering the curriculum. Knowing that resources were limited helped the task forces arrive at a solution that was feasible and easily implemented. Of course, the resource constraints limited the available options; it was not possible to simply add content and more resources to introduce the three principles into our core curriculum. Interestingly, the resource constraints actually forced the task force members to rethink the current curriculum, to creatively redesign courses, and to think about the learning experiences both inside and outside the classroom.

Data collection and analysis   As we revised our curricula, we wanted to gather input from a variety of stakeholders. Fortunately, our institutional research center regularly conducts surveys on college applicants, entering students, graduating students, alumni, and recruiters for all of our undergraduate and graduate programs. We used past data and, in some cases, revised our surveys to gather new information about the perceptions of our current and proposed curricula. We also supplemented the survey data with focus group discussions with a variety of stakeholders. Through data collection and analysis, we were able to understand the views of our current program and assess how well our new ideas resonated with the various stakeholders.

While a prediction approach helped inform our curricula revision efforts, it was also important to engage a creation approach to co-create innovative teaching materials and courses.

A Creation Approach to Management Education Reform

In the uncertain and at times unknowable world of management education, a creation-oriented approach to introducing curriculum change can be valuable. Engaging a creation approach enables educators to introduce new curricular ideas in a way that enables them to build relationships, gain feedback, and further refine the idea before launching. The following three examples highlight how we have used a creation-oriented approach to introduce new educational initiatives.

Global partnerships　One system-level approach to ensuring ongoing experimentation and learning is to work directly with global partners who can test and co-create with local populations. Such initiatives not only help improve partners' teaching competencies but also ensure ongoing institutional learning. For instance, the Global Consortium for Entrepreneurship Education (GCEE) is a collaborative group that aims to prepare entrepreneurial leaders to create opportunities "for a better world." This group is experimenting with "serious play," a pedagogical approach discussed in chapter 1. GCEE's Serious Play Studio designs and creates new products and processes pertaining to management and entrepreneurship education.

Low-risk experiments　Experimentation with new course materials or course content can also be done in low-risk situations within current degree programs. For example, new materials or courses can be tried out with a small group of students. When we first rolled out our

Fast Track MBA degree program, we began with a small number of students (30 to 60 per entering class). This enabled us to experiment with the content and the process of delivering management education in a low-risk situation.

This was our first program, for example, that used a hybrid approach to learning that included both online and face-to-face classes for its delivery. This allowed us to test the effectiveness of using video presentations, online discussions, social media, and other tools. The program also allowed us to experiment with new course material. For example the Managerial Assessment and Development course, highlighted in chapter 8, was developed, tested, and refined in our Fast Track MBA program and is now being introduced into our traditional two-year MBA program. We also used an experimental approach when expanding the geographic footprint of the Fast Track MBA program into San Francisco. Rather than invest in substantial market research, we simply launched a pilot program to determine demand directly. This pilot shows strong demand, is allowing us to quickly scale the program based on student feedback, and actually costs less than market research.

Ecosystem experiments   Another approach to experimentation with new course content is to develop, deploy, and test new concepts in nondegree courses and research projects. One example is the Babson Entrepreneurship Ecosystem Project, led by Daniel Isenberg. This is an action-focused research project to develop the entrepreneurial capacity in specific areas by bringing together the policies, structures, programs, and climate that foster entrepreneurial leadership and venture creation. As Isenberg described in the *Harvard Business Review* (2010), the project offers "rules for revolutionaries"—down-to-earth guidelines for leaders who want to foster entrepreneurship. As we work with cities, nations, and different regions of the world, we experiment with new concepts, gauge engagement with and effectiveness of those concepts, and learn more about the global environment. This real-time learning helps us to develop new course content for our degree programs.

Conclusion

We have laid out a comprehensive paradigm for how to revise, and perhaps even reinvent, management education and development to train entrepreneurial leaders who will shape social and economic opportunity. We have offered examples at the class, course, and program level and have discussed approaches for management education reform in general. Our aspiration is that these ideas will incite other educators, policymakers, and professionals to explore how to create new educational opportunities for developing entrepreneurial leaders. If we as management educators don't collaborate and consider new paradigms, we are unlikely to meet the challenge of educating the next generation of entrepreneurial leaders who are capable of creating social and economic opportunity.

References

Ahren, C. S. 2009. "Detangling the Unique Effects of Co-Curricular Engagement on Self-Reported Student Learning Outcomes." Doctoral dissertation, Indiana University. Department of Educational Leadership and Policy Studies.

Isenberg, D. J. 2010. "How to Start an Entrepreneurial Revolution." *Harvard Business Review,* June.

Khurana, R. 2007. *From Higher Aims to Hired Hands: The Social Transformation of American Business Schools and the Unfulfilled Promise of Management as a Profession.* Princeton, NJ: Princeton University Press.

Moffatt, M. 1988. *Coming of Age in New Jersey: College and American Culture.* New Brunswick, NJ: Rutgers University Press.

Acknowledgments

T HIS BOOK BEGAN IN 2008 WHEN BABSON COLLEGE'S LEADERSHIP team challenged the community to consider what it would mean to develop the next generation of management education. We begin by thanking Len Schlesinger, president of Babson College, and Shahid Ansari, provost of Babson College, for presenting this challenge, for having confidence in our abilities to engage faculty in these discussions, and for encouraging us to write this book. We also want to acknowledge the work of the deans and the administrators at Babson who are championing our continued work with the ideas that are introduced here.

This book is the commencement of efforts to formally codify and elucidate how Babson is developing its next generation of management pedagogy. By introducing these new ideas to the wider academic community, we are inviting those who are passionate about the potential of management education to join the conversation.

The ideas herein would not be possible without the energy and the intellect of our task force colleagues, who worked for six months to address the question *What do we need to integrate into the Babson pedagogy if we are going to be educating a generation of students who will have the passion, understanding, knowledge, and analytical skills to create great economic and social value everywhere?* The task force members included Julio DeCastro, associate professor of entrepreneurship; Stephen Deets, associate professor of history and society; Mary

Gentile, senior research scholar; Laurie Krigman, associate professor of finance; Dessi Pachamanova, associate professor of math; Anne Roggeveen, associate professor of marketing; Janice Yellin, professor of arts and humanities; Diane Chase, director of academic resources; and Eliana Crosina, manager of international alumni programs. We would also like to recognize Saras Sarasvathy for her research on effectuation (see *http://www.effectuation.org*) and for taking the time to talk to our task force about entrepreneurial thinking.

This task force analyzed global environmental changes, demographic shifts, and technological changes as we considered how we could prepare our students for their future endeavors in large businesses, startups, nonprofits, NGOs, and all types of organizations. We conducted an extensive literature review, we interviewed top management educators inside and outside of Babson, and we surveyed data from management students, employers, recruiters, and our alumni. Needless to say, the task force engaged in many heated discussions about the needs of our students and the ways to proceed. Six months later, after extensive physical, intellectual, and emotional effort, this task force developed and presented a white paper, which is the basis for the introduction of this book. Our Faculty Senate accepted the white paper and asked the curriculum redesign committee to consider how to move forward on the ideas it presented. We each have continued our work to move these ideas forward by serving on the task forces that are working to incorporate these ideas into our undergraduate program (Danna), graduate program (Kate), and executive education program (Jim).

At the same time, we want to recognize our colleagues and students throughout Babson. The colleagues who contributed chapters to this book are dedicated educators whose innovative pedagogy is putting these concepts into practice as they develop entrepreneurial leaders. As we assembled the contributor team for this book, we requested a level of involvement and flexibility that is often not asked of contributors. As true entrepreneurial leaders, their flexibility and willingness to engage both action and analytics in the process of writing this book created an infinitely more insightful manuscript.

Other colleagues and students have also made contributions to this book in less visible ways. Babson's history of innovative pedagogy has yielded a unique culture that is open to change and thus was a safe place to introduce and pursue these ideas. In addition, through ongoing conversations, some more heated than others, the engagement of our colleagues with these ideas has further strengthened the pedagogy that we lay out. We know that our colleagues will continue to challenge the Babson community to improve tomorrow's management education. Most importantly, they continue to inspire us to rethink management education.

When we brought this book to Berrett-Koehler, we were immediately struck by the energy and the engagement the editorial team had for a manuscript on rethinking management education and the need to develop entrepreneurial leaders. Neal Maillet and Jeevan Sivasubramaniam invited us to reconsider the book's structure, and in so doing we believe the ideas are clearer and more engaging. The hands-on involvement of the entire BK team is unusual in today's publishing world, and we are deeply grateful for the opportunity to work with an editorial team who are entrepreneurial leaders.

At the end, and at the beginning, we deeply acknowledge the support, love, encouragement, and patience we receive every day from our partners (Michael, Mark, and Susan) and our children (Micaela, Jonah, Seth, Maya, Marcos, Benjamin, and Brooke). To our children, we hope that each of you will become entrepreneurial leaders in whatever endeavors in life you choose.

Index

Kate McKone-Sweet

Kate McKone-Sweet is an associate professor of operations management and the chair of the Technology, Operations, and Information Management Division at Babson. She teaches operations management and supply-chain management courses to both undergraduate and graduate students.

Professor McKone-Sweet's current research focuses on supply-chain management. The results from her research have been published in numerous academic books and journals, including the *Journal of Operations Management, Production Operations Management, Journal of Supply Chain Management,* and *Supply Chain Management Review.* She has also published numerous operations management cases and management education papers. She has a strong interest in teaching materials that consider social, environmental, and economic value creation as well as hands-on simulations and exercises that engage students in the learning process.

Professor McKone-Sweet holds BS and MEng degrees from Cornell University and MBA and PhD degrees from the Darden Business School, University of Virginia.

H. James Wilson

H. James Wilson is senior researcher and senior writer at Babson Executive Education. His research appears regularly on Harvard Business Review Online and focuses on knowledge worker performance, strategy, and managerial innovation. In the past year, he has led research projects, on such topics as business model innovation, social media strategy, leadership in uncertain times, and how global firms focus their collaboration strategies. Prior to joining Babson, he led thought leadership and research initiatives at Bain and Company and at Accenture's Institute for High Performance Business.

About the Authors

Danna Greenberg

Danna Greenberg is an associate professor of management at Babson College, where she holds the Mandell Family Term Chair. Her field of expertise is organizational behavior, where she teaches core and elective courses at the undergraduate, graduate, and executive levels.

Professor Greenberg's primary area of research focuses on the intersection between organizations, family, and community. Currently, she is involved in two large research studies related to pregnancy in the workplace and the negotiation of flexible work arrangements. She also actively engaged with research on the scholarship of teaching a learning. She has published more than 30 articles and book chap with writings in such journals as *Administrative Science Quan Academy of Management Learning and Education, Journal of C zational Behavior, Journal of Management Education,* and *Jo Applied Behavioral Science.*

Professor Greenberg serves on the editorial boards of emy of Management Learning and Education and the *Journ nizational Behavior* and as an ad hoc reviewer for *Hum Management.* In the community she serves as a consultar member to a number of nonprofits focused on edu social and emotional development of children.

Wilson has authored articles for the *Wall Street Journal, MIT Sloan Management Review, Harvard Business Review,* and numerous other business publications. He is co-author of *What's the Big Idea? Creating and Capitalizing on the Best New Management Thinking* (Harvard Business Press, 2003), which *Fortune* magazine described as one of the best business books of the season. He has also edited and contributed to more than 10 other leadership and management books.

Babson Faculty Contributors

Janice Bell

Jan Bell is a professor of accounting and holds the Weiner Family Term Chair for Accounting. Her expertise is in strategic management accounting and financial reporting. She is the co-author of a modular series, *Management Accounting: A Strategic Focus,* which won the American Accounting Association and the Institute of Management Accountants' award for innovation in management accounting education. Professor Bell hosted the Global Accounting and Organizational Change Conference held on the Babson campus in July 2010. The theme of the conference was "accounting's role in promoting social change," and academics from 16 countries presented research papers.

Richard Bliss

Richard Bliss is an associate professor of finance at Babson College. He teaches at the undergraduate, graduate, and executive levels, specializing in corporate financial strategy and entrepreneurial finance. Prior to coming to Babson, Dr. Bliss was on the faculty at Indiana University; he also taught extensively in central and eastern Europe, including at the Warsaw School of Economics at Warsaw University and at the University of Ljubljana in Slovenia. He has developed and delivered customized corporate training programs for Lucent Technologies; the

Slovak American Enterprise Fund in Bratislava, Slovakia; the Foundation for the Establishment of the Futures Exchange in Warsaw; and Bright China Management Institute in Beijing.

Tom Davenport

Tom Davenport holds the President's Chair in Information Technology and Management at Babson College. He has taught at Harvard Business School, the University of Chicago, Dartmouth's Tuck School of Business, and the University of Texas at Austin. He has directed research centers at Accenture, Ernst and Young, McKinsey and Company, and CSC Index.

Professor Davenport has written, co-authored, or edited 13 books, including the first books on business process reengineering, knowledge management, the business use of enterprise systems, and analytical competition. He has written hundreds of articles and columns for such publications as *Harvard Business Review, MIT Sloan Management Review, California Management Review, Financial Times, Information Week, CIO,* and many others. His most recent book is *Analytics at Work: Smarter Decisions, Better Results* (Harvard Business Press, 2010). In 2003 he was named one of the top 25 consultants in the world by *Consulting* magazine, in 2005 he was rated the third most influential business and technology analyst in the world (after Peter Drucker and Tom Friedman), and in 2007 he was the highest-ranking business academic in Ziff-Davis's list of the 100 most influential people in the IT industry.

Stephen Deets

Stephen Deets is an associate professor of politics at Babson College, where he teaches courses on international and comparative politics, ethnic conflict, Soviet/post-Soviet politics, and society and entrepreneurship in Ghana. He has published more than a dozen articles on various issues concerning post-communist democratization, including electoral reform, minority rights, healthcare, and environmental politics. Currently, he is finishing a book on new models of minority governance across Europe, and he is starting a project on social welfare reform in Lebanon.

Prior to becoming a professor, he spent a decade at the National Academy of Sciences, where he organized cooperative programs with the academies in eastern Europe on a wide variety of topics, including environmental issues, energy efficiency, higher-education reform, and commercializing university research.

Lisa DiCarlo

Lisa DiCarlo is an assistant professor of anthropology in the Entrepreneurship Division at Babson College. Her research areas include transnational migration, consumption and sustainability, entrepreneurship and creative economy, and the intersection of ethnographic research and social entrepreneurship. She is the recipient of two Fulbright Research Fellowships and the author of *Migrating to America: Transnational Social Networks and Regional Identity among Turkish Migrants* (I.B.Tauris, 2008). Her current projects include social impact assessment of environmental initiatives in Turkey and examining state support of, and public reactions to, Attila Durak's book *Ebru: Reflections of Cultural Diversity in Turkey*.

Sebastian K. Fixson

Sebastian Fixson is an assistant professor in the Technology, Operations, and Information Management Division at Babson College. His research, teaching, and consulting focus on innovation management. In recent work he has studied the impact of product and process characteristics on product development performance. His research has appeared in books and journals, including *Journal of Operations Management, Research Policy, IEEE Transactions on Engineering Management, Concurrent Engineering,* and *Technological Forecasting and Social*

Change, and he has worked with various corporations, such as Boeing, Ford, General Motors, Harley-Davidson, Alcoa, Raytheon, and others. Dr. Fixson teaches in both the undergraduate and graduate programs at Babson and has also taught at both business and engineering schools, including MIT's Sloan School of Management, the University of Michigan's College of Engineering, and Northeastern University's School of Technological Entrepreneurship.

Mary C. Gentile

Mary C. Gentile, PhD, is a senior research scholar at Babson College; a senior adviser, the Aspen Institute Business and Society Program; and an independent consultant based in Arlington, Massachusetts. Previously, she was a faculty member and the manager of case research at Harvard Business School.

Currently, Dr. Gentile is director of Giving Voice to Values (*http://www.GivingVoiceToValues.org*), a business curriculum launched by the Aspen Institute and the Yale School of Management, with ongoing support from Babson College. GVV is a pioneering approach to values-driven leadership that has been featured in the *Financial Times* (twice), *Harvard Business Review* (twice), *strategy+business,* Businessweek Online, *Change* magazine, *Business Ethics* magazine, and *BizEd* and is being piloted in more than 100 business schools and organizations globally. She is the author of *Giving Voice to Values: How to Speak Your Mind When You Know What's Right* (Yale University Press, 2010). As an independent consultant (*http://www.MaryGentile.com*), Dr. Gentile works with corporate, nonprofit, and academic institutions on leadership development, social impact management, ethics, business education, and diversity.

PJ Guinan

Patricia J. Guinan is an associate professor in the Information Technology Management Division and teaches in the Management Division.

She teaches multidisciplinary courses in information technology, cross-functional teamwork, organization design, organization change, and management strategy.

She is the author of the international award-winning book *Patterns of Excellence for IS Professionals: An Analysis of Communication Behavior* (International Center for Information, 1988). Dr. Guinan received two awards for teaching excellence from Boston University, where she taught prior to joining Babson's faculty. In her executive education career, she has worked with numerous Fortune 500 companies on topics related to technology and innovation.

Karen Hebert-Maccaro

Karen Hebert-Maccaro is a visiting assistant professor of management at Babson College. She is also the former associate dean of the F. W. Olin Graduate School of Business at Babson. In this capacity she served as the chief operating officer of the graduate school, with overall responsibility for admissions, program management, and career development. She has held several positions at Babson since joining the college in 1997, including director of strategic initiatives and assistant dean and administrative director of the MBA programs. Prior to her career in higher education, she worked in the financial services industry.

James Hunt

James Hunt is an associate professor of management at Babson College. He teaches management, talent management, talent development, and leadership at the undergraduate, graduate, and executive levels. He was a co-founder of Babson's Coaching for Leadership and Teamwork Program and Babson Executive Education's Coaching Inside the Organization: The Certification Program for Internal Coaches.

Professor Hunt is the co-author (with Professor Joseph Weintraub, also of Babson) of two books on coaching, the best-selling *The*

Coaching Manager: Developing Top Talent in Business, second edition (Sage, 2010) and *The Coaching Organization: A Strategy for Developing Leaders* (Sage, 2006). He is also the author or co-author of numerous articles on developmental coaching and leadership development. He has consulted with numerous corporations and healthcare organizations throughout the United States.

Julian Lange

Julian Lange is the Governor Craig R. Benson Professor of Entrepreneurship and Public Policy at Babson College. He is also founder and president of Chatham Associates, a management consulting firm that assists businesses in building competitive advantage. He was president and CEO of Software Arts Inc., creators of the first electronic spreadsheet (VisiCalc), and was a founding trustee of the Massachusetts Software Council. He has taught in numerous executive education programs and has served as assistant professor of finance at Harvard Business School.

Dr. Lange has been a management consultant to startup, midsized, and Fortune 500 companies and has developed and implemented training programs for companies in computer hardware and software, financial services, and the healthcare industry. His research is concerned with the financing of high-growth entrepreneurial ventures and the challenges and the opportunities for entrepreneurial firms presented by the Internet.

Nan S. Langowitz

Nan Langowitz is a professor of management and entrepreneurship at Babson College and served as the founding director of Babson's Center for Women's Leadership, the first comprehensive center dedicated to advancing women in business and entrepreneurship at a leading school of management. Her research is focused on the entrepreneurial leadership of women as well as the challenges and the opportunities that organizations and managers face when developing and leveraging talent.

In the classroom Professor Langowitz teaches professional development and leadership through courses in Babson's MBA program as well as at Babson Executive Education. She was awarded the Dean's Teaching Award for the graduate program in 2009. Professor Langowitz has more than 20 years of experience in executive development design and delivery, having worked as a consultant, a researcher, and an educator with organizations ranging from complex global corporations to new startup ventures. She has also served on corporate and nonprofit boards.

Toni Lester

Toni Lester is a professor of law, culture, and society and holds the Kelly Lynch Term Chair at Babson. She chairs the Teaching and Curriculum Development Initiative on Environmental Sustainability at Babson, which promotes the development of faculty teaching and research on sustainability issues. This has included introducing faculty to companies and nonprofit organizations with programs designed to promote greater environmental awareness and approaches to developing best business practices that reduce global warming and the negative impacts of climate change. The initiative also hosts a discussion series featuring cross-disciplinary teams of faculty members who present cutting-edge environmental topics to their peers.

Professor Lester also co-designed and teaches a course with science colleague Vikki Rodgers called Eco-tourism, Biodiversity, and Conservation Policy in Costa Rica, and she designed the first advanced elective at Babson on animal rights, called The Role of Animals in Law, Technology, and Society. She has also served on the steering committee that helped shape a new and exciting cross-disciplinary, collaborative certificate program on environmental sustainability offered by Babson

College, Wellesley College, and the Olin College of Engineering, which commences in the fall of 2011.

Heidi Neck

Heidi Neck is the Jeffry A. Timmons Professor of Entrepreneurial Studies at Babson College. As faculty director of the Babson Symposium for Entrepreneurship Educators, she passionately works to improve the pedagogy of entrepreneurship education because new-venture creation is the engine of society. In addition to entrepreneurship education, Professor Neck's research interests include social entrepreneurship, corporate entrepreneurship, and creativity.

Recognized for her contributions to innovative teaching and curriculum developments, she's received numerous awards, including Babson's Deans' Award for Excellence in Teaching, the Gloria Appel Prize for entrepreneurial vitality in academe, the United States Association for Small Business and Entrepreneurship (USASBE) Outstanding Entrepreneurship Course, USASBE's Best Practice Pedagogy for theatrical improvisation, and USASBE's Best Workshops for Social Entrepreneurship Development and Entrepreneurship Pedagogy.

Salvatore Parise

Salvatore Parise is an associate professor in the Technology, Operations, and Information Management Division at Babson College. His research focuses primarily on using social network analysis to understand innovation, talent management, technology-mediated networks, and worker performance. His other research work focuses on how organizations are using social media applications both internally among employees and externally among customers and business partners.

Professor Parise has worked directly with managers and executives across a wide range of industries, including management consulting, technology, consumer products, healthcare, financial services, petroleum, and government. He teaches multidisciplinary courses at both the undergraduate and graduate levels on information systems, knowledge management, and social network analysis. He also teaches executive education on such topics as social media applications and social networks.

Jay Rao

Jay Rao is a professor of operations management at Babson. His research and consulting focus is in the areas of innovation, implementation of innovation programs within firms, and customer experience innovation. He teaches at the graduate and executive education levels. Prior to Babson, Dr. Rao taught at the University of Kentucky and at the University of California, Los Angeles.

His research has appeared in *MIT Sloan Management Review, Academy of Management Executive, Journal of Innovative Management, Production and Operations Management Journal, Quality Management in Health Care,* and the *Cornell Hotel and Restaurant Administration Quarterly.* He has written more than a dozen business cases that range in topics from innovation, customer service, and operations strategy to strategic alignment, supply-chain management, and quality management. He has extensive consulting and executive education experience with complex global organizations as well as new startup ventures on topics related to operations management, innovation, and new-product development.

Vikki L. Rodgers

Vikki L. Rodgers is an assistant professor of environmental science in the Math and Science Division of Babson College. She received her BS degree in biology, ecology, and evolution from the University of New Hampshire in 1999 and her PhD in forest ecology from Boston University in 2007, studying the impacts of invasive plants on soil nutrient cycling and native plant diversity in the forests of New England. Her main areas of interest include ecology, botany, climate change, and biogeochemistry. Professor Rodgers has published articles in the *Journal of Ecology, Bioscience, Biogeochemistry, Oecologia,* and *Canadian Journal of Forest Research.*

Keith Rollag

Keith Rollag is an associate professor of management and the chair of the Management Division at Babson College. His teaching focuses on organizational behavior, teamwork, and leadership, and his research focuses primarily on newcomer socialization and training, organizational culture, social networks, and leadership development.

Professor Rollag has published articles in *MIT Sloan Management Review, Journal of Organizational Behavior, Journal of Occupational and Organizational Psychology,* and *Journal of Management Education.* His research has also been featured in *Harvard Management Update, Stanford Social Innovation Review, Wired News,* and *Boston Business Journal.*

In 2005 he received the New Educator Award from the Organizational Behavior Teaching Society, a national organization focused on management education. He currently serves on the organization's board of directors. Prior to obtaining his PhD in industrial engineering from Stanford University, Professor Rollag was a product development manager at Procter and Gamble.

Virginia Soybel

Virginia Earll Soybel teaches financial accounting and financial statement analysis at the F. W. Olin Graduate School of Business at Babson College. She has participated in multiple curriculum design initiatives there, focused primarily on integrating functional disciplines so that students learn how to combine concepts and tools most effectively to solve complex business problems.

Professor Soybel earned her MBA and PhD degrees at Columbia University and her BA degree in American history at Williams College. Before joining the Babson College faculty, she taught at the Amos Tuck School of Business at Dartmouth College. Professor Soybel's research focuses on the effects of alternative reporting methods on corporate financial statements and ratios, the time series behavior of financial ratios, and the political process of accounting standard setting.

Robert Turner

Robert Turner, associate dean of MBA Programs, is an associate professor of accounting at Babson College. He previously taught at Boston College, Boston University, and LeMoyne College. His teaching interests are in the area of corporate and nonprofit financial reporting. He has taught financial accounting at the undergraduate and graduate levels and in the Intermediate Management Core. Professor Turner has published numerous articles on financial reporting, primarily in the area of reporting by nonprofit organizations, and on teaching accounting.

Berrett–Koehler
Publishers

Berrett-Koehler is an independent publisher dedicated to an ambitious mission: *Creating a World That Works for All*.

We believe that to truly create a better world, action is needed at all levels—individual, organizational, and societal. At the individual level, our publications help people align their lives with their values and with their aspirations for a better world. At the organizational level, our publications promote progressive leadership and management practices, socially responsible approaches to business, and humane and effective organizations. At the societal level, our publications advance social and economic justice, shared prosperity, sustainability, and new solutions to national and global issues.

A major theme of our publications is "Opening Up New Space." Berrett-Koehler titles challenge conventional thinking, introduce new ideas, and foster positive change. Their common quest is changing the underlying beliefs, mindsets, institutions, and structures that keep generating the same cycles of problems, no matter who our leaders are or what improvement programs we adopt.

We strive to practice what we preach—to operate our publishing company in line with the ideas in our books. At the core of our approach is stewardship, which we define as a deep sense of responsibility to administer the company for the benefit of all of our "stakeholder" groups: authors, customers, employees, investors, service providers, and the communities and environment around us.

We are grateful to the thousands of readers, authors, and other friends of the company who consider themselves to be part of the "BK Community." We hope that you, too, will join us in our mission.

A BK Business Book

This book is part of our BK Business series. BK Business titles pioneer new and progressive leadership and management practices in all types of public, private, and nonprofit organizations. They promote socially responsible approaches to business, innovative organizational change methods, and more humane and effective organizations.

Berrett–Koehler
Publishers

A community dedicated to creating
a world that works for all

Visit Our Website: www.bkconnection.com

Read book excerpts, see author videos and Internet movies, read our authors'
blogs, join discussion groups, download book apps, find out about the BK
Affiliate Network, browse subject-area libraries of books, get special discounts, and more!

Subscribe to Our Free E-Newsletter, the *BK Communiqué*

Be the first to hear about new publications, special discount offers, exclu-
sive articles, news about bestsellers, and more! Get on the list for our free
e-newsletter by going to **www.bkconnection.com**.

Get Quantity Discounts

Berrett-Koehler books are available at quantity discounts for orders of ten or
more copies. Please call us toll-free at (800) 929-2929 or email us at **bkp
.orders@aidcvt.com**.

Join the BK Community

BKcommunity.com is a virtual meeting place where people from around the
world can engage with kindred spirits to create a world that works for all.
BKcommunity.com members may create their own profiles, blog, start and
participate in forums and discussion groups, post photos and videos, answer
surveys, announce and register for upcoming events, and chat with others
online in real time. Please join the conversation!